A Few Degrees from H.

ACKNOWLEDGEMENTS

Thanks to all of the runners and crewmembers who toed the starting line of the 2003 Badwater Ultramarathon, arguably the toughest of the "toughest footrace on the planet." To the 25 runners who contributed to this book, my deepest appreciation. Please share my gratitude with your crews, because without them there would be no stories for any of us to tell.

Thanks to Susanne Thurman, enhancer of numerous photographs and opener of countless computer files towards the construction of this book.

Thanks to Denise Jones for her wisdom and insight. I know Ben is glad to have you in his corner.

Thanks to Stephanie Robinson for helping me put everything between the covers once again (Stephanie worked with me on my first two books as well). I'm glad to have you in my corner.

Thanks to Al, Gary, Paula, Eric and Josh. I wouldn't have a story to share without you all.

Finally, thanks to my wife Cindy, who gave me the video *Running on the Sun*, the story of the 1999 Badwater Ultramarathon. The first time I watched it I knew one day my running shoes and I would find our way to Death Valley. If anyone asks who is responsible for this book, I'm pointing in her direction. She'll deny it, of course... *but you'll know*.

White Hot Tales from the
Badwater Ultramarathon

By Scott Ludwig

A FEW DEGREES **FROM HELL**

DEDICATION

*For those with the passion
to pursue their dreams…*

Meyer & Meyer Sport

British Library Cataloguing in Publication Data
A catalogue record for this book is available from the British Library

A few degrees from hell
Maidenhead: Meyer & Meyer Sport (UK) Ltd., 2013
ISBN: 978-1-78255-003-7

© 2013 by Meyer & Meyer Sport (UK) Ltd.
Auckland, Beirut, Budapest, Cairo, Cape Town, Dubai, Hägendorf, Indianapolis,
Maidenhead, Singapore, Sydney, Tehran, Wien
Member of the World
Sport Publishers' Association (WSPA)
www.w-s-p-a.org
Printed by: Color House Graphics
ISBN: 978-1-78255-003-7
E-Mail: info@m-m-sports.com
www.m-m-sports.com

© Thinkstock/iStockphoto/Fluid Illusion

CONTENTS

FOREWORD

"I really regret that run." Said no one. Ever.

I saw this on a marketing poster and thought truer words were never spoken. After all I should know, as I've had well over 13,000 chances to say it.

You see, I've run every day since November 30, 1978. Every. Single. Day.

In fact, on many days during a 13-year window from 1994 to 2006 I ran two, three and on occasion four times in a single day. My average daily mileage during that time was 13 miles. Again: Every. Single. Day. I took pride in my running regimen that I simply referred to as "training to exhaustion." If I had a spare moment and/or an ounce of energy, I would find myself running. I wasn't sure why; I just knew when the opportunity presented itself I wanted to be ready for it.

Then one day I realized what I was preparing myself for. It was Father's Day, 2001. I was watching the documentary *Running on the Sun*, chronicling the 1999 edition of the Badwater Ultramarathon, a 135-mile race through Death Valley and up and over three mountain ranges and finishing at the Portals of Mount Whitney. Forty runners competed that year and many of them were featured in the film. I was fascinated, no – *mesmerized* every second the images of runners being put to the ultimate test of physical endurance flashed on the screen. (Much to my wife's chagrin; ironic in a way as she was the one who gave me the video as a gift) I knew less than halfway into the film that I too would one day find my way to the starting line in Badwater, California.

After all, how could I *not*? The comments spoken by the competitors were in perfect harmony with my "training to exhaustion" running regimen. Every word they spoke was so familiar to me there was no doubt whatsoever that one day (or night) I would be crossing the finish line at the Portals of Mount Whitney.

- *Do you have the right stuff?*

- *I can be dying and an hour after I can be flying!*

- *Mind over matter.*

- *That's why so few people do these endurance races: they hurt.*

- *Competition is between the runner and the course.*

- *What a hell of a journey!*

Fast forward to an extremely hot July morning in 2003. I was on the starting line of the Badwater Ultramarathon, seconds away from beginning the most incredible, most rewarding, most incredible adventure of my life.

About nine years to the day later I watched *Running on the Sun* again on a hot, steamy 95-degree July afternoon in my home in Peachtree City, Georgia, a mere 1,830 miles from Badwater (and about 35 degrees cooler!). When the images of the competitors crossing the finish line began flashing on the screen, my allergies kicked in* (*code for "eyes began welling up") and I immediately started to analyze why.

Then it suddenly dawned on me:
With my ever-advancing age and a body slowly moving in the opposite direction it is highly doubtful I will ever have the opportunity to run the Badwater Ultramarathon again.

THAT, my friend is something I *do* regret!

The last line in the film – ruminating on the allure and attraction of competing in the Badwater Ultramarathon sums it up nicely:

• *Life becomes so much richer.*

Indeed.

WELCOME TO DEATH VALLEY *By Al Arnold*

A picture is worth a thousand words.

My favorite depiction of Death Valley is in an old cartoon.

Visualize a large luxury convertible automobile as it passes a sign that reads:

"You are now entering Death Valley"

Its occupants – oblivious as to where they are going – merrily enter this forbidden spot in the bowels of the United States.

The next – and appropriately the last – illustration shows this same vehicle as it passes another sign:

"You are now leaving Death Valley"

However, the automobile is now "sun bleached" beyond recognition, and the once-festive occupants are now merely parched bones.

That, my dear reader, is just one small stretch of the imagination that contributes to the various historians and their input in designating this "different world" as Death Valley.

There's no other place like it.

And... I love it!

In the incredibly hot summer of 1977, with air temperatures exceeding 135 degrees, Al Arnold, at 225 pounds and 50 years old became the first person to successfully trek – continuously – from Badwater, Death Valley (the lowest point in the Western Hemisphere) to Mount Whitney Summit (the highest elevation in the contiguous United States). His route was 200 miles and the total vertical elevation was almost 25,000 feet. It took him 84 hours

When the Badwater Hall of Fame was created in 2002, he became its first inductee.

HELL ON EARTH

My truck is adorned with University of Florida paraphernalia – bumper stickers, decals, and a license plate, all of which is fine for another story for another day for another book for, well, quite frankly another audience (unless you happen to be a fellow Gator in which case – *Go Gators!*). The decal in the back window resembles the very familiar "26.2" oval decal found on virtually every vehicle driven by anyone who has ever completed a marathon. However, my oval decal is different, as the number inside the black oval is 134.4, the distance of the greatest adventure I have ever been a part of. The license plate frame on the back reads "Badwater Ultramarathon... The Toughest Footrace on the Planet."

The hottest temperature ever recorded in North America was 134 degrees on July 10, 1913 in Death Valley, California. It was a day that inspired generations to pass along the legend that those who experienced it were heard to say *"this is what Hell must be like."*

A little over 90 years later, on July 22, 2003, 73 hearty souls ventured into this same desert on a mission to run, walk or (if need be) crawl from California's Badwater Basin to the portals of Mount Whitney. The trek would take them from the nation's lowest elevation to the portals of the highest peak in the continental United Sates. As they crossed Death Valley, they would encounter temperatures as high as 125* degrees.

The Badwater Ultramarathon repeatedly lives up to its reputation as the toughest footrace on the planet. In 2003, only 46 of the aforementioned 73 hearty souls would complete the journey from Badwater to Mount Whitney, a finishing rate of only 63% (in the other 20 years of the 134.4-mile event from 1990 to 2010, there has been an overall finishing rate of 81% – 827 finishers out of 1,019 starters). The heat on the first day of the race (the race has a 60-hour time limit, so runners will actually complete the race on their second or quite possibly *third day*) allegedly reached the low-to-mid 130's, according to reports from many of the competitors and crewmembers who were there.

In this book you will hear from those who were there to cross the desert – or at least to give it a shot on a day that the temperature was literally *a few degrees from Hell*.

---

* A note of appreciation to Marshall Ulrich, Ben Jones and Emily Pronovost for their efforts in verifying this statistic. You will read about Marshall and Ben in the coming pages, and Emily is the archive technician for Death Valley National Park. Thank you all for your help.

INTRODUCTION – BADWATER

The Badwater Ultramarathon is a 135-mile invitational running race starting in Badwater in Death Valley (elevation 280 feet below sea level) and finishing at the Whitney Portals on Mount Whitney (elevation 8,360 feet).

The course runs through Death Valley – where runners could face temperatures reaching 130 degrees – and over three mountain ranges with a finish on the highest mountain in the contiguous United States.

Runners are required to make their presence known at five checkpoints during the course: Furnace Creek, Stovepipe Wells, Panamint Springs, Darwin and Lone Pine.

Badwater is recognized as "the toughest footrace on the planet."

In 2003 seventy-three determined runners set out to conquer the Badwater Ultramarathon. Forty-six of them would ultimately reach the finish line on Mount Whitney. The others would give it everything they had, only to fall short of the ultimate achievement in running.

In this book you will read about 23 of the runners who were successful in their quests, as well as about two who were not. Their stories are all intriguing and inspiring, yet each one distinctly unique. The runners came from all walks of life: doctors, lawyers, teachers, engineers, corporate executives, photographers, managers, consultants, computer programmers, race directors and small business owners. Yet, as different as their backgrounds were they all shared the same dream: to finish the Badwater Ultramarathon.

The majority of the runners you will meet in this book wrote their own account of the race. The others were written by me based on telephone interviews and E-mail correspondence I had with them.

It is my distinct honor to present their stories in the pages ahead. Before you turn the page, you might want to pour yourself an ice cold drink:

This is going to be one hot read.

Scott Ludwig
Peachtree City, Georgia
July 2012

BADWATER ULTRAMARATHON CHECKPOINTS

Checkpoint	Distance	Elevation (+/- sea level)
Badwater (Starting Line)	0	-282 feet
Furnace Creek Ranch	17.4 miles	-165 feet
Stovepipe Wells	41.9 miles	0
Panamint Springs	72.3 miles	+1,970 feet
Darwin Turnoff	90.1 miles	+5,050 feet
Lone Pine	122.2 miles	+3,610 feet
Whitney Portal (Finish Line)	134.4 miles	+8,360 feet

Total Flat Miles – 69
Total Downhill Miles – 20
Total Uphill Miles – 46

For a more descriptive portrait of the Badwater Ultramarathon course, refer to Chapter Twenty-Six.

CHAPTER ONE – PAM REED

From Pam's 2003 Badwater Application

Age: 42
Tucson, Arizona

Why I want a slot on the start line of the 2003 Badwater Ultramarathon:

I want to break my own record and make sure the whole thing was real.

SOME LIKE IT HOT BY SCOTT LUDWIG

Pam Reed stood at the starting line of the 2003 Badwater Ultramarathon with a huge target on her back. As the defending champion, that's to be expected. But the figurative target on her back wasn't her primary concern. Pam had more important issues to contend with.

For the past year Pam had to contend with the rumors circulating on the Internet that her 2002 Badwater victory was a "fluke." After all, she did have the good fortune of the "easier" 6:00 a.m. start which allowed Pam four hours of running before the hot desert sun was out in force later in the day – which made the conditions more difficult for the 8:00 a.m. and 10:00 a.m. starters (the latter group theoretically containing the faster runners in the race). Running virtually alone (i.e. no other competitors in sight) the entire race, Pam did not feel the regular pressures of actually competing head to head with anyone in the field. At least that's what the rumormongers would have you believe.

The fact that Pam's winning time a year ago (27:56:47) was a new women's course record by almost two hours didn't seem to have an impact at dispelling the "fluke" theory circulating around the world. Neither did the fact that the second place finisher (first place male) in the 2002 race finished over 4 ½ hours behind Pam. Or that Pam's 2002 time would have been fast enough to win Badwater seven times in the past decade. Or that Pam ran 12 hours faster than the 2001 women's champion. No, it was easier to simply discount Pam's 2002 victory as a fluke than to actually analyze the evidence and realize that Pam was indeed something special.

As Pam Reed stood at the starting line of the 2003 Badwater Ultramarathon, she had something to prove. It would be tough, as talented runners Dean Karnazes and Chris Bergland were lined up with her in the 10:00 a.m. starting group. At least the Race Director realized that Pam was a force to be reckoned with, assigning her the top-seeded bib number 1 and placing her in the third and final starting group, a solid four hours behind the "easier" 6:00 a.m. starters. Prior to the starter's pistol, Pam was relying on her pre-race thoughts that doing well would be "an easy thing to do." After all, she knew that 2002 was no fluke.

Pam had the utmost confidence in her crew, headed by Chuck Giles. Giles served as a marshal for the Badwater Ultramarathon and witnessed a Russian woman break the course record by several hours. Through his experiences in Death Valley, Giles designed a spraying system that could be installed in a runner's support van to keep the runner cooled off as they ran through Death Valley (he also designed a sprinkler system for cyclists competing in the Race across America).

He approached Pam prior to the 2000 race and encouraged her to participate; she politely declined. However, Pam thought about his offer and in 2002 she simply "showed up and ran." After her historic victory, Pam felt that she believed she ran "a perfect race." Along the same lines of the internet rumors about her victory, television reporters from Brazil and Germany asked her point blank if she had cheated. How could she explain that such a simple thing – getting cooled down while she ran – played a significant role in her 2002 victory? Didn't anyone realize that no one else was doing it, which set her apart from everyone else in the race?

Pam had prepared well for this year's race. She had been running three times a day totaling 100 to 115 miles a week near her home in Tucson, Arizona. Her training called for incremental training runs to prepare her for longer distances: 13-mile training runs to prepare for marathons, marathons to train for 50-milers, and 50-milers to train for 100-milers. For this year's Badwater, Pam had run a 100-kilometer (62 miles) race – a mere 10 days before!

Pam, attired in her traditional shorts, cotton T-shirt and white running hat, was ready to defend her title. She wore her iPod every step of the way. (Oddly enough, the iPod didn't work during the race; however she was in a "zone" and didn't want to change anything, so she wore it anyway.) During the race Pam's diet consisted of a steady supply of Ensure, Red Bull and club soda. There would be no solid food until the race was over. Her crew worked around the clock throughout the race: provided her with much-needed calories, telling her stories as they bicycled next to her, and giving her the emotional support one needs to run through an incredibly hot desert and over unforgiving mountain ranges. The importance of a crew is summed up in the words of Chris Giles: "A crew can't win it for you but can certainly lose it for you." Pam, on the other hand attributes 100% of her success to her crew.

Once Pam ran the first few miles, she ran comfortably in third place behind Dean and Chris. Two thoughts – which are significant since Pam believes that Badwater is 90% mental and 10% physical – were going through her mind at this point:

I can't believe I'm doing this.

It's OK not to win.

Imagine her surprise when first Dean and then Chris were in Pam's rear-view mirror.

It didn't come easy, however. Pam had to live through her "lowest point" in the race as she was trying to catch up to the two front-runners on the second major climb. Mentally she had settled for third place. She was feeling low emotionally, wondering "what the hell was I thinking" when she decided to return to defend her championship.

But her perseverance and training paid off.

As Pam passed Dean around the 80-mile mark, she thought Dean "was done" as the heat really seemed to be taking its toll on him. She exchanged pleasantries with Dean as she moved into second place and wished him good luck. Now to find Chris.

Ironically, she caught up with Chris Bergland at almost the same spot in the race – around 110 miles – that she realized she would win the 2002 race as she was so far ahead of the field. Poetically, she realized that she would repeat as champion at virtually the exact same spot as she passed Chris.

However, her second victory wasn't secure. The Race Director caught up with Pam five miles from Lone Pine (approximately 117 miles into the race) and told her that Dean was only 25 minutes behind her.

In a race of this magnitude, 25 minutes can equate to something as simple as a bad spell requiring a short recuperative rest on the side of the road. But there would be no resting for Pam. Amazingly, Pam did not stop at all during the race. Most runners opt to rest periodically – some as frequently as once every mile – by sitting in a canvas chair placed on the side of the road by a crewmember. (Note: Pam did not sit during either of her two Badwater victories.). Her "game plan" for the 2003 race was to win by running relaxed for most of the race with the exception of walking that "last hill" (only someone from the west coast would refer to the intimidating Mount Whitney as a "hill"). She executed her game plan to perfection, and finished the race in 28:26:50, a few seconds shy of 25 minutes in front of Dean Karnazes. Pam's steady approach to navigating that 'last hill' was successful, as Dean was unable to make up any of his 25-minute deficit on the 13-mile climb up Mount Whitney.

After Pam Reed's historic victory in the 2002 Badwater Ultramarathon, her life changed as people respected her more and she in turn was able respect *herself* more as well. Winning provided her more confidence and helped her to become a better runner.

Following her (perhaps even more) historic victory in 2003, the name of Pam Reed was receiving universal acclaim and recognition. Pam appeared on television (the David Letterman show, the Wayne Brady show, the Tony Danza show), in magazines (*Running Times, Runner's World and Outside*, among others), and spoke at the ISPO, the famous annual winter sports forum in Germany.

When asked which victory meant more – 2002 or 2003 – Pam opted for the latter. In Pam's mind, she had faced and conquered the greatest challenge of her life.

Pam Reed was indeed no fluke. She was a champion. The confident, two-time champion of the toughest footrace on the planet.

2003 Finishing Time – 28:26:52
2003 Badwater Champion

CHAPTER TWO – DEAN KARNAZES

From Dean's 2003 Badwater Application:

Age: 40
San Francisco, California

My Weirdest Experience:

On the second night of running 199 miles nonstop, I fell asleep while running and continued to run for quite some distance while sleeping. We've all heard of sleep walking, but this was something new: sleep running.

TOO LITTLE TOO LATE *BY SCOTT LUDWIG*

When Dean Karnazes took his spot on the starting line at Badwater in July of 2003, he had only one goal in mind. It certainly wasn't to win the race. It wasn't even to finish in the top five... or ten, for that matter.
Dean's goal was simply to finish the race.

After all, his entire support crew consisted only of his friend Jim Vernon – who paced him only for as long as he could during the race – and Dean's father Nick. The three were looking for an experience that offered the opportunity for some good old-fashioned male bonding in a unique environment that only Death Valley could offer.

It wasn't until the three of them made the turn in Lone Pine – just 13 miles from the finish line of this 135-mile race – that the thought of actually *competing* entered into their collective minds. It seems that the leader of the race, Pam Reed, was less than an hour ahead of Dean. And as treacherous as this last climb to the finish line at the portals of Mount Whitney is, a deficit of an hour can be made up rather easily should the leader take a turn for the worse. And after running 122 miles in 130+ degree heat and crossing two mountain ranges, stranger things have happened.

Dean's first foray into Death Valley was in 1995, the only time he failed to reach Badwater's finish line. At that time the race began at night, and when Dean stopped at a gas station in Furnace Creek early in the race to drink some water, he failed to see the sign above his head which read "Non potable" until his headlamp illuminated it, but it was already too late. Ironically, Dean had literally *consumed* bad water. Later in the race his support vehicle broke down, and by the time he reached Panamint Springs (mile 72), Dean literally broke down as well when he passed out and ultimately dropped out of the race.

A year later Dean and his father – Dean's sole support for the race, returned to Badwater and completed the race in 51:23, which included an eight-hour stop at the Dow Villa (mile 122) so Nick could take a much-needed nap before the finishing climb up Mount Whitney.
Getting back to the 2003 race, Dean recalls the climb out of Stovepipe Wells into an incredibly hot headwind he describes as "savage" as one of the highlights of the race, with another being the amazing solitude he experienced running all alone in the desert in the middle of the night.

Dean completed the last 13 miles of the 2003 Badwater Ultramarathon in an impressive three hours and 26 seconds, ultimately finishing in second place a mere 24 minutes and change behind winner Pam Reed. Dean is proud he was able to push Pam at the end of the race, and admires her ability to focus and persevere in an event in which "finishing strong" means a little more than the finishing kick you may have witnessed during the last 385 yards of s standard 26.2 mile marathon.

Dean returned to Badwater in 2004, again with only one goal in mind. This time the goal was to win. In one of the most exciting finishes in the history of the race, Dean found himself racing against time rather than an actual person as Ferg Hawke, who had started the race in the 8:00 a.m. wave (Dean started in the 10:00 a.m. wave) crossed the finish line as Dean was just beginning the final 13-mile climb. Dean was made aware of Ferg's time and knew he had to finish strong to win the race (note: at the 122-mile checkpoint in Lone Pine, Ferg had a two-minute lead on Dean). Dean did just that, completing the last 13 miles in 3:08:48 and winning the race by seven minutes and 32 seconds, posting a fine 27:22 finish and winning the race.

Dean loves running Badwater, a race which he rates as "an 8.5" on a 10-point difficulty scale. He rates the Atacama Crossing – a six-day self-supported race covering 155 miles as a "10." Dean competed in the 2008 event, finishing in a commendable 31:49:44 and winning the event, or "surviving the fastest," as he puts it. Chile's Atacama Desert is 50 times more arid than Death Valley, and offers a wide fluctuation of temperatures from day to night.

But for Dean, it seems the more difficult races stir his competitive fires. His best finish at Badwater was in 2008 (27:11), the year he competed all four desert races (the other three being Gobi, Sahara and Antarctica). In fact, Dean was the first person to finish *all* of them in a single year.

Dean admits his most difficult Badwater was in 2009. His father had undergone massive open heart surgery right before the event, and when Dean went to see him in the hospital Nick wanted to know if he "was ready" to run Badwater. When Nick learned Dean wasn't planning on running, he insisted his son compete. Dean listened to his father and participated, but his head wasn't in the race and he finished in (for Dean) a pedestrian 34:51.

Through his competition over the years at Badwater and other ultra distance events, Dean has adopted an almond butter sandwich with bananas and honey as his "go to" food. Another? Soy sauce on bread. As for fluids, he relies on Pedialyte (an electrolyte replacement drink for children suffering from diarrhea and vomiting). During his 2004 win at Badwater, Dean's crew recorded his fluid intake: a whopping nine gallons of fluid (he knows he drank even more in 2003 at Badwater but no one kept track).

Dean believes the hardest part of Badwater is the climbing. He says "the heat is a given, but the severity of the mountains is another thing."

A staple for most participants at Badwater is "the chair." Most runners will utilize a chair throughout the race for intermittent breaks – some as frequently as every half-mile. The crew will set up the chair along the course and the runner will stop and sit in the chair to drink, eat, change shoes or to simply take a break from the relentless forward motion that is the core of ultrarunning. In fact, a common mantra heard at Badwater is "Beware the Chair," an implication that over time the chair becomes more of a "mental crutch" than a physical necessity. In 2003, Dean used a chair only to change shoes. He did his eating and drinking "on the run," and didn't take any rest breaks, all of which leads to Dean's best piece of advice for the budding Badwater competitor, a phrase which originated with Winston Churchill:

When you're going through hell, don't stop.

2003 Finishing Time – 28:51:26
First Place Male
Second Place Overall

CHAPTER THREE – MONICA SCHOLZ

From Monica's 2003 Badwater Application:

Age: 36
Ontario, Canada

My Most Challenging Race Experience:

San Diego One Day. 24 hours around a track proved to be the most daunting mental and physical challenge I've ever experienced. Staying focused and injury free proved to be tough.

Why I want a slot on the start line of the 2003 Badwater Ultramarathon:

Badwater became my favorite race when I ran it last year. I made a lot of mistakes that I would like to try to correct this year.

NIGHT FEVER *BY SCOTT LUDWIG*

People enjoy being around Monica Scholz.

How else would you explain people virtually lining up to accompany Monica to Death Valley – during the hottest month of the year – to spend the better part of two days waiting on her hand and foot – that is, if you aren't summoned to run by her side for several miles in temperatures as high as 130 degree,

Such is the case with Monica, whose actions speak louder than words as she celebrates life as one big wild, wonderful party – with the whole world as her guests.

Monica Scholz made her Badwater debut in 2002, finishing as the third place female in a time of 38:33. Prior to her Death Valley debut she had already completed 46 100-mile races in an incredibly short span of time: 45 months. In her first full calendar year of running ultras (2000), she posted 16 100-mile finishes including first female honors in four of them (Lost Soul, Haliburton, Heartland and Ancient Oaks). In 2001 she upped the ante and completed 23 100-mile events (which at the time was the most 100-mile finishes in one calendar year by either man or woman; more on that later in the book), including being the first female in nine of them: HURT, Umstead, Mount Rushmore, KISS, Heartland, Dan Rossi, Canadian Rockies, Ancient Oaks and San Diego.

It should be noted that in four of those nine Monica was not only the first female but also the first overall finisher as she continued to improve her standing in the ultrarunning community. An indication of her improvement is seen in her finishing times in two events she won both years: Heartland – 23:18 in 2000 and 20:32 in 2001 – and Ancient Oaks – 23:30 in 2000 and 22:23 in 2001). Two of her more impressive finishes in 2001 were a 19:35 finish at Rocky Raccoon and 23:53 at the Western States Endurance Run, which placed her as the 11th female in the latter in a very competitive field of elite women.

Monica first became intrigued with the thought of running Badwater when she met Lisa Smith-Batchen several years prior at Western States. Monica listened intently as Lisa told tales of Badwater as well as the Marathon des Sables (another race Monica would run in 2002, an event she entered after additional encouragement from Angelika Castaneda, the 1999 Badwater Women's Champion). After all, Monica had already decided that 2002 would be her "Year of Doing Something Different."

The 2002 Badwater Ultramarathon was not what Monica had anticipated. She expected it to be hot, she was familiar with the road surfaces she would be running on, but she didn't realize the severity of the mountains she would be encountering. Using the crew who had supported Angelika in 1999, Monica began the race with one strategy in mind: Keep doing what has worked in the past.

But Badwater is different, and what may work in a 100-mile event sometimes doesn't translate to 135 miles across a blistering desert and up three mountain ranges. The sleep breaks she had lined up were an exercise in futility. Monica vividly recalls scheduling a sleep break (with cot!) at Father Crowley (around mile 80); even though the sun was going down and she was physically and mentally tired, she simply could not sleep. So after lying on the cot for literally seconds, she got up and said "I'm running." As Monica began to experience a rush of anxiety as she neared the finish, she received an assist from an unlikely source: her 72-year old mother, who calmed Monica down and accompanied her for the first five miles of the treacherous 13-mile ascent to the finish. To this day Monica says that experience prepared her for handling the grueling demands of the final 13 miles of the race on Portal Road.

Monica admits she made many mistakes in her initial Badwater, and sought to improve on her performance in 2003. She enlisted the aid of her friend and coach/mentor/runner extraordinaire Lisa, who provided Monica with a wealth of advice she took to heart (The one that stands out the most? Putting ice in your hat and scarf to keep cool). Lisa arranged for Marie Boyd (an operating room nurse from Bishop, California) to be Monica's crew chief. Marie would later go on to be Monica's crew chief the next five Badwaters in which she competed. The arrangement, obviously, worked.

A better-prepared, more 'under control' Monica – complete with a "super crew" – comfortably finished Badwater in 2003. Monica approached the race competitively, and knew there were several runners ahead of her in the latter stages of the race. She understood Pam Reed and Dean Karnazes were 'battling somewhere up ahead' and ran alone for quite a while until she caught up with Chris Bergland (*Look! A runner!*), who had led the race for 100 miles, on Portal Road. Monica and Chris hit it off and stayed together for several miles. As is wont to happen in the throes of competition as intense as Badwater, the two would soon become fast friends. In fact, in time Monica and Chris would both be sponsored by (Badwater sponsor) Kiehl's and at one time they contemplated competing in the "Race across America' as a two-person team (alas, the idea fell through, but what a team the two would have made!).

Monica ultimately crossed the finish line of the 2003 Badwater Ultramarathon as the second place woman and third place overall finisher.

Getting back to the "people enjoy being around Monica Scholz" part: In 2003 Monica was supported by 10 crewmembers and four vehicles (in a later Badwater her "high water mark" would be 12 crewmembers and six vehicles!). A contingent this large allows for crewmembers to be "on duty" for six hours, and to sleep and/or party in the reserved hotel rooms along the way when they are "off duty." As for the "one big wild, wonderful party" part, each year Monica adopts a "theme" for Badwater. In 2003, the first year Monica adopted this festive approach to the toughest footrace on the planet, the theme was the music of the popular pop group the Bee Gees. Other runners and crewmembers from Badwater in 2003 can still hear Monica and members of her crew singing "Staying Alive" as her rolling party made its merry way over the mountains well into the night. (In 2009 the theme was "So Divine." Imagine big burly male crewmembers dressed in drag singing, hooping and hollering across Death Valley in the middle of a dark summer night – that, my friends, is ONE BIG PARTY!)

Monica returned to Badwater in 2004 with an even more definitive game plan in mind: she would implement a strategic "walk/run" method suggested by none other than her friend Lisa. The approach was simple: on the flats run for eight minutes and walk for two; on the hills run for four minutes and walk for one. Even though she admits Pam Reed "blew by her" early in the race, Monica stuck with her game plan from the very first step. Ultimately it paid off: Monica, in only her third attempt at Badwater, was the first female finisher in an impressive 29:22:29. Perhaps even more impressive is that Monica was the third overall finisher, and was less than two hours behind Dean Karnazes and Ferg Hawke, who endured one of the most memorable battles in history for first place! Monica would go on to be the first female finisher again in 2006. In 2007 Monica saw "how the other half lived" and crewed for one of her former crewmembers who was competing in his first Badwater.

Badwater will always be one of Monica's favorite events. She believes the key to success lies not in overcoming the heat ("you know it's going to be hot, so you can prepare for it"), but in finding a strategy to handle the mountains. She must be on to something: How else do you explain her incredible improvements at Badwater in her first three attempts?

- **2002:** 38:33   *3rd Female, 7th Overall*

- **2003:** 33:41   *2nd Female, 3rd Overall*

- **2004:** 29:22   *1st Female, 3rd Overall*

Also, be sure to remember you're on this planet to celebrate life – one big wild, wonderful party.

2003 Finishing Time – 33:41:29
Third Place

CHAPTER FOUR – CHRIS BERGLAND

From Chris' 2003 Badwater Application:

Age: 37
New York City, New York

Qualifying Standard:

I have won the Odyssey Adventure Racing Triple Ironman (7.2 mile swim, 336 mile bike, 78.6 mile run) for the past three years.

Why I want a slot on the start line of the 2003 Badwater Ultramarathon:

I guess I could say that the reason I want to do Badwater is I have done the Triple Ironman for the past three years and I am looking for a new challenge. The truth is I don't have an intellectual reason for wanting to do the race. I just kind of feel it in my bones. I love Death Valley. I love the desert. I like heat. I keep imagining about what they sky would look like at night. And how bright the sun will be during the day.

ROOKIE MISTAKES *BY CHRIS BERGLAND WITH SCOTT LUDWIG*

Until Chris Bergland heard the word "Badwater" from the gentleman who owned Zoot Sports one year while competing at Kona, he had no idea what was in store for him. Chris remembers the descriptions of the Grand Pianos in Death Valley and became instantly intrigued.

After competing in triathlons for several years, Chris had the good fortune of having a sponsor support him in official trademarked Ironman events all over the world. As an athlete Chris was sponsored by Kiehl's; after all, the Kiehl's store was right around the corner from where he lived and – coincidently, he happened to work there.

It just so happens that the sponsor of the Badwater Ultramarathon was none other than Kiehl's. So it was a natural evolution for Chris Bergland, triathlete extraordinaire, to represent his company in the toughest footrace on the planet.

In 2003, the owners of Kiehl's, Jami Morse and Klaus Von Heiddeger were both incredible athletes. The store, a small family-owned apothecary, had been located on the same corner since 1851. Chris asked Jami and Klaus if they would send him to compete at Badwater. Since both had a deep love for adventure, they agreed.

Chris flew into Los Angeles prior to the race and was met by his life-long friends Bobby Lavelle and David Ketterling, who had both flown in from New York. They stocked up on what Chris calls "real" food (i.e. not Powerbars or Gu which had a habit of jump-starting Chris' gag reflex during Ironman competitions): grapes, cantaloupe, watermelon, salt-n-vinegar potato chips, pretzels, and the necessary fixings for ham and Swiss cheese sandwiches.

Prior to the race Chris had prepared well mentally; however, he never examined a map that would have shown him what the Badwater Ultramarathon had in store for him. It was evident, though what the *heat* had in store for him, as while he was attending the pre-race meeting in Furnace Creek, all of the suntan lotion and water bottles in his support vehicle exploded.

ESPN the Magazine followed Chris at Badwater. The experience resulted in a memorable article, "The Road to Hell," which describes what Chris was going through physically as well as psychologically at various checkpoints along the course. Here are a few of the highlights:

- At the starting line, Chris is "eerily calm." However, his rookie support crew – big sister Renee, little sister Sandy, Bobby Lavelle and a writer from the magazine – are not quite as calm. Prior to Chris' start in the 10:00 a.m. wave, he makes one last attempt at tying his running shoes "just right" and, of course, clearing out his bowels.

- At the first checkpoint in Furnace Creek (17 miles) Chris has problems with a charley horse in his right knee –oddly enough brought on by the long flight to California to compete, and a cracked rib courtesy of a collision with a fellow cyclist a mere month ago. As Chris reaches the first checkpoint in first place, the 128-degree heat doesn't appear to bother him and he asks his crew innocently, "is it hot?'

- At Stovepipe Wells (mile 42) the crew is busy dousing Chris in water as the temperature has climbed another two degrees. Chris tells them he doesn't feel the heat within his body; just a "warm glow" from how well the race is going. Nine miles later he coughs up most of the apricot energy bar he just ate.

- At Panamint Springs (mile 72) it begins to get dark. Chris is still in first place and singing "Up Where We Belong." The temperature is now a cool 110 degrees and Chris is satisfied with his downhill pace. However, once the imminent climb begins, sleep deprivation and darkness consume him. The lights on the horizon produce a mirage effect; in reality, the lights are *much* farther away than they appear. In fact, so much that this illusion begins to sink Chris' spirit.

- At 90 miles Chris remains lucid; however the race is beginning to extract its revenge from the Badwater rookie: fallen rocks pose a distraction and the camber of the road is abusing his legs. Chris is torn between running and walking: *Which is better for me at this point?* He learns that the defending Badwater champion, Pam Reed is close on his heels; however, he also learns that she is struggling as well. Chris opts for walking, and his elation is now being replaced with dejection.

- After 111 miles, Chris stops without warning, drops his shorts and empties out his intestines "in one explosion." Pam Reed takes the lead at this point, but Chris continues along until yet another "accident" (read: *explosion*) fills his shorts with "burning acid." Big sister and little sister tend to him, wet-wiping him clean. Twenty-four miles remain.

- Four miles later Chris collapses into the back of his support vehicle. His face is ashen white and his lips are a death-like blue and green. The rookie crew fears a fatal heatstroke, but once his temperature is known to be fluctuating between 97 and 101.3 degrees they know Chris is out of serious danger. Chilled soda cans are applied to his groin and armpits. As Chris shivers from the cold and his body becomes engulfed in goose bumps, a medic advises him to relax and rest. Within an hour Chris is back on his feet and back on the course.

- At Lone Pine (mile 122) Chris' spirit is now broken. The recent rest sessions have caused his leg to swell. Falling out of first place has affected his will. The altitude has become suffocating, and his body appears as if it has been artificially inflated. He repeats the 9/11-inspired motto of "Stay Strong: We are New York."

- It takes Chris an agonizing five hours and 15 minutes to cover the remaining 13 miles to the finish. An hour later his crew helps him into bed. Chris is too tired to either eat or move at this point. He admits that he feels like he has been "ripped in half."

- Three weeks later Chris' legs are still numb. Four toenails have fallen out. He's removed a large patch of skin from his severely blistered foot. Another week later he is still having nightmares about his physical and psychological breakdown. Yet, he is having dreams about returning to Badwater in 2004 to "conquer hell."

Chris returned to Badwater one year later, but dropped out of the race at Stovepipe Wells.

In 2005 Chris again competed at Badwater. He finished in 8th place with a finishing time of 34:23. Chris completed the final 13 miles in five hours.

As for the 2003 event, Chris realizes he went out too fast, but still had "the best experience of his life."

If he were to compete at Badwater again, he would look for a way to minimize the water getting into his socks and make amends for having one of the slowest climbs over those last 13 miles to the finish line on Mount Whitney.

Three very positive things Chris took with him from Badwater in 2003 are the friendships he forged with fellow competitors Pam Reed, Dean Karnazes and Monica Scholz – friendships still as strong as the Death Valley sun is hot.

2003 Finishing Time – 33:58:37
Fourth Place

CHAPTER FIVE – SCOTT LUDWIG

From Scott's 2003 Badwater Application:

Age: 48;
Peachtree City, Georgia

Why I Run Ultras:

I've been successful at them over the years (I kind of sensed this in high school because in 10th grade I could run the 600 yard run better than anyone in my class that didn't throw up afterwards). Running 5-10% slower than I do in marathons makes an incredible difference in what I'm able to accomplish over distances of 50K and up. As I'm getting older and losing my speed, ultras are more and more appealing to me.

JUST CREW IT *BY SCOTT LUDWIG*

My wife Cindy gave me the movie *Running on the Sun*, a documentary of the 1999 Badwater Ultramarathon for a gift on Father's Day 2001. As I watched it and saw the variety of pain and discomfort the runners experienced running across Death Valley, all I could say was "been there," "been there" and "been there." When the movie came to a close, I said in no uncertain terms "I'm doing it." (Cindy, who had been in the kitchen, noticing what the runners in the movie were going through quickly replied "no you're not." She didn't have a prayer.)

For me to one day run Badwater was, as they say a "no-brainer." A couple years later when I signed the Badwater Ultramarathon waiver, specifically the statement "I realize I may die participating in this event," I couldn't help but think that "no-brainer" took on an entirely new meaning.

From my perspective, I knew that deep down inside I had been training for almost a decade for something special; I just wasn't sure exactly what. I'd been putting in well over 90 miles a week during that time while maintaining a requiring 50-hour-a-week job and a household with a wife, two sons and our black Labrador "Magic." I learned to survive on five hours sleep, literally (as I called it) "training to exhaustion." I knew that one day my decade-long sacrifice had a purpose: I just didn't know it would take me to Death Valley to compete in the planet's toughest footrace.

Now for the really hard part: finding a few people who would be willing to crew for me. Not only would they need to sacrifice a week of their respective lives; they would need to be in top physical (not to mention mental) shape to endure the challenges of the harshest environment they had ever encountered.

Surprisingly, the search for a crew didn't take long at all:

Al Barker

Al Barker and I had been running 20 miles every Sunday morning together since Thanksgiving 1993. We had been to hundreds of races together during this time and became great friends. Ten years my senior, Al sported personal bests that mirrored mine in races of virtually every distance from the mile to the marathon (Al is quick to point out that he ran a sub-five minute mile – I never did, but I always counter with me breaking 2:50 in the marathon – which *he* never did). I'll have to give him credit, though: After running with him for ten years I wasn't running anywhere near the fast times he had been running ten years earlier – back when he was my age.

Asking Al if he would crew for me at Badwater was (yes, I'm going to use the phrase one more time) a no-brainer. He eagerly accepted and we both decided we needed to focus on increasing our mileage and getting acclimated to the conditions we would face in the desert. We increased our mileage, occasionally putting in 30 or 35 miles on Sunday. We also believed our training in the heat and humidity of Atlanta,

Georgia would probably translate well to the *extremely* hot yet arid conditions in Death Valley. In time we would discover that our assumption was correct. The desert heat would ultimately be one of the least of our worries, however.

Gary Griffin

I met Gary Griffin at the three-mile mark of the Callaway Gardens Marathon in January 2002. He was sporting a Gulf Winds Track Club singlet – a club Al had been a member of when he lived in Tallahassee, Florida before he moved to Atlanta – and I introduced myself and asked if he knew Al. Gary didn't know Al, but after Gary and I ran the remaining 23 miles of the marathon together – talking every step of the way (in all honesty Gary did most of the talking and I did most of the listening), I did know that in time the two of them would become friends. You see, I did manage to mention to Gary that one day I wanted to run the Badwater Ultramarathon and he said he wanted to be a part of it.

Eighteen months later Gary would get to know Al; in fact he'd get to know Al very well.

Paula May

I met Paula May at a summer track meet in Peachtree City, Georgia in 1999. Less than a year later she became part of our regular Sunday morning 20-mile group and became quite an accomplished masters runner in the southeast, regular winning her division in distances from 5K to the marathon. A physician's assistant anesthetist by trade, Paula – knowing I would need a person in the medical in-the-know at Badwater – volunteered her services. I quickly accepted and in time Paula developed an elaborate plan to ensure I would be getting the proper nutrition, fluids and calories as I made my way across Death Valley.

I asked Paula to be my Crew Chief. She gladly accepted.

Eric Huguelet

I met Eric Huguelet by way of Paula May. You see, Eric is Paula's husband. At first I'd see him every once in a while – usually at the annual Peachtree Road Race where we'd meet in Piedmont Park after the race and drink a few beers. In time Eric would occasionally join us on Sunday mornings as well as for an occasional marathon. However, in time what Eric and I enjoyed most was playing Darkside (the name of our running club) golf, which meant one of two things: (1) there are no rules and/or (2) rules can be made up along the way. Don't like that five-iron you just hit into the woods? No worries; try another. Just missed that two-foot putt? No worries; keep putting until you make it. Hit your drive out of bounds? No worries; I'm dropping a ball next to your drive you put 250 yards down the middle of the fairway. You get the idea.

Eric was the first to suggest I practice *walking* – and more specifically *walking uphill* in preparation for Badwater. One of my biggest regrets to this day is that his suggestion was made less than a month before the actual race.

Josh Ludwig

I have known Josh his entire life. Since the day he was born, in fact. Josh is the youngest of my two sons, and the only one who took an interest in running. He started running when he was six years old, and by the time he was 10 was running 18 minute 5K's, 40 minute 10K's and one memorable 76:36 10-miler that would have bettered the Georgia state age group record by over nine minutes – had the course been certified.

Josh took an interest in other sports as well. He was particularly adept at soccer and basketball, but managed to find time for a little baseball and football as well. As children are apt to do, in time he experienced a "sports burnout" in high school, which served as the perfect time to ask him to be on my Badwater crew. After all, isn't that the dream summer vacation for most 17-year olds?

Well, maybe "dream" isn't quite the right word, but Josh reluctantly became the fifth and final member of my Badwater crew.

The Crew

Overall my crew was in excellent physical condition. Al and Paula were accomplished marathoners, and Eric was not far behind. Gary was a talented and experienced ultrarunner; and Josh was in great physical shape and had the added advantage of youth on his side.

The crew and I met several times to go over our Badwater game plan. We met with a veteran Badwater crewmember, Andy Velazco, as well as with an experienced Badwater crew chief, David Sowers: both had successfully supported their respective runners in the past. The advice and information was invaluable, and quite honestly I don't think we would have had as good an experience in the desert without their help.

I knew the crew was just as committed and excited about Badwater as I was – if that's possible. They quickly adopted the slogan "Just Crew It."

I couldn't help but think that if you said the slogan really fast it could just have easily been "Just Screw It." Just in case, you know.

The Runner

I'll be the first to admit that once I received my official acceptance into the 2003 Badwater Ultramarathon, every day as I finished my run I would visualize myself crossing the finish line on Mount Whitney. I knew in my heart and without a doubt I would make it – I just didn't know if I would be competitive or if I would be bringing up the rear. But I was absolutely confident in the fact that I would finish.

I gave my crew a simple list of **Badwater Don'ts**:

Don't:

*   Tell me my injuries (if I have any) are bad (downplay them, please!).

*   Tell me where I stand relative to others in the race (in my mind, if I was running well and no one was in sight, I wanted to believe everyone else had dropped out and I was winning).

*   Feel sorry for me.

*   Complain (*not in front of me*, anyway).

*   Let my shoes and/or socks get wet.

*   Force me to eat (you *can* force me to ingest liquid calories, however).

*   Question what I want to eat (trust me – it won't be much).

*   Let me start out too fast.

*   Panic if I fall behind my game plan/time table.

*   Allow me to waste energy/motion.

*   Allow me to look at any blisters, etc.

*   Share our team goals with others.

The Badwater *Do's*? Didn't have any.

How did the crew fare, you ask? One at a time, here's how they did:

Al

Al was responsible for driving the backup support vehicle, a four-door sedan. The backup vehicle was essential for critical errands (ice, emergency popsicles when I craved them) as well as being on standby should anything happen to the primary support vehicle, a large van. Fortunately it was never needed for the latter. He also accompanied me as a pacer on several occasions.

Al would later admit that it took a full month for him to recover from the Badwater experience, only to add that he didn't regret it for a minute and loved every second of it.

The moment the other members of the crew talk about all the time is something Al said in the middle of Death Valley. Paula was meticulously recording the "input" and "output" of both me and the members of the crew to ensure we were all properly hydrating and eating. At one point both vehicles drove ahead to a predetermined spot where they waited for me to take my next break. Once they got there Al walked off into the desert, bent behind a bush and returned to the vehicles uttering the most memorable line of the adventure: "Put me down for a turd."

However, the most notable comment from Al was something he wrote after our week out west:

> *Being a part of it, even in such a small way is one of those times in life that*
> *I will never forget. Someone once said that "going for a run with good friends*
> *is one of life's greatest joys." And what a run it was!*

Gary

Gary had a secondary motive at Badwater: He wanted to determine if one day he would be willing to give it a try himself. With that in mind Gary volunteered to run most of the race with me from Furnace Creek to Townes Pass – a distance of over 40 miles (Gary would ultimately accompany me for approximately 60 miles). In Gary's role as "spiritual advisor" (which I anointed him with), he lived up to his job description doing everything he could to keep my spirits up and keep my body moving. Gary ran beside me carrying two water bottles: one for me to drink and the other to pour on me to keep me cool. What Gary *didn't* use much of the water for was for *him*, which ultimately led him on a desperate search for medical assistance in Panamint Springs. After consuming some water and sodium, Gary was eventually able to return to pace me through some of the faster miles we covered between the Darwin Turnoff (mile 90) and Lone Pine (mile 122).

During the stretch leading to Stovepipe Wells Gary proved one of the myths of the Death Valley heat to be true when the sole of one of his running shoes melted while he was pacing me through the desert.

So, after all that what did Gary say to his wife Peg when she asked him after we finished if he would one day give Badwater a shot? An emphatic "NO!"

But, as Gary wrote afterwards: "as is often the case in ultrarunning, (in time) it always gets better. Never say never."

Paula

Paula was a masterful crew chief. Keeping the peace amongst a crew of five in the most undesirable and inhospitable environment imaginable – while ensuring that the runner is supported every step of the way during a 135-mile odyssey is indeed quite a challenge. But Paula pulled it off.

In fact, Paula knew that it would be "detrimental to the mission"(as she called it) if any of my aforementioned "Don't-s"were not followed. She also realized that it was not in my best interest to tell me anything negative – regardless of how big or small.

Which is why she didn't allow anyone in the crew to tell me someone temporarily lost my credit card which they were using to purchase gas, ice and whatever else we needed along the way. Or that she and Gary had a slight "disagreement" about my hydration plan immediately after the pre-race meeting at Furnace Creek the day before the race. Or that I had fallen behind my time/game plan during the long uphill climb from Panamint Springs to the Darwin Turnoff. Way behind.

Paula was a rock from start to finish. I think the only break she took was when we were at the Panamint Springs Resort. I requested a five-minute nap once we had covered 72 miles (it was now pre-dawn on the second day) so that I could mentally divide the first day from the second day. Paula and I each took one of the twin beds, and although I'm not sure if Paula ever dozed off, I *do* know that in what seemed like a lot less than five minutes Paula was telling me "that's it – time to go.' And off we went.

When I developed the only blister of the race (picture in your mind a cherry tomato balanced between the second and third toe on the *top* of your left foot), Paula did a masterful job doctoring it. I also learned that Paula is arguably the best sock-changer-for-someone-else in the world. At Lone Pine, after 122 miles, Paula made the best cup of Ramen noodles anyone has ever cooked on the radiator of a car. Paula May: Crew Chief Extraordinaire.

Eric

Eric was the primary driver of the team van, a thankless job requiring him to drive usually one mile at a time, pull over on the side of the road, open the back of the van and help the crew get any fluid, food and/or gear ready for me once I got there. However, through it all his sense of humor and positive attitude remained a breath of fresh air.

Eric was also assigned the role of "designated uphill walker." Officially the Badwater Ultramarathon has 46 miles of uphill with a total elevation gain of 13,000 feet. Eric was by my side for most of them, ironic in a way as he was the one who mentioned I should have done more walking (specifically *uphill* walking, remember?) in my preparation for Badwater.

Eric also made sure I didn't waste any motion late in the race when I wanted to retrace my steps to check out a dead animal (a bat, I believe) on the side of the road.

Lastly, Eric was the videographer of our desert adventure. A few months after Badwater the crew and I were all treated to the premiere of the 55-minute film *Running on the Sun Redux*, "starring" none other than yours truly and a supporting cast of five.

Josh

Josh was the anchor of the crew, and outside of one minor mistake when he informed me at the Darwin Turnoff that we were in 8th place ("Don't tell me where I stand relative to others in the race'), his performance was peerless.

Josh paced me for one incredible mile around 100 miles into the race. Eric, after driving ahead mentioned there was another runner about a mile in front of me, and at our current pace we would catch him in about five miles. I looked over at Josh and asked him if he wanted to run hard until we caught him. Josh, chomping at the bit to run hard replied yes, and after an 8:15 mile we caught him (Charlie Engle) and took over 7th place. (About 30 minutes later this entire sequence played out again almost identically – although this time I was running with Gary, and soon we were in 6th place.)

Paula may have said it best in a note she wrote to Josh afterwards:

I know your dad is as proud of you as I am for being a great team player, always having a positive attitude, being available to run, pacing your dad through some of those difficult hot miles before Lone Pine, and being my go-fer. There were so many tedious tasks that I needed done, and you were always there to handle them. I'm so glad you were part of the crew.

So was I, Josh. So was I.

The Finish

The crew made one critical mistake near the end of the race: They failed to reset the odometer of the van when we began the final 13-mile ascent up Mount Whitney. In all of our preparatory meetings we had been advised that the runner would want to know *precisely* how much distance was left to the finish line during this final stretch. I'm here to tell you that we had been advised correctly: I must have asked every 45 seconds or so "how much now"(i.e. how much further to the finish line)? When you're progressing (notice I didn't say "running," or even "walking," for that matter) up Mount Whitney after covering 122 miles across Death Valley and over two mountain ranges, you want to know exactly how much is left until it's over.

Finishing at night made matters worse, as every headlight of any vehicle driving down the mountain appeared to be the lights that in my tired mind indicated the finish line. Of course they weren't, so for the final 90 minutes of the race I saw what I thought (*wished!*) was the "finish line" at least three dozen times.

With two miles to go Eric drove to the finish line, parked the van and promised to run back to the "one mile remaining" point so that we could all run the final mile together. Eric left the video camera with someone at the finish line to record our finish. Eventually we met up with Eric and 25 minutes later we finally... *finally* were crossing the finish line together at the Whitney Portal. No more 133-degree heat. No more mountains. No more Ramen noodles, lost credit cards or *Running on the Sun*.

We did it.

Footnote: I couldn't have done it – any of it, without my crew. To this day whenever I talk about our Badwater adventure I refer to the experience with the pronoun "we."

It was the ultimate team effort, pure and simple.

2003 Finishing Time – 36:32:46
Sixth Place

CHAPTER SIX – LUIS ESCOBAR

Age: 40
Santa Maria, California

From Luis' 2003 Badwater Application:

Why I Run Ultras:

Most people never get the chance to do something really big. Most of us live a prepackaged, freeze-dried, artificially sweetened, predictable life. Get up, go to work, drive home, go to bed, get up, go to work, drive home, go to bed… Ultrarunning is not predictable. Ultrarunning is real. Ultrarunning has taken me across the country, to the highest peaks, to the lowest valleys, through steamy swamps and dark tropical jungles. I have seen a lot but there is much more yet to see. Distance running is part of my life; I do it, because I like it!

Why I want a slot on the start line of the 2003 Badwater Ultramarathon:

Like any craftsman, a runner is never fully satisfied. One lesson must lead to the next. Badwater is the next logical step in my progression as a long distance runner.

AN EXTREME ADVENTURE *By Luis Escobar*

I write this a mere two days after my crew and I walked across the finish line of the Badwater 135-mile Ultramarathon. We are home now and back to normal life. My face is peeling and the swelling in my feet and legs have gone down and I am once again able to walk unassisted up and down the stairs to my bedroom. I have been running and racing for more than 15 years. I have seen a lot of races and been to a lot places, but I have never seen anything quite like Badwater! Everything about the Badwater Ultramarathon is extreme and larger than life. The people, the places, the conditions and the event are all served up in epic proportions.

Between the start and finish there could be a 60-degree temperature difference. As if that's not enough of a challenge for you, there are three windswept desert valleys; three gigantic mountain ranges; 135 long, hot, and unforgiving miles; and enough running experiences to last a lifetime. Badwater is a big league racecourse with approximately 69 flat miles, 20 downhill miles and 46 uphill (up-mountain?) miles. All of them share one element: They are undoubtedly *hot*! The temperature in Death Valley seems to vary from place to place and is based on the season, time of day, wind speed and direction. It is always hot, but some places are hotter than others. As my crew and I sat by the pool in Stovepipe Wells two nights before the race, the air temperature was 110 degrees. At midnight! It was already well over 110 degrees when we started running on Tuesday morning at 10:00 a.m.

My fellow competitors were a qualified collection of elite ultra distance athletes from around the world. Race Director Chris Kostman hand selects each athlete from resumes submitted to him months in advance. On the starting line I could hear people talking in several different languages. In the race was a diverse collection of athletes from Germany, Monaco, Tahiti, England, France, Canada, Switzerland, Brazil and Mexico.

As diverse as their backgrounds may have been, they had a few things in common: They were all big time, hard ass, no-nonsense kind of people. The extremists of the extreme. Each one touted an impressive biography and a list of credentials a mile long; some arguably 135 miles long. These people meant business. It was more than a little intimidating to line up with runners of this fine caliber. Everyone at Badwater is talented. Polished. Trained. Eager. My heart rate was a pounding 161 beats per minute as I stood on the starting line. I was surrounded by an excited group of international running celebrities. These are the same people I had been reading about for months and now, here I was lined up with them about to start the longest and most challenging running event of my career.

We are standing in the deepest pit of Death Valley. It is 9:59 a.m., 115 degrees, my heart is pounding, the stage is set, and it is now time to run. This is Badwater. The racecourse is paved and runs point to point. The road seems endless before you; a long black ribbon on a bed of white sand fading into the horizon miles and miles away. We are required to run on the left side of the road (towards traffic), while our pace vehicles were required to drive along on the right side.

My crew consisted of my wife Beverly, Major Mark Johnson (2002 Badwater- 5th place in 36:30) and his wife Lynn, and my buddy Doug Rich.

Anyone who has ever run an ultra will tell you it is definitely a team sport. The Badwater event supplies no aid, so obviously your crew is essential. Without two reliable vehicles, a good pacer and a solid support team one has no chance of crossing the finish line on Mount Whitney. While the mind-numbing heat, incredulous winds and majestic landscape are distractions, the road becomes the runner's primary focus.

I was attired in white from head to toe. Long sleeves, long pants, a sun hat, dark glasses and a wet towel pinned around my head and neck. The bill of my hat and the towel pulled tight around my face served to create an illusion of tunnel vision. For hours at a time I would be looking straight down; seeing only the black road and endless white line that would eventually lead me to the finish.

About 15 miles from Stovepipe Wells, our little desert caravan had a surprise: My friend and fellow distance runner Greg Pirkl and his girlfriend Evelyn appeared on the course. Greg is in the service and had just returned home from a five-month tour of duty in Iraq. Greg and Evelyn took turns running with me through the hottest part of the day. It was a thrill to see Greg and hear about his time in the war.

As we approached Stovepipe Wells the thermometer in one of our pace vehicles read 134 degrees! The air temperature is one thing, but the surface temperature of the black asphalt road is another and usually much higher. Some race veterans say that the surface temperatures can reach 200 degrees! My feet were cooking inside the shoes I had lined with heavy-duty aluminum foil. Until that day in the desert blisters had never been a real issue for me. Naturally I've had blisters in the past, but nothing like this. The blistering started around 60 miles when the course begins a long decent into the Panamint Valley. The heat and friction from running downhill caused the skin on my heels and toes to slowly rub off. The pain was nearly unbearable.

At several points throughout the race we were forced to stop and repair my feet. Lynn had taken the time to learn all she could about foot injuries and blister care from race veteran Denise Jones. Without Lynn's help I would have never finished the race. The idea is to cut the blister open with a knife or razor blade. The opening has to be big enough so the skin can't reconnect. Then she would squeeze out all of the hot bloody fluid, apply some antibacterial ointment, followed by a coat of adhesive, a very thin fabric bandage, more glue, and finally tape on top of everything. The entire process would take about 10 minutes per blister. It was very frustrating, time-consuming and painful.

The Montrail Shoe Company was very supportive and generous with me. They were generous enough to supply me with shoes for the run. The shoes were working fine but my feet had swollen and needed relief. Eventually we cut off the top, front part of my shoes, exposing my throbbing blistered toes. Having fun so far?

At night it is very dark in the desert. This night was lit up by lightning storms far off in the distance. Running at night is always a challenge. It is sometimes difficult to stay awake. We stopped twice during the race for 20 to 30 minutes at a time to sleep. We would sleep on the ground or on the tailgate of the truck.

When the sun came up on day two we were somewhere around 90 miles and just past the Panamint Mountain Range on our way to the Darwin checkpoint. An early morning rainstorm cleaned the road and temporarily cooled things down a bit. It was a welcomed surprise that didn't last long; soon the temperature shot back into the low 100's. We had been on the course for nearly 24 hours and the blisters, long miles, relentless heat and sheer exhaustion were taking their toll.

I never considered quitting, but at this point all I wanted to do was finish.

We continued through the Owens Valley, eventually reaching the town of Lone Pine and the final 13-mile assent to the Mount Whitney finish line. There are only three major climbs on the course and they saved the best for last. It is just shy of a 4,000-foot climb to the finish line and by this point all I could do was to hike. At a very slow pace.

We finally arrived at the Mount Whitney Portals at 11:19 p.m. on Wednesday, July 23. We had been on the course long enough to see the sun rise and set twice. But now it was over. Doug, Mark, Lynn, Beverly and I crossed the finish line of the Badwater 135-Mile Ultramarathon together. It was the moment we had been working towards for months.

The Badwater 135 Mile Ultra Marathon is an ambitious but reasonable goal. If you are interested in attempting this epic run, here is my advice:

DO:
- Become familiar with the course.
- Contact Ben and Denise Jones.
- Blister Prevention: tape your feet.
- Arrive prepared for anything.
- Become familiar with the course

DON'T:
- Run shirtless.
- Try anything new.
- Underestimate the course.
- Overestimate your abilities.

2003 Finishing Time – 37:19:18
Seventh Place

© image sportfotodienst/Norbert Schmidt

CHAPTER SEVEN – LOUISE COOPER

From Louise's 2003 Badwater Application:

Age: 49
West Hills, California

Why I want a slot on the start line of the 2003 Badwater Ultramarathon:

To experience the desert, the people, and the race… once again.

THE FIGHT OF MY LIFE *By Louise Cooper*

Badwater!

The name alone should make you wonder, or at the very least catch your attention. Most people I know still refer to it as "that Badlands race." Perhaps that is a more appropriate name for an event that has the power and ability to destroy the mightiest of men and women.

I had heard of the event, wanted to do it, but had not paid much attention to it as it conflicted with my competitions in adventure races in more exotic locales around the world. Death Valley, while being an amazing place to visit with a beauty and intrigue of its own, was still not on my radar as I planned my race schedule in places on other continents I deemed more appealing at the time.

In 1998 I was sidelined from racing as I started the biggest race of my life – a race against time after being diagnosed with a very aggressive form of breast cancer. An inconvenient illness at its best, it frustrated me as it upset my happy and active lifestyle. As I watched my friends leave for events in which I was entered, I realized I needed another goal, something to help keep me focused as I battled my way though months of heavy chemotherapy and radiation. Enter my good friend Lisa Smith-Batchen. "The timing is perfect" she stated with authority. "You'll be finished with most of your treatment and will have about five months to train." Her enthusiasm and encouragement led me to the start line of Badwater in 1999, while still undergoing weekly IV infusions of the drug Herceptin to hopefully keep my type of cancer from recurring. I was smitten. There was definitely something to this insanity. Happy to be active and racing again, I returned to my adventure racing life and rejoined my team. Life was good.

Badwater (there's that name again) was always in the back of my mind. *Hmmmm, five months after chemo, I built my body back, rebuilt my muscles, and was able to compete in that monstrous race finishing in 40 hours and 14 minutes. I wonder if I could do better not coming off of that horrid treatment.*

The fact I was four years older never entered my mind! Of course, registration was already closed, and I had to beg, plead and make promises I could never deliver to the Race Director to allow me to enter this late. Finally he relented, and now I had a bib number. With mixed feelings of both excitement and doom, I approached my friends. The same people who had leaped at the idea of crewing for me in 1999 now looked at me with total horror! All voiced the same sentiments. "You're kidding! Why? Didn't you learn the first time?" were common ones. Then I heard words like insane, loony, deranged, demented, crazy, and idiotic. Knowing what a commitment it is, I was treading lightly as I made my plans. I knew friends would step up to the plate. All I had to do was show my own commitment. Sure enough, they did.

I had plenty of support training for the event, as long as I was running in the cool of the day. Why would anyone want to run in the San Fernando Valley after 9:00 a.m. during the summer? I had learned from the first time that getting acclimated to the heat was key, so once again I started running in the heat of the day, driving around the valley with my heater on and the windows closed at midday, and sitting and often running in the sauna at the gym.

The air conditioner in my home became a piece of non-functional artwork, and the ceiling fans went on sabbatical. Before the school year was over, the air conditioner in my classroom kept malfunctioning. Contrary to some suspicion amongst my friends, I had not tampered with the unit, but did take delight in the malfunction, as it certainly helped me with my heat training. My poor students sat fanning themselves as I assured them I had reported the problem and it would be repaired soon. How could I have deceived my poor babies? Apparently, quite easily! They prayed for cooler days, as I prayed for record heat. How was I jinxing myself? Be careful what you wish for, Louise...

The experience of having done the race before taught me I needed significantly less gear and food than I had the first time. Two cars were essential, a change of clothes, foot care, ibuprofen, many water bottles, sponges, towels, ice, a variety of fluids, my electrolytes and a few choices of soup, crackers and fruit were all I really needed. The extra things thrown in the car were for the comfort of the crew. I hoped to be somewhat low maintenance.

Living in Los Angeles made the preparation infinitely easier logistically. All we had to do was load up the cars and head to Death Valley. We arrived there two days before the start, allowing ourselves some time to "adjust" to the desert heat. How quickly one can forget the difference of a desert heat. Isn't it supposed to be a "dry" heat? What was up with the humidity?

A race briefing was held to remind runners of all the rules you wouldn't remember after the first mile of the race. I caught a glimpse of all the other competitors: some old friends, some now-terrified soon-to-be friends. I couldn't help but notice the poor crewmembers, unlucky enough to be suckered into spending an inordinate amount of time in a car in grotesquely hot conditions. A few hours later and we were off for dinner and a final organization of the cars.

I think I slept well, I really don't remember; but I awoke ready for battle. I was in the 8:00 a.m. starting wave and couldn't wait to get going. My plan was to run to Furnace Creek, walk any inclines, and then start a run/walk pattern where I would run for eight minutes and walk for two until Stovepipe Wells. I remember thinking that it was really warm already, but tried not to focus on something over which I had no control anyway.

Furnace Creek couldn't come soon enough, and my crew kept me well hydrated. My run walk strategy worked well for me as I tried to take in the views of the magnificent dunes on the way to Stovepipe. Georgene ran with me at different times, and Marcia would jump in on occasion. Always good to have someone along side, feeling their energy.

I don't recall too much conversation – somewhat of a rarity for me, but perhaps because the heat was sapping a lot of energy. I noticed that Bill, my photographer friend, usually full of humor and conversation, was becoming quieter as well. I frequently thought about my crew in the heat, in and out of the car, catering to all my needs, and hoped they were doing OK and taking care of themselves. Bill wasn't used to the heat, and little did I know at the time that he was headed towards heat exhaustion.

My crew dangled the carrot of the pool awaiting me at Stovepipe. The idea of jumping into cool water was like a powerful magnet pulling me in. I quickly removed my shoes and socks, and lowered my weary, steamy, sweaty, and altogether disgustingly gross body into the pool. The fact that the "cool" water was probably 90 degrees did not diminish the joy of being off my feet. I didn't stay submerged for long, as I was afraid of my skin wrinkling, a potential for blisters. With the help of my crew, I changed into a fresh set of running clothes, declined the offer for a rest, took a water bottle filled with broth and headed up the hill. At that time, unbeknown to me Bill was resting in a cool hotel room, trying to recoup from the effects of the heat. No one wanted to tell me.

As the sun slowly settled behind the mountains and the sky began to darken, I hoped for cooler air. However, a strong wind appeared like a herd of stampeding buffalo, undeterred by anything in its way. "Great" I thought. Let's see how much more misery we can add. I must admit though, that psychologically, not having the sun beating down on me was a huge bonus. It gave me a moment to regroup and settle in for the night. Multi-day events lasting 24 hours and more had prepared me for long, exhausting nights, but it also taught me to expect visions and hallucinations. What would this night bring? What would I see? It becomes a game. Stopping to sleep was not an option for me. I prefer to keep moving. I hoped my crew would take some time to rest, and while they did take turns, they never left me. Apart from the occasional gremlin that reached out to drag me down, the unicorns that danced in front of me, and the gun toting rabbits shooting at some unrecognizable objects, there weren't too many exciting hallucinations to mention. I guess the heat was keeping them at bay as well. And so, I continued to plod up the hill, hoping to reach Panamint before sunrise and the next onslaught of heat.

Noticing the reduced number of crew vehicles on the road should have clued me in that the heat was affecting more and more people. Perhaps I was being naive, or perhaps I was too oblivious. My crew just humored me, encouraged me, and gave me everything I needed to get to the next bottle exchange. Fatigue and heat can do interesting things to the brain. I don't recall being really aware of others around me. Maybe I was just too focused on that darn white line!

The stretch from Darwin to Lone Pine once again proved to be the most difficult stretch for me. The sun was beating down furiously, frontally, and totally encapsulating me. Nothing was cooling me down. I had been walking for quite some time at this point; running seeming like a distant and past memory and a future impossibility.

I tried to think of Meagan, a past student of mine who was undergoing treatment for ovarian cancer at the tender age of 15. I was racing for her. It gave me strength. That and the addition of friends who showed up to relieve my now exhausted crew. Craig and Kathy, willing me along, gave me new energy and hope. Jef and Harry, keeping me moving and insisting on more nourishment. Who can eat in that heat?

Passing the Dow Villa in Lone Pine made me realize that the end was approaching. Hell, I can do this... *again*! The final leg of this torturous journey was in sight. The air was cooler, the sun was setting and I began the last climb. Georgene, always positive and full of humor and love, encouraged me with words and a gentle hand on my back. Bill drove the car, and I could feel his joy and pride as he parked the car and joined us as we crossed the finish line together; a weary, overworked, overheated, overjoyed team.

How quick we forget. The next day dawned and life continued as usual. Only later did we find out about the record temperatures. Would it have made a difference? Who knows? I finished in 39 hours and 22 minutes. So much for being in better shape than when I did the race post-chemo! I don't think it was the heat: I blame it on the additional four years to my age! Imagine if I did it now!

2003 Finishing Time – 39:22:14
Ninth Place

CHAPTER EIGHT – BILL LOCKTON

From Bill's 2003 Badwater Application:

Age: 55
Santa Monica, California

Why I Run Ultras:

I don't know if I know why. I like pushing to see what my limits are, but I'm not sure I know what the motivation behind that is. I'm finding that I've been enjoying ultras more than shorter runs (marathons and lesser distances) and fun is a big motivating factor for me. I have also really like everyone I've met in the ultra world. It seems to attract a better class of athlete.

FUN RUN *By Bill Lockton*

I started running again in August 1999. Seven years before that two different orthopedic surgeons had independently told me that it was physically impossible for me to ever run again – that the damage I had done to my Achilles tendons in both ankles was too severe to overcome and if I were foolish enough to try, the tendons would snap.

Yet seven years later it seemed to me I had regained some range of motion, and that started me wondering if a different future could be in store for me. One day – simply on a whim I went out to the grassy median in front of my apartment to test my ankles and I heard a car horn blowing and my name called out. An old girlfriend from 13 years ago was waving. She pulled over and while we caught up she told me she had just joined the L.A.LEGGERS, a marathon-training club I had heard about. As she was describing how they organized in pace groups, most of whom took walk breaks, the thought came that this sounded pretty gentle and that maybe I could run with them. I didn't care how fast I ran – I just wanted to see if I could run again, regardless of the speed.

I joined them in August 1999, with no clue that four years later I was going to be nationally ranked at some insanely long distances.

It took a while to develop. My conditioning was terrible. My Achilles protested a lot. I spent a lot of time going to physical therapists (I have to acknowledge how extremely helpful LA-based Steve Paulseth was. A sponsor of the Leggers, he was a master at taping me up so that the aches and pains I was experiencing didn't sideline me. If you watched beach volleyball during the Sydney Olympics, you would have heard Kerri Walsh and Karch Kirali rave about how terrific and necessary he was in keeping the U.S. team on the field of play). I became a student of proper running form, figuring that the laws of physics apply to running just as much as they apply to everything else in the world, and that if I ran in harmony with the way the body is supposed to work, that would put less stress on my Achilles. I also became an advocate of effort-based training after discovering I had over-trained much of my first season.

At that time there was a video passing around the club, spoken of only in whispers. There was something seemingly clandestine about it. Overhearing some of those whispers, I managed to borrow a copy of it – and was blown away! *Running on the Sun* depicted a race that seemed idiotic, crazy, scary, and fascinating all at once. Watching it in the comfort of my air-conditioned apartment, there was no way to conceive of what the experience of running through Death Valley must be like, but it seemed pretty crazy. It was the most ridiculous thing I had ever heard of. If you're wired like me, that's incredibly attractive!

Months later, a club member approached me about booking Shannon Farar-Griefer as a speaker after one of our training runs. Shannon had just done a "Badwater double," going from Badwater to the summit of Mount Whitney and then returning to Badwater. I ended up booking her, and remember turning to a friend as Shannon was speaking and saying "Why would anybody ever want to do an ultra? 26.2 miles is too long! 18 miles. 20 Miles... I don't get tired until then... Half marathon – a brilliant race! You can race one of those every month if you want. But an ultra? Forget it!"I remember the statement word for word!

However, when Shannon invited me to crew for her at the next Badwater, I jumped at the chance. See the event up close? I'm there! I didn't know what I was doing between then and July, but my July was now officially booked! Unfortunately, Shannon suffered an injury and her coach wouldn't let her enter. As sorry as I was for her, I still planned on going; I was fortunate to meet someone else running Badwater, and I joined her crew.

So in 2002 I had my first taste of Badwater, crewing for Angela Brunson. We went out over the 4th of July for one of the Heat Training Clinics hosted by Ben and Denise Jones. I thought it was important for me to experience what my runner would be going through, otherwise how would I be able to relate to what it would be like for her? When I ran 20+ miles the first day and another 18 the second, it was an eye-opener for me. Until then, I thought you had to wait two weeks between long runs; I did not know you could do them back to back.

I spent a lot of time asking people questions about how to train for the heat, but stopped after a couple of days. It's not just that lots of people contradicted each other; I found most people also contradicted themselves. Right or wrong, I was left with the impression that no one really knew exactly what worked but they knew that once upon a time something had worked, so they threw everything at me they had done at the time. Buried in among the myths and superstition was the real factor, but no one really seemed to be quite sure what it was, and even if they were, it was tough to sort out of all the disparate opinions I received. In retrospect, I see that everybody gave me some good advice. In the face of so much contradictory information, however, there was no way for me with my limited knowledge to figure out which advice to take. That was interesting, and something I filed away in my memory bank.

Angela was brilliant in her race. Her body never gave out, and her resiliency was amazing. She was nothing short of inspiring! At the end of the race, I remember saying to some of the finishers that when I came out there, I was already incredibly impressed by them all, but now – now I thought they were gods and goddesses!

I was also left with the impression that the race was totally doable, the question now being could *I* do it?

There were reasons to think I could not. I have already mentioned the chronic Achilles tendonitis. That was still going on. There were other reasons to question my ability. I had only been running three years at that point. There were other health considerations as well. Not to mention I had never done well in the heat, much less on hills.

But I was intrigued, so I set about starting to test myself. If I could meet the minimum requirements, that would be proof of some degree of preparedness, so I started training seriously. I had just started competing in triathlons, so I upped my workouts as if I were entering an Ironman, thinking that if I weren't accepted into Badwater, an Ironman would be my backup. Because of my Achilles issues, I was sure that running 100+ miles a week wasn't good for me. I figured I could cap my training at around 50-60 miles per week and spend the rest of my time working aerobically on my bicycle and in the pool, getting up to 20 hours per week of serious training. I was hoping the trade-off in order to reduce the risk of injury would be worth it.

It was truly a delight to see how readily my body responded. Some friends organized a 12-hour run around the Rose Bowl in September that I was able to use as a test of running strategies. It hit 100 degrees that day, and I felt fine doing 52.7 miles. That was the first time I had ever done more than 26.2 miles, and it was easy and fun.

Then I did the San Diego 1-Day in November. Even though it rained for the first 17 ½ hours, friends told me I had the biggest grin on my face every time I came around the track! How could I not, doing something as patently ridiculous as running around a college track for 24 hours, most of it in the rain?

For Badwater's purposes, all I had to do was hit 100 miles in 24 hours, so when I reached that mark fairly quickly, I stopped and took pictures with everybody under the clock, phoned my son in college who was staying up with his fraternity brothers to follow my progress, phoned everyone else I could think of around the country, and then started walking, talking to everyone else on the course. It suddenly hit me that this was no way to be in a race, so I looked at my watch, saw how much time I had left, did some quick math in my head to see if I could beat a friend's result of 107 miles the year before, and decided to give it a shot. I finished with 109, and that ultimately got me into Badwater.

I probably had the lightest resume of any applicant. I had only been running for 3 1/2 years at the point of applying. I had only officially completed one ultra: the San Diego 1-Day. The good news was that the only applicant with a recently posted 24-hour result better than mine was Scott Ludwig, so that made me look like a relatively strong candidate. I will always suspect that the friends I made out there, crewing for Angela and at the Heat Training Clinics helped me, too, but I'll never know for sure.

The invitations went out late that year. All of the Ironmen I might have gone to if I wasn't going to Badwater sold out, and I still hadn't heard whether or not I would be participating in Death Valley. Was I going to get in? Was I going to have a race at all? Several of us still waiting to hear started signing off our E-mails to each other with "BOB" for "Badwater or Bust." It was nervous time...

Finally... *I got in*! The invitation came and along with it the realization that the work had only just begun. Since I was wary of the training advice others had given me, I started reading original research on training and heat training. My master's degree had a lot of biochemistry in it, so I knew how to read research and separate the wheat from the chaff. I even bought medical texts on heat-induced illnesses and their treatment. I figured that we all share a common, human physiology, and the principles at work in you are the same ones at work in me, so all I needed to do was uncover them and apply them. What I learned ran counter too much of what I was told by veterans of the race, but I went with the science, and it seemed to have worked for me. (*The particulars are recorded in my race report below.*)

Also along the way, I met someone who played a huge factor in what has happened to my life since the race. I had organized a Monday night Track Program for the Leggers, which was at that time being coached by professional triathlete Jamie Murphy. One Monday afternoon I got a call from Jamie asking me if I could cover track for him that evening as he was still in Nantucket and not likely to make it. He suggested a workout; I gave it to them, and afterward found myself the focal point of a semi-circle of people who knew I was training for Badwater and wanted to know all about it. There was a cute girl who was new to the track since I had last been there grinning from ear to ear while I was talking. The next day I got a call from her. She introduced herself as Amy Berg, a producer for one of the networks. She told me she was at the track because she had met Jamie in the context of a show she was involved with about extreme sports, and wanted to know if she could film me. She said that the whole time I was talking, all she could think of was "I have to get THIS guy on MY show!" She explained that it was a 30 minute show for Sunday Sport's Spectacular, that I would be one of five clips, and each would also be aired during Extreme Week on the news...and asked me if I would like to do it? I didn't pause for even half a second. "NO. Not a chance. I'm not interested."

That took her a bit aback. I think people in the entertainment world assume that everyone wants a shot at 15 minutes of fame. I could not have cared less. Badwater was potentially life threatening, and I wasn't about to compromise my training just so she could have something to air. She protested and countered with saying I had complete control – that if at any point I found it was too intrusive, I could pull out. That eventually got me to agree to participate.

She was wrong. It was intrusive. It was disruptive. It did interfere several times. Mostly, though, we were able to work around it. It was originally scheduled to air before the race, so they were only going to show my training, but the airdate of the show kept being postponed. Eventually, it was put off long enough that it became possible to include the race itself. I suggested that to them, and their boss gave the approval. The segment, which was originally scheduled to be just 2 ½ minutes of the show was extended to 4 ½, which they thought was huge, and eventually became the piece of the show the producers submitted for Emmy consideration. *They won!* Amy told me I can tell everyone I won an Emmy, but ... isn't saying "I am an Emmy Award-winning Athlete" a little like saying "I'm an Oscar-winning Plumber?" The award doesn't quite go with the profession.

I have to say the first time I saw it I didn't like it. I was aware of all the material that wasn't used, and was a little perturbed that so much of what ended up being really a pain in the neck at the time ended up not being used at all. After seeing it a few times, though, I accept that they did a really good job. The focal point of the piece ended up being the race itself, using me as just the entry point for the viewer to experience the race. It was nicely done.

There was a funny result from it as well – for more than a year, friends would tell me they'd be at a sports bar, hear my voice, look around to find me, and instead see me on the bar's TV screens as the clip was being re-broadcast. Too bad I wasn't getting royalties!

The race had another effect on me as well. Up until then, I had always been athletic, but never considered myself an athlete. Even the 109-mile performance at the San Diego 1-Day, while good enough to be the 25th best performance in the country that year, didn't alter that view of myself; it was easy to dismiss by saying that not a lot of really good people participated in 24-hour runs that year. But finishing as the 6th man (10th overall) at Badwater in its hottest year and coming in ahead of several world-famous endurance athletes – that DID cause some psychological upheavals. I had to come to terms with the fact that now I was an *"athlete"*– whatever that means. And along with that came the thought that if I could be this good at something just goofing around, what could I do if I actually trained to compete?

Maybe it's my New England WASP upbringing raising its ugly head, but... if you discover you have a talent at something, aren't you supposed to develop it and see how good you can be at it? The truth is, I would have preferred to be better at something easier to train for, but those weren't the cards I was dealt. A few years later, I came in 8th American Male at the 24-Hour National Championships with a personal best of 122+ miles, and at the end of the year Ultrarunning magazine listed me as the 10th best American at that distance (I came in 9th Male at the race and 11th on the list because one person who beat me was a Hungarian national – Akos Konya – and as a Hungarian national, didn't figure into the list of Americans).

The following is a race report I wrote immediately after completing the 2003 Badwater Ultramarathon. It was my description of the race and probably holds truer to my thoughts and feelings at that time. Since then, I have more perspective. I will always love the people who crewed for me, no matter what happens in the future. (Laurie Woodrow and my son, Andrew Lockton were one team, and the other was Dan Manns and Rodney Basset. Laurie has since become an ultramarathoner herself with thoughts of doing Badwater. My son became a professional triathlete. Dan and Rodney have become coaches.) I've been back to crew for Xy Weiss and Fred Pollard since then, and will probably do more. I like crewing. I want to run it again myself. I just really love it out there. I love being able to see from horizon to horizon. I love being able to see as far as the eyes can see, knowing that in a few hours I will have actually covered all of that distance on foot; that never ceases to impress me. I love how severe it can be, and yet even in that most austere of those surroundings, if you look closely you see Life teeming. I find the whole experience incredibly moving.

One final point before my race report: When we were out there, our thermometers measured a peak temperature of 130 degrees, and that's what I had been repeating as part of my story. A few years later, crewing for someone else, Race Director Chris Kostman and Ben "The Mayor of Badwater" Jones overheard me telling someone my race hit 130 degrees, and they both jumped up and exclaimed like it was important that I wasn't taking enough credit – that in 2003 the temperature reached 133 degrees. I saw somewhere that the "official" temperature had been downgraded, but the differing numbers can be reconciled when considering that the "official" temperature is just the temperature that was recorded at that one site, wherever it was – Furnace Creek, Stovepipe Wells, or wherever; it could have been a very different temperature out on the course. Whatever it was, it was Hot!

Here's my race report:

Badwater is over and done with, and I've had a little time to try to put this all together. I've been having difficulty. There's too much to say, and there's too little to say. In reality, all I did was run, drink, go to the bathroom, and finish. My crewmembers have all the stories to tell, not me. *(They were great, and a ton of fun. Because there are no bathrooms out there in the middle of the desert, one of them coined the phrase "The world is my toilet." It was funny at the time. It was amazing how many sentences he was able to squeeze it into. They also wanted to make up T-shirts for themselves with the slogan "The Lockton Crew: Only Slightly Less Crazy!")*

I'm also having trouble coming to grips with the fact I did so well. By my own definitions, I've always been athletic, but never an athlete. I refer to my performances in events as "my usual, slightly-better-than-average-mediocre-results." That my goofing-around performance at the 24-hour run I used to qualify to apply to Badwater was ranked the 25th best performance in the country last year (male) seemed to be a fluke.

I ran Badwater with expectations of my usual results, just hoping to earn the belt buckle by breaking 48 hours while having a secret and unspoken desire to break 45. Imagine my surprise when I broke 40 hours with a time of 39:39:32! Then the next day I found out I finished 10th overall and was the 6th male finisher. I'm still kind of in shock. You have to realize who I was competing against, and how much of a chance the Race Director was taking in extending me an invitation. To quote Luis Escobar, the 7th place finisher on his website: *"These runners are big time, hard ass, no nonsense kind of people. The extreme of the extreme. Each one has an impressive bio and a list of credentials a mile long. These people mean business. It was more than a little intimidating to line up with runners of this fine caliber. Everyone at Badwater is good."* Out of all the qualified applicants, Race Director Chris Kostman handpicked the entrants. Luis' estimation of the quality of other entrants really did not apply to me because I had no track record to speak of. Of the American men, I had the 2nd best 24-hour performance last year, but many had better performances in years past. (Scott Ludwig, the one who beat me last year, also beat me at Badwater, finishing three hours and seven minutes ahead of me, taking 6th overall and 3rd male. He had the 4th best 24-hour performance in the country last year, and I felt honored to run part of the race with him.)

During the race, I couldn't figure out where all the fast runners were. Only a few passed me, and I kept wondering where all the famous names behind me were. Now I realize that the reason they didn't pass me was that I was beating them. This is causing severe distress to my self-image! It's being forced to recreate itself.

The Conditions: As you know by now, the race is 135 miles long, goes over two mountain ranges before it reaches Mount Whitney for a total vertical rise of 13,400 feet (It also has descents of close to 4,700 feet – tough on the quads!) and goes through Death Valley in the heat of the day at the end of July. This year there was a lot of debate about exactly how hot it got. The consensus seems to be 130 degrees, although many people told me they got higher readings, all the way up to 135! The humidity, typically around 4-6%, was in the 15-18% range, which was even more of a factor since every increase in humidity makes you feel the heat even more. I was blown away last year by its 125 degrees and 6% humidity. This year was epic! Several veterans told me it was the most extreme conditions they had ever experienced.

The Training: The only way I could figure to train for the race was to make my workouts so much more grueling than anything I would expect to experience at the race, so that the race would seem easy in comparison: the "Train Hard, Race Easy"-formula. It worked.

For the athletes reading this, a typical weekend towards the end would be to run 18 miles of hard hills on Saturday, then on Sunday take those aching quads on a 55-mile bike ride that had some significant hills in them and try to hold on to the wheel of the leader as long as I could (impossible for me even when I'm fresh), and then after the ride, go run another 20 miles of hills. One of those routes was 10 miles straight up an incline steeper than anything at Badwater but the finish, followed by 10 miles back down. I hurt more any given Sunday night than I did during the entire race, and not only taught myself how to continue on but to do surges when my body was already beat. For heat training, I went out to Death Valley over both Memorial Day and Fourth of July weekends and after the latter, came back and trained in the sauna for 12 days. That was the worst! I'd go in for 90 minutes, keep the temperature around 165-170 degrees, and eventually worked up to doing a 5 + 5: five minutes rest followed by five minutes doing anything to get my heart pumping hard: pushing off the walls, modified pushups off the bench, jumping jacks, running in place, etc. As a consequence, although I was clearly aware that it was hot during the race, I was surprised to find out it was hotter than anything I had ever experienced out there. It worked.

Prerace: People kept asking me if I was scared, nervous, or anything. I wasn't. It seemed perfectly natural that I was about to do this thing, and there was no sense of trepidation at all. I was aware of the fact that people tend to drop like flies, but there's no use anticipating some Act of God coming along to wipe you out, and I had done the work. I felt strong and confident, with only a slight concern that I had tapered too long, I hadn't. It takes at least two and maybe three weeks for your body to recover from the kind of damage my training had done while strengthening me.

The Race: In many respects this is the most boring part in that there really isn't much to report. I ran it as a fun run, and I think that is confirmed by the facts that I stopped at mile 41 to jump in the pool at Furnace Creek and took a two hour break (90 minutes of it a nap) at Panamint Springs (mile 72). That was my only down time. Other than that, I did have a fun run. I ran within myself, and met a lot of really nice and interesting people along the way (mostly as I passed them). I had stomach problems once, but that cleared up quickly. I ended up taking no solid food whatsoever, getting my calories from Accelerade and Slim Fast, which for some reason went down (and stayed down) really easily. Sure, I got tired, and every time my crew would work on me (feet, legs, etc.) I'd lay back and close my eyes until they were done.

Fortunately/unfortunately, that only lasted about five minutes each time. There was one point where I thought I'd have to stop running. Starting up after a walk break, I got a sharp shooting pain in my left calf that stopped me cold. Trying it again after a couple of paces, that shooting pain went across the back of my knee. At that point I could have walked the rest of the way and still earned the buckle, so it wasn't the end of the world, but I wanted to run and I think we spent close to 45-minutes working on it. This happened shortly before the Darwin Checkpoint, which is why if you look at the charts you see that a lot of people who I led into Panamint checked into Darwin ahead of me. It took an hour or so for my leg to let me get back up to my regular pace, at which point I was able to catch almost all of them.

The Numbers:

First leg from Badwater to Furnace Creek: 23rd fastest out of 73 runners, 23rd overall, covering the 17.4 miles at an 11:19 pace.

Second leg from Furnace Creek to Stovepipe Wells: 10th fastest of 58 runners still in the race, which moved me up to 10th place. This was the hottest stretch and my time slowed to 14:18 for the 24.5 mile leg, 13:10 overall. Note that 15 competitors had already dropped out.

Third leg from Stovepipe Wells to Panamint: 12th fastest of 50 runners still in the race (lost eight more), which dropped me to 11th place. 20:18 pace for the 31-mile leg and 16:06 pace overall. This time includes the hour stop at Stovepipe Wells for a swim and an ice bath, then an 18-mile hill that climbed 5,000 feet: deducting the hour of "down time," and I ran it much faster.

Fourth leg from Panamint to Darwin: 29th fastest of 47 runners still in the race (three more dropped out), dropping me to 18th place. A 25:34 pace for the 18-mile leg, and a 17:58 overall. The time for this 18-mile leg included both the two-hour stop at Panamint and the time working on my cramp. It was also mostly all uphill.

Fifth leg from Darwin to Lone Pine through the Owens Valley: 10th fastest of 46 runners still in the race (the final person dropped out), moving me up to 13th place. Even though I had to start slowly for the first hour because of the cramp, I averaged 16:26 for the 32-mile leg, for an overall pace of 17:34.

Final leg from Lone Pine to the Whitney Portals: 7th fastest of the 46 runners still in the race, moving me up to 10th place overall. This mountain just continually gets steeper the further you go. I burned out my pacer and had to have him relieved. I did this 13-mile leg at an 18:13 pace, for a final overall average pace of 17:37.

Then, the next day, three of us climbed Mount Whitney – another 22 miles. At the top, the clouds rolled in to bless us with hail, and when the thunder and lightning off in the distance started coming closer, we ran most of the way back down.

After the Race: I was very lucky. I had no blisters to speak of except for a very tiny one my crew insisted needed fixing. I think they were just bored and needed something to do. I will eventually lose two toenails from the run and another for sure from our Mount Whitney excursion, but as many of you know that is a fairly common occurrence in long distance running; not a big deal.

I don't feel like running much, but I have led pace groups for Nike's Club Run LA for the past two nights without difficulty, and it has only been a week from the start of the race, not the end. I'm losing more weight after the race than I did during it, where it didn't really change much. My body fat dropped three percentage points from the day I left for the race to the day I returned. Interestingly, it makes me look fatter. Go figure! Because everywhere else is slimmer, the deposits that remain actually stand out more than they did when their appearance was smoothed by the presence of more body fat around them.

I'm going to cool it for a while, mostly biking and swimming for the first month before I gear up to start training again.

The Future: Would I do it again? *Absolutely!* I could have completed this one faster by shortening the breaks. Will I do it next year? We'll have to see. My business partners are very glad it's over; they were feeling neglected because of all the attention I had to put on preparing for the race, and were concerned it was eating into my productivity. They are right. There is no doubt that it was. This kind of training can be destructive on relationships in general, something most Ironman competitors are well aware of.

Death Valley is incredibly beautiful. While running through it, I kept being struck by the utter tenaciousness of life. No matter how extreme the conditions, no matter how apparently barren the surroundings, if you looked closely you saw life teeming everywhere. It was truly magnificent.

My crew was brilliant. They were all rookies out there, but I had taken three of them with me over the Fourth of July Heat Training clinic. They developed into a good crew while they were there. At the race, they became a *great* crew. I fell in love with every single one of them, and their devotion to getting me through this event was nothing short of humbling. One of those crewmembers was my son Andrew, and that was especially great. I was thrilled to have him there helping me through this. His Ironman training made it a fairly easy task for him to keep up with me.

And that's it! That's what I did for my summer vacation. How was yours?

Final Thought:

About a week after the race I was visiting my new primary care physician with the new health plan for my company, and he gave me a physical. At one point, he asked me to put my arm out so he could draw some blood for blood work and I said no. He gave me the most interesting look – I had to laugh! I explained that I had just run Badwater, at which point I then described the race to him, that I had finished the race a week ago today and that the products of tissue breakdown from that race were probably at their highest level in my blood that day, so no – I wasn't going to do a blood test; he'd get nothing but false readings. He paused for a moment, smiled, and said, "OK. We'll reschedule for two weeks... and should I also book a psych consult?"

2003 Finishing Time – 39:39:32
Tenth Place

© Thinkstock/iStockphoto/Fluid Illusion

CHAPTER NINE – JOE DESENA

From Joe's 2003 Badwater Application:

Age: 34
New York City, New York

My Weirdest Experience:

My weirdest ultrarunning experience has got to be during a race in Santa Monica. This was actually what inspired me to get into adventure racing. This was my first race and the run was 50 miles. One of my good friends had asked me to do this with him. My friend at the time was a little on the chunky side so I figured if he could do it so could I. To my disbelief he was in such good cardiovascular shape and I was dying: gasping for air, dizzy and feeling so out of shape. We finished the race and I knew from that minute forward that I was going to train and continue to race.

TAKING IT SLOW *By Joe DeSena*

I was working on Wall Street. 9/11 had come and gone, almost as if the world hadn't changed. We worked just a few blocks from Ground Zero and virtually at the exact same elevation the planes had struck the World Trade Center.

I remember thinking on that fateful day "I should go and help the firefighters by running stairs." Thankfully one of my coworkers talked sense into me before I ran into what would certainly have been the end of me.

As a profession, Wall Street is extremely hectic even without magnificent towering buildings collapsing and people dying all around. It was high energy and high stakes every minute of every day.

As an escape I needed long distance challenges to clear my mind. When people would call and ask me if I was interested in running the Sahara or competing in an Eco-Challenge, the standard reply was "yes."

Later I would have to figure out how to make my hectic schedule work. There were many times when I had to exclude events I really wanted to participate in for the sake of work. Then a few years later Lisa Smith-Batchen asked if I was interested in competing in the Badwater Ultramarathon. As I wasn't familiar with the event, I had Lisa explain it to me... and then sign me up. I didn't realize I had committed to the Lake Placid Ironman and the Vermont 100 already, or that all three events were within a seven-day period.

At some point soon after signing up I realized what I had done. My first reaction was to figure out which event to back out of. Then it occurred to me this might very well be a challenge of the highest level.

Not being a runner and not knowing anything about the Vermont 100 or Badwater and having already finished several Ironmans made the decision easier. I knew I needed to take my training seriously; however, the problem was I still had this demanding job on Wall Street and had to continue to deal with all the stress that comes with it.

I figured as long as I ran and continued my yoga two or three times a week I would be fine.

So two months before I began a regimen of running 10 miles and finishing it with yoga class twice a week. I would run 10 miles in about 90 minutes, finishing just in time for yoga. It was a great way to acclimate myself to the heat and do some "body maintenance" after the runs.

Fortunately, one year earlier I had met the girl of my dreams. We met at a race in Nantucket and falling for her was as easy as signing up for all of my crazy endurance challenges. Our first date was an eight-hour kayak through the Long Island Sound. To accentuate my training, I opted not to bring any fluids or foods.

Courtney turned out to be quite the trooper. She paddled for eight hours with me, without any food or water, and I thought to myself "this would definitely be the girl to marry." She could handle seven children if this was her approach to life; if was important for me to find someone who could deal with anything... and she appeared to fit the bill. Did I mention that Courtney was also quite stunning? Well, she most certainly was.

During my training for the "triple-witch" (Badwater, Vermont 100 and Lake Placid Ironman), I now had Courtney in my life. She met me often at my yoga classes.

About six weeks before Badwater I thought it was time to step up my training. On weekends Courtney and I would drive to Vermont. I would head out on Saturday mornings with a 35-pound pack on my back and attempt an eight-hour run. Distance didn't matter; I just thought I needed to be on my feet for that amount of time. For four straight weeks that was my routine; Sundays allowed me to "pay for it."

Courtney's dad was an FBI agent as well as a Naval officer. I thought "who better to convince to help crew me at Badwater than he and Courtney?" I asked him to make all the arrangements, including finding a tub large enough for me to sit in and fill up with ice.

As the final weeks approached, he and Courtney were working with Lisa who just happened to be doing the "Grand Slam' – something about six 100-milers in a row –so she would be in Vermont with me.

Lisa had a friend named Heathe Gosslin who lived near our house in Vermont. He would also be running the Vermont 100. I asked Lisa if she could get Heath and me together for my last "back pack run" two weeks before the race.

The logistics of being in Vermont on a Saturday and Sunday, Las Vegas and Badwater on a Tuesday and Wednesday and Lake Placid the following Saturday proved to be difficult. That is to say, difficult without factoring in a Friday night wedding; a family affair that Courtney and Bob (her dad) informed me that I would be attending.

I thought "Come on, guys – how can I possibly squeeze a wedding in? Friday night? In Massachusetts?" Impossible! But, in this new world of engagements *(I forgot to mention that we had gotten engaged and planned on marrying two months later)* I had to make concessions.

After all, they were supporting this whole trip: from ice tubs to logistics to making peanut butter sandwiches to just dealing with this crazy person on a mission that seemingly made no sense.

We were only two weeks out when Bob informed me of major problems with the "tuna tub." We could use it in Vermont with no trouble, but flying it and getting it to Badwater would be a problem. He additionally had heard from Lisa that the race organization might not allow us to use our tuna tub at Badwater for fear that the tub full of ice in the extreme heat could cause me to be crushed.

This was obviously a problem. I was dead set on the tub idea. I was at a point that I had convinced myself that I could not compete if I didn't have my tub.

The last two weeks I decided 10 straight days of 10 mile runs were in order, followed by four days of rest. I would run before or after work –rain or shine –on the Brooklyn Bridge several times or if I had to, on the west side of the highway. Anything to get my 10 miles in.

Another problem: I needed to get my bicycle to Lake Placid in advance since the only way for me to get from the wedding was to fly a puddle jumper from Massachusetts to Lake Placid late Saturday afternoon. I thought since I had not ridden my bicycle this season I would just ride it the weekend before to Lake Placid to get in shape. I wasn't sure how far it was but it had to be 200 miles, which would serve as a great tune-up.

I had a friend who said I could leave my bicycle at his house, so now the only issue appeared to be getting back from Lake Placid. I would have to convince a friend to drive me back.

I always thought no matter how long the challenge, your mind and body typically get tired about 70% of the way into it. So if you are running a marathon you get tired at mile 20; if you are running 100 miles it's at 70 miles. I had no idea if this logic would hold true at Badwater. I did know, however, that if I could soak in my ice tub every 25 to 30 miles for five minutes I would get stronger as the days passed.

Lisa showed up at our house in Vermont and we both went to check in for the 100 miler. As I suspected, the race was easier physically and mentally because I had Badwater on my mind. This race was my warm-up to the hell I would encounter later next week. I still wanted to break 24 hours in Vermont, but didn't want to beat myself up doing it.

Heathe, Lisa and I began the race with a few friends of ours, Noel and Lynn Hanna. It was Lynn's first 100 and since she was married to Noel, she would attack the course like a gazelle.

Noel was an all-around tough guy, completing races all over the world; most recently he had climbed the highest peaks on each continent and then raced to sea level. Being shot at while in Papa New Guinea or losing friends on Everest became a normal part of his existence. Needless to say, we only saw Noel and Lynn for a few minutes at the start.

Lisa set the pace; she was the vseteran. She knew exactly when we should be at each aid station. She had gotten me through my first 100-miler a year earlier at Old Dominion. I remember seeing someone passed out at Old Dominion face-first in the dirt at mile 70; after Lisa and I tugged at him for a few seconds we heard a groan and the words "leave me alone." We did, and went on to finish in respectable times. During Vermont we were on a good pace when we ran into a huge man at mile 50 with no shirt. He had muscles everywhere and wasn't carrying a water bottle.

He was perspiring like mad. As we were running Lisa asked him why he didn't carry water. He said he opted to "leap frog" from station to station. Lisa mumbled that it was quite a bit of leapfrogging so she asked him about wearing a camelback. He said he didn't like getting the tubes tangled around his neck. He did admit to carrying a water bottle in a backpack on occasion. This made absolutely no sense to us. Then suddenly "leap frog" sprinted up a massive hill and he engaged in more conversation with other runners about his race strategy.

Meanwhile, Heathe was under strict orders from Lisa to walk all of the hills.

At mile 70 there was a weigh-in station. If a runner had lost a certain percentage of their weight since the start of the race they would not be allowed to continue. Around mile 69 we saw "leap frog"face down on the ground. When he saw us he immediately jumped up and explained he had attempted 18

100-mile runs and never completed any of them. He went on to say that he hated running and all of his training consisted of nothing but lifting weights.

Just as we pulled into the weigh-in station "leap frog"asked us to stop as he needed to do something. Once "leap frog"got on the scale, we were surprised to learn that he had actually *gained* weight since the start of the race.

He then proceeded to unload rocks from his pockets once we left the station...

Around mile 80 Heathe began having big problems. I suggested he need to get into my ice tub, but I was outvoted by Lisa who thought it was silly. I, however was feeling great but at the same time looking to get this race over with and get in my silly ice tub to prepare for Badwater.

The Vermont 100 is also a horse race, so as you run horses will occasionally pass you. Horses also tend to stop quite often for water and rest.

Around mile 85 Heath blew up and had to be taken away in an ambulance. Lisa suggested I continue; she would see that Heathe is taken care of. We later discovered his kidney had failed.

In time Heathe would be OK. I eventually crossed the finish line, breaking the 24-hour mark with 20 minutes to spare. Bob was waiting patiently with my tub; I jumped in and began my recovery. While sitting there I got to watch some of the remaining runners... and horses finish.

As the 24-hour mark approached I heard race organizers scream to get ready, as another horse was coming in. It appeared to be a horse of considerable size, but it was hard to tell for sure as it was very late at night. Just then out of the woods came "leap frog" and Lisa; it was the former that everyone thought was a horse. This guy was so big and carrying two head lamps, so in the dark...

"Leap frog" finished his first 100-mile run.

Cars, planes, hotels and 36 hours later and we were at the start of Badwater. It was HOT... wow... we were so stiff. I remember the race meeting. I was handed a bib number, a wooden stake and a few odds and ends. I must have been completely out of it as I honestly thought the wooden stake was to stab yourself with should you get to a point where you could no longer continue.

I remember there was another person from New York City. There may have been more but this was runner was representing the race sponsor, Kiehl's. I remember seeing Pam Reed and other than that I remember the hotel rooms where we stayed across from a gas station and next to a pool. I remember the heat being unbearable.

Badwater

I had no idea what to expect, but I was happy I had something in the distance to focus on: an Ironman competition immediately afterwards. I found that focus helped me through the 130-degree wind bursts smashing in my face as we approached this devilish part of America.

Was that a golf course? I started to think that just like in the old movies in which the victim in the desert starts to "see things;" maybe it was happening to me. Maybe I was in fact "seeing things." Was there a golf course out here?

I was in a hot hotel room reviewing race strategy with Lisa and a team consisting of enough experience to get us through Hell. Lisa thought I was crazy with the ice tub idea, but she had given up fighting me on it as she had her own demons to deal with.

Bob was his name. He was part of the experienced crew Lisa had assembled. He had run Badwater before and was going to provide lots of experienced help. Heathe, who was with us in Vermont and whose kidney had failed was with us, as was my future wife and father-in-law who rounded out my support team.

I grabbed a pillow and sat on the floor of the room and listened while I stretched. It sounded very complex and strategic, but all I could think about was getting this thing started. I just wanted to get it over with, and the more we talked about it the less I wanted to do it.

After the meeting Bob pulled me aside the night before the race and in a serious tone said: "I am not sure this will work." I was confused. He went on to say that I had sat on his pillow in the room during the meeting, and that simply wouldn't work.

I was absolutely baffled and was waiting for the punch line. I went to the maid, who coincidently was in the room at the time, and asked for another pillow that I in turn gave to Bob. We were heading to Hell and this guy was flipping out over a pillow? *This* was my support crew?

The countdown begins. Lisa and I were both slated for the 10:00 a.m. start. I didn't question Lisa when she instructed me to dress in white Arabian gear. I felt like an Arab as we drove to the starting line.

Once we arrived at the start it was HOT... painfully hot. I looked down at my long-sleeved shirt and it was melting as it clung to my body. This couldn't possibly be good.

Lisa turns to me as we start and says not to run; we are going to walk the first 26 miles. I was completely confused and wanted to run; after all, it *was* a foot race.

I had no reason to question Lisa, as she had finished Badwater several times and must know what she is talking about. We walked, and I thought perhaps it was a means to get my shirt to stop melting. We walked and walked and walked some more. We put ice on our head and ate small quarter-sandwiches and drank fluids... and walked and walked and walked.

All I cared about was my ice tub. I wanted to sit in it every 26.2 miles, and I wondered if my support crew would be able to get enough ice for it.

It was very disheartening to be in last and next-to-last place walking in a running race. I had to keep mumbling that Lisa knew what she – and I were doing.

About nine hours into the race we reached the hotel with the swimming pool; I just had to jump in to get refreshed! I wasn't sure if we had the time to spare for me to jump in, so I didn't ask as I plunged into the water. I was shivering and actually cold when I got out of the pool, so I knew I was adequately hydrated.

We resumed our journey, only now it was about 10 degrees cooler since the sun had gone down. It felt great! I think at this point my crew started to have problems; in retrospect they weren't paying enough attention to the heat and their own hydration. But how could they? They were so focused on Lisa and me.

At one point I looked over at the support car and noticed no one was driving but yet the car was keeping pace with us. The crew had gotten delirious and gone to the back of the car to make sandwiches and left the car in "drive" while doing so; they didn't even notice that no one was driving!

whaatt

The first night was inspiring. We were climbing one of the long mountains and every few minutes we were passing runners and support crews on the ground either vomiting or altogether passed out; the strategy of starting slow appeared to be working out as we continued to press on. We felt great and were now moving at a great pace while people were battling hosts of issues ranging from dehydration to heat stroke.

That night we found ourselves amongst the leaders of the race. We hadn't really even started running yet, and I found it amazing how things were playing out.

We hustled through the next day and kept moving toward a less-hot environment as we headed to Mount Whitney. We had our ups and downs but by and large we were still moving. I had some breakdowns along the way but I kept thinking if I had the choice between Heaven and Hell, I was going to Heaven so I needed to find a way to escape Hell.

We were at mile 100 when the arch in Lisa's foot collapsed, forcing us to stop. Lisa and the crew worked for hours trying to fix the foot issue. It was now fairly cool and provided me a great rest while the crew duct-taped a pillow (no, it wasn't Bob's) around her foot and then tried to put a larger pair of running shoes on her feet.

Every minute runners were passing by and it was driving the competitive side of me crazy watching this happen. Finally after about four hours Lisa said "Joe, I have to put my stake in the ground; you need to go on.'

I literally thought the wooden stakes were meant to use should you want to end your misery; perhaps some form of medieval technique to end your own life. My mind was clearly messing with me, but when Lisa pounded the stake in the sand and said it was her marker for her to return to the course later I thought "Wow, that makes sense."

Heathe said he would get me through the next 25 miles leading to the final climb up Mount Whitney. I needed music and I needed to fix my shoes. Up ahead I could see the lights of the dozen or so runners who had passed us by. I duct-taped my shoes together, turned up the music and left with Heathe.

We started RUNNING... we were really moving and I remember tall grass on both sides of the road for literally four solid hours. I was convinced some large creature was stalking us from behind the tall grass.

We reached the final checkpoint in Lone Pine and Heathe was finished. He said good luck and was off to find our hotel. All that remained for me was the final 13 miles up Portal Road. It was quite a climb to the finish, and I still had a lot of people to catch.

I asked my crew for some coffee beans, cranked up the music and started to run. I was definitely out of my mind at this point. I believe I noticed a sign warning about bears. I begged my crew to keep the lights burning for me. Like I said, I was borderline delirious.

I pushed absolutely as hard as I could and as fast as I could and finally... FINALLY reached the finish line!

I couldn't have done it without my crew, Lisa and believe it or not, "Pillow Bob," who had made me so mad it drove me to the finish line to escape from Hell.

2003 Finishing Time – 42:03:13
Thirteenth Place

© imago sportfotodienst/Norbert Schmidt

CHAPTER TEN – ROGER KLEIN

From Roger's 2003 Badwater Application:

Age: 57
Hassel, Luxembourg

Why I want a slot on the start line of the 2003 Badwater Ultramarathon:

I think it's the TOP of the ultra races. To finish Badwater must be the highlight in a runner's life.

ONE ROAD, ONE GOAL *By Roger Klein*

I was a late bloomer. I didn't start running until I was 39 years old.

In Luxembourg City there is a 10-kilometer race every year. Times are not officially recorded, so after promising a colleague I would participate I finally entered the world of running. The date? July 7, 1985. I had never run farther than one kilometer in my life, but I lined up next to my colleague and took off in my first "ultra." After all, 10 kilometers is a long way for someone who had never even run an entire mile.

One hour later I finished, slightly ahead of my colleague. I felt every single muscle in my body, because every single one of them was aching. However, I had the satisfaction of achieving a goal. It was the start of a beautiful relationship, and from that point on I was running two or three times a week in my neighborhood.

One year later I ran my first half marathon, and felt I could do more. One more year, and I was lining up for my first marathon, which turned out to be a successful debut at 26.2 miles as I finished in a respectable 3:17, and my muscles felt just fine. What's next?

I was watching television one day and saw coverage of two women who had run through Death Valley. At first I thought they were crazy; after all, why would anyone voluntarily put themselves in such a miserable environment for a prolonged period of time?

For the next six years I competed in several marathons and ventured into the ultra ranks in locales such as the Island of Reunion, Jordan (The Desert Cup), as well as several mountain races in Switzerland.

In 2001 while competing in the Desert Cup I saw some pictures of a competition in Death Valley. I recalled seeing the two women on television several years ago running through Death Valley. I searched the Internet and ran across details of the competition known as the Badwater Ultramarathon. After a brief conversation with my wife and children, it was clear that one day I would be going to Death Valley to voluntarily put myself in a miserable environment for a prolonged period of time. I was hooked and there was no denying me my appointment with the toughest footrace on the planet.

My friends were (obviously) surprised, and wondered the same thing I had wondered about those two women not so long ago. Undeterred by the discouraging words from several of my friends, I began making my initial plans to run Badwater.

My first order of business – lining up a support crew – turned out to be quite simple. My wife Nicole, my parents Anna and Gilbert, my children Sven and Natasha and Alain, a friend of my children all agreed to follow me to the desert. The second order of business was submitting an application to the Race Director and waiting to see if I would be given an invitation. The waiting was difficult, but in time I would receive my official invitation to compete at Badwater.

Now for the logistics: I booked flights and hotel accommodations for the seven of us. I rented two cars. I scheduled two weeks of vacation after the race. From this point forward my mind was firmly entrenched in thinking about Badwater. Any time, every day – I was thinking about Badwater. Every conversation in our family or among my friends ultimately concluded with a Badwater update.

Next in line: some serious training. I increased my mileage from 100 kilometers a week to 250 kilometers a week, which meant that I was using virtually all of my free time to run. During my training the temperatures were regularly in the high 80's in Luxembourg from March until June. This was unusually warm for the area, but I considered it an opportunity to acclimate to the temperatures I would experience in Death Valley. Secretly, I thought it might not be too much warmer in the desert. I would find out that I was greatly mistaken.

As added incentive for my upcoming participation in the race, I started a campaign in Luxembourg to raise money for disabled children. I encouraged others to support this "crazy runner" who wanted to help others who aren't able to run; to help make their lives better. The campaign was a great success; in time a special playground for handicapped children was built through the donations raised by my run through Death Valley.

Slowly but surely my date in Death Valley approached, and I was becoming increasingly nervous. So many questions were running through my head: Can I run that far? Has my diet been adequate? Have I trained too much? Too little? Were my friends who told me running 135 miles through the hottest conditions imaginable was impossible right? I would soon know the answers to these questions and many, many more.

Friday, July 18, 2003

At 8:00 a.m. it was time. Finally, after many weeks of intense preparations my crew and I headed to the airport. We flew to Frankfurt where we changed planes and flew to Los Angeles. At 4:00 p.m. we were in California, and we immediately checked into our hotel. We were exhausted from our long day traveling through the sky. Plus, we knew we needed to put any rest possible in the next few days "in the bank.'

Saturday, July 19, 2003

We rented two cars and purchased a few items that were difficult to bring with us from Luxembourg. At 1:00 p.m. we headed out to Death Valley and were checking in at the hotel in Furnace Creek around 9:00 p.m. When we stepped out of our air-conditioned cars, we were overwhelmed by the oppressive heat. My morale immediately took a nosedive. Negative thoughts overwhelmed my mind: What am I doing here? Why am I doing this? I can't run farther than one kilometer in this heat! After a quick dinner I managed to fall asleep relatively fast – despite the ominous heat of the desert.

Sunday, July 20, 2003

We woke up at 8:00 a.m. The sun was already doing its thing, the temperature quickly rose, and by 10:00 a.m. it was already 113 degrees. In the shade. After breakfast we tried a short walk to get used to the temperature, but the heat was still rising and before long we were back in our hotel room, where we could set the air conditioner on high.

In the afternoon we drove the 17-mile stretch from Furnace Creek to Badwater to check out the starting area of the race. We took some photos and after 15 minutes or so we had our fill of the heat and headed back to the hotel. I decided on the way back I wanted to get out of the car and run the last five miles. My wife Nicole was driving and she reluctantly let me out of the car on the lonely stretch of road to fend for myself. We agreed that if I weren't back at the hotel in one hour she would return to look for me. It was 4:00 p.m. in the afternoon and I shocked quite a few tourists as they drove by and snapped a photo of me – *who was this crazy person running through the desert in the middle of the afternoon?*

One hour later I was back in my room at the hotel, perspiring profusely. Many thoughts were running through my mind, most prominently this one:

If I am broken after only five miles, how am I going to complete 135 miles?

I focused on the confidence in me by those who had supported my run through their generous donations to support the disabled children. I had to have that same degree of confidence in myself.

Monday, July 21, 2003

I was awake by 6:00 a.m. and immediately went outside for a one-hour run. The temperature was in the high 80's, which felt surprisingly cool and gave my morale a much-needed boost. At noon I picked up my racing packet and met with several of the runners who would be competing in tomorrow's race. At 3:00 p.m. my crew and I attended the pre-race briefing. Despite the oppressive heat in the auditorium (*no air conditioning!*) there was a positive, uplifting atmosphere shared by everyone during the two-hour meeting outlining the rules and recognizing several prominent people in the Badwater community. The rest of the day was spent preparing our supplies and organizing them in the car. We purchased more water and ice, and after dinner I was in bed by 9:00 p.m. and, thankfully, fell asleep immediately.

Tuesday, July 22, 2003

I slept well and was awake by 4:00 a.m. After a lukewarm shower, I got into my running attire. At 5:00 a.m. Crew #1 (wife Nicole, daughter Natasha, mother Anna) and I drove to the starting line in Badwater. We were one of the first teams to arrive. I rubbed cream on my feet and carefully put on my socks, paying particular attention to making sure there were no "wrinkles" that could lead to blisters later on. I then put on my running shoes and tied them with the same care. More teams were arriving as I made my last-minute preparations.

It was already 95 degrees and the sun was still hidden behind the mountains. I was assigned the 6:00 a.m. start, and after the obligatory group photograph, we were ready to compete.

Adam Bookspan, a participant in the race played the American National Anthem on his trumpet. This was a very emotional moment as the melody echoed through the valley. At precisely 6:00 a.m. Race Director Chris Kostman started the 2003 Badwater Ultramarathon.

Early on I was running a steady pace, holding firmly on to seventh place amongst the runners in the first starting group. By 8:00 a.m. the last shadows of the mountains were gone and the sun was now shining brightly in a clear blue sky. The temperature rose relatively fast, and I quickly changed into a running outfit sporting both long sleeves and long pants to protect my limbs from the brilliant sunshine. I changed my shoes and socks regularly throughout the day (a practice I would dismiss albeit unintentionally – the next day, which would ultimately result in three blisters). My crew was doing a good job of supplying me with fresh water and solid food. At 9:12 a.m. I reached the first checkpoint in Furnace Creek, firmly entrenched in second place and with no physical problems to speak of. I was amazed at how fast I had run the first 17 miles. Had I run too fast? I maintained my pace and before long I was running in first place (remember, there were still two other starting groups to follow at 8:00 and 10:00 a.m.). I was beginning to doubt my performance, or should I say my *restraint*? As there now weren't any other runners in front of me, I slowed down my pace. Meanwhile, the temperature was now above 120 degrees. Nicole put an ice cold wet towel over my head and across my shoulders to cool down my body. My morale was still good and my body felt well.

At noon Crew #2 (son Sven and friend Alain) took over. By 3:00 p.m. I was experiencing my first physical crossroad – spasms in my left leg. This concerned me because I was only 35 miles into the race. Even more importantly, there were still 100 miles remaining. To compensate for the spasms, I altered my running style so as to take some of the pressure off of my left leg. A medical team patrolling the course stopped and asked if I had any problems. I told them of my spasms and they advised me that if I wanted to finish the race I would need to drink even more water as well as regularly take salt tablets. I followed this advice and in time the spasms would disappear.

While I was dealing with my spasm problem, two runners had passed me by so when I arrived at the second checkpoint in Stovepoint Wells at 4:23 p.m. I was now in third place. We had booked a hotel room here so my crew encouraged me to go to the room to get something fresh to eat. Twenty minutes later I was back on the course. We were now at sea level and over the next 17 miles we would climb approximately 5,000 feet. I transitioned from running to walking in an effort to sustain my energy. To make matters worse a very hot wind was blowing across my path, making progress up the mountain difficult. At 6:00 p.m. Crew #1 was back in action. Physically I didn't have any problems with the exception of a small blister on my right heel, which Nicole promptly treated. The wind was taking its toll, so I took a short break around 9:00 p.m. I spent 30 minutes inside the car to escape the wind, and by the time I returned to the course the wind had abated somewhat. I arrived at Townes Pass around midnight.

Wednesday, July 23, 2003

Crew #2 was back on the job as I began my 11-mile descent into Panamint Springs, the third checkpoint. Shortly after 1:00 a.m. something happened we had not anticipated – a sharp stone had flattened the front left tire of our car. My spirit was dampened immediately, and several thoughts ran through my mind: Do we have a car jack? Is the spare tire OK? What happens if we suffer a second flat tire? All of these negative thoughts accomplished nothing, and the fact remained that we had to change the tire. To do this, we had to remove the coolers, supplies and gear that were in the trunk of the car. Fortunately we found the jack and the spare tire, and after an hour we had the tire changed and the trunk reloaded and I was able to resume my run. However, my spirits were still low and my morale didn't seem to be improving, so I opted for a sleep break around 3:00 a.m. I fell asleep in the passenger seat where I remained for the next 60 minutes. Once I woke up, every muscle in my body ached as I tried to put them back in motion. A few minutes later I made a decision: There would be no more sleep breaks.

I reached Panamint Springs at 6:48 a.m. By now, at this – the third checkpoint, many runners from the second and third starting groups had passed me. I was now in twentieth place, and I was experiencing my mentally lowest point in the entire race. Over the next 16 miles – all uphill – my spirit was coming alive. I was beginning to feel better and better. My morale was on the rise and I thought that in this crazy race I still might – with a little luck – finish under 48 hours which would reward me with the coveted belt buckle awarded to all sub-48 hour finishers. Crew #1 returned during this climb when suddenly two F-16 fighters flew quite low through the valley. The loud sounds created by the planes unsettled the women, but not me – I welcomed the entertainment! It's great to see F-16 fighters flying through the desert!

At 11:46 a.m. I reached the top of the mountain – and the fourth checkpoint, after another 5,000 foot climb. However, what I saw in the distance was not encouraging: a large, wide valley with a blurred mountain range behind it.

Somewhere in that blurred mountain range was my goal, which meant that for the next 32 miles the road moved like a worm through the valley. All I had to guide me was the black asphalt in the middle of two painted lines leading me to the finish line. Despite this seemingly endless road in front of me, I focused on the goal I desperately wanted to achieve. I calculated over and over in my head how much longer it would be before I would reach Lone Pine... and the finish line on Mount Whitney.

I asked my crew – repeatedly – how I was doing. Would I finish under 48 hours- Numbers became more and more confusing. My calculations were interrupted when the Race Director stopped in his car and asked if I wanted an ice cream. I accepted it without hesitation, and the cool, soft and delicious ice cream was a welcome change from the food and drink I had been forcing down over the past few hours.

At 6:00 p.m. Crew #2 returned. I was making good progress, still intently focusing on my next two destinations. I was beginning to see houses, which meant Lone Pine, the fifth checkpoint, was near. Dark clouds were gathering behind me and I feared that a severe storm was approaching. But apart from a few drops of rain that evaporated instantly once they reached the hot asphalt, the storm never developed. It was becoming quite dark, so I put on my reflective vest and headlamp as we arrived in Lone Pine at 9:20 p.m. Thirteen miles remained: the long, lonely 13-mile climb to the portals of Mount Whitney.

It may sound unusual, perhaps even unbelievable, but I was looking forward to this final climb of 8,000 feet. The long 32-mile stretch was now behind me, and I was on the precipice of finishing my long journey that started almost two days ago. I grabbed a flashlight and asked my crew to reset the odometer in the car to zero so I would know exactly how many miles I had left to walk to reach the finish line. Again and again I asked how much I had left to complete the race; so much, in fact that I was not only getting on the nerves of my crew but on *my* nerves as well.

I decided that my wife should advise me as each mile counted down by giving me a cup of Coke. This helped the miles pass by and oddly enough, my crew had actually been giving me a cup of Coke after every *one-point-two* miles (a scheme devised by my crew to provide me with a pleasant surprise later in the race, as I would actually be much closer to the finish than I had been calculating). But what the heck: After four hours and 17 minutes I finished my climb and arrived at the finish line at precisely 1:37:09 a.m. My finish time was officially 43 hours, 37 minutes and 9 seconds. The coveted belt buckle would be mine!

I had achieved the unthinkable goal that had existed in my head for years, and what I had prepared myself for over the past several months. I owe my success to my crew, who has my unending praise and thanks. A novice crew all, they had performed admirably in the most difficult of conditions. They were always there for me, and I know in my heart that without them I could not have done it.

A big thank you goes to all of the people and the sponsors who placed their trust in me and supported my campaign for the disabled children.

Three small blisters on my feet and legs that felt as if they were made of lead reminded me the next morning of what I had accomplished over the past two days.

I've never felt better.

2003 Finishing Time – 43:37:09
Eighteenth Place

© imago sportfotodienst/Norbert Schmidt

CHAPTER ELEVEN – JANE BALLANTYNE

From Jane's 2003 Badwater Application:

Age: 48
British Columbia, Canada

Why I want a slot on the start line of the 2003 Badwater Ultramarathon:

The reason I want to compete in the 2003 Badwater Ultramarathon is because I feel this is the ultimate physical and mental challenge. I have wanted to do this race for several years, and I was especially motivated to do it after Steve King did so well in 2001. That, plus Steve's account of how wonderful this race is, how well organized it is, how great the people are and what an incredible experience it is to complete this event. Steve and his wife Jean will be part of my crew and I know they are looking forward to returning for another Badwater experience.

A LOT OF HELP FROM MY FRIENDS *By Jane Ballantyne*

I have been trying to figure out what made me decide to apply for Badwater. If you've read the description of the race, it is not something that you might think "Oh this will be fun!"

Think of the hardest thing that you have ever set out to do. Now think of how you felt when you finished. I believe that feeling is what made me take on the Badwater challenge.

You begin every adventure with a picture in your mind of what it is going to look like; the actual reality of the journey either confirms or shatters that preconceived picture.

I went off to Badwater with the knowledge that it was 135 miles of highway with some steep climbs in very hot conditions. Hot was an understatement; "a few degrees from hell" is far more accurate!

All the preparations, the training, the sauna time, watching the documentary of the 1999 Badwater Ultramarathon *Running on the Sun* (about five times), reading Kirk Johnson's book *To the Edge* (only three times) – nothing could have prepared me for the race; you just had to experience it to understand.

My Story

The crew and I arrived in Furnace Creek two days before the race was to start. As we got out of the air-conditioned car, we quickly realized why they called it "Furnace Creek." The heat was unbearable and we all decided to make our first stop the pool! We threw our bags in our rooms and headed over to the spring fed pool. Doesn't that sound refreshing? We dove in only to find out that the water temperature was over 100 degrees- Again the name should have given us some indication!

After dinner on the first night the crew decided they should stay out and have a few drinks...sort of a bonding session. I was glad to excuse myself and get to bed early. I guess a few drinks turned into quite a few drinks...needless to say the next day no one was too keen on our prearranged morning run. Even early in the morning, the sun was already high in the sky and the temperature was already over 120 degrees. The short run gave us all clear insight into why they call it "Death Valley!" The crew, looking a bit – shall we say *green*, had their first taste of what the next two days were going to be like: they looked a bit terrified!

On that fateful Tuesday, I started in the 8 a.m. group; I had two vans and six crewmembers. The vans were loaded with everything but the kitchen sink. "Just in case we need it" was our packing motto. That turned out to be a big mistake. What we ended up needing, we couldn't find!

My coach was Lisa Smith-Batchen, who has completed Badwater many times. Her training program had me in the best shape of my life. I planned to run most of the 135 miles. After all, I didn't know exactly what I was getting into.

The race plan that had been laid out for me was thrown out the window after the first 20 miles. The smile that I had embarked on this journey with faded as I realized the magnitude of the challenge that lay before me. With almost 115 miles left to go, it struck me that this was going to be much more difficult than I had expected! The heat and the awesome reality of how long 135 miles really was took over. I was reduced to fast walking after the first check-in at about 17 miles. I could no longer keep up the "run" portion of my alternating walk/run routine.

I felt like I was cooking from the inside out – as well as the outside in. I had to keep checking my skin to see if it was being scorched by the burning sun. Only 17 miles... I already had blisters and was slowed to a walk.

This wasn't right.

I trudged on, doing the best I could to power walk and occasionally run in what was turning out to be the hottest Badwater race day ever...

As the miles went slowly by, the morning turned into afternoon, and the temperatures continued to soar, I felt discouraged and started to have doubts. With all the blisters that had already formed on my feet, would I be able to hobble my way for another 100 miles? The race had really just begun and I already felt beaten.

Luckily I had the most amazing crew: Steve King, his wife Jean, my husband Lanny and three good friends: John, Areef and Eric. They were there at every mile with smiles, encouragement and taking orders for any kind of food or drink I wanted. I know they were feeling the heat as well, but not once did I hear them complain about it or about the ridiculously slow pace I had adopted. They were my team and supported me every painful step of the way! Not once did I see any doubt in their eyes as they continued to reassure me with the consistent encouragement of "you are doing great!"

This was not the picture I had in my mind of how things were going to go-

Then I realized: this is what Badwater is for me. It is like life: You plan, you set goals, you prepare, but it is never quite like you planned because it is not all in your control. The true test of fitness, both physical and mental, is to adjust to how things unfold and to make the best of what you get.

I realized I had to change my plan and my attitude. I had to accept this was not going to be the run I had hoped for, but it was going to be more than the challenge I had bargained for! I had to figure out how to continue moving forward. The blisters were not going to go away and the sun was going to be up for many more hours.

Some of the crew was already experiencing heatstroke. The clipboard that was to be used for recording my calorie and fluid intake only had two entries on it at the end of the race. Nausea had prevented the record keeper from writing while the car was moving. I knew nothing of this until the race was over.

For two days, I was the only one that mattered. I would ask how everyone was doing and they would just say "we're doing great...keep going, Jane."

Someone had recommended bringing a water sprayer to cool the runner down. Because it played into our motto of "in case we need it" we had brought one along. I thought they meant a small plant sprayer, which was not quite the size required! The crew enthusiastically sprayed me at every opportunity, but it was like trying to put out a fire with a squirt gun and eventually we gave that up. We started putting small towels in the coolers with the melted ice; I would drape one over my shoulders and wrap another one around my waist like a skirt. In a matter of minutes they would both be dry and we would do it over again. It kept me from frying in the sun and made the hot wind bearable.

The blisters were accumulating and there was one very large one on my heel. Every step was agonizing. I decided to try switching to open-toed sandals.

I had thrown them in "just in case;" I had never intended to wear them. After all, I wouldn't be walking, remember? As it turned out I wore them for many, many miles. I couldn't really run in them, but I could walk with much less pain.

So, now in sandals and alternating cold towels regularly, I plugged on in the heat; the sun felt like it was burning a hole through my skin. There was lots of wind; it was loud and very, very hot. I had to stop many times to try to relieve the blister situation, but we didn't really have the equipment or the "know how" to treat them, so I would eventually decide just to go on.

As the sun started to set we pulled into the second check-in at Stovepipe Wells. Only 42 miles down and so many miles left to go... and the first day was nearly over.

I have to admit that I felt a bit down, even though I had resolved to stay positive. Seeing that there were other runners at the check-in gave me a lift as I had assumed I was so far behind I was probably last! After a swim in the pool and some chicken soup I began to feel a bit better. Luckily Doctor Andy (a fellow runner in the race) kindly agreed to work on the worst blister on my heel, and another crew provided tape and supplies. The other crews were all willing to help other runners in any way that they could, a good spirit of "kokua."

As we prepared to set out again, the crew went to get ice. Stovepipe Wells was out of ice; a very serious problem. Areef, John and Jean decided to drive back to Furnace Creek to get the ice while we started the climb up Townes Pass. It was getting dark at this point and although we had been told it got cooler in the desert at night, that was not the case on this particular night. The temperature stayed around 110 degrees all night. Eric and I walked for hours toward the top of Townes Pass, Eric got a back spasm a little after half way and Lanny relieved him and continued the climb with me.

The other crew had returned with the ice and met us at the top with a chair ready along with food and drinks. I rested while the crew tried to put my sore and swollen feet into running shoes again. They thought I would be able to run the downhill section that was coming up. It was hopeless, so I continued on wearing my sandals. All I could manage was a fast walk. Areef, John and Jean took the first sleeping shift, returning from Panamint Springs around 3 a.m. Steve, Lanny and Eric went back to the motel at the shift change. Areef and John took turns walking with me during the night, but I have to admit I wasn't very talkative; I had hit a really low spot.

As the night wore on and the sun started to creep up, I felt truly exhausted. I felt irritated I couldn't run and frustrated I could see Panamint Springs, but it wasn't getting any closer. At one point I caught up to another runner and his crewmember said he thought it was about three miles to Panamint Springs. It looked so close, but in reality there were still 10 miles to go! The lights had been visible in the distance for hours and it seemed like they never got any closer; it turned out there was a valley you had to cross in between which created the illusion of Panamint Springs being closer than it really was.

Lanny appeared back around 6:30 and walked the last six miles with me into Panamint Springs. I was walking at a good clip and he said he was having trouble keeping up.

That made me feel better, as I had been feeling like I was moving at a pace slower than a snail for hours, making very little progress; or so it seemed. But finally I could really see Panamint Springs and knew I would make it before I fell completely apart.

Arriving at the check-in at Panamint Springs was a huge relief, which only lasted for a few minutes when I realized I still had half of the race remaining! Exhausted and blistered I stumbled to our motel room for a shower and a change of clothes. Alone inside the room I burst into tears and had a really good cry.

Trying to be brave for 24 hours had taken its toll. My husband walked in and tried to console me. I asked him, "Do you think anyone will mind if I stop here? I just don't think that I can go on." He replied "Well, I only know one person who will mind, and that would be you." In my condition, I couldn't imagine that I would care, I only wanted to climb into bed and sleep forever! But I knew Lanny was right: I had worked very hard to earn a place in the prestigious Badwater field, and I knew I had to continue to push on.

After a shower and a fresh wardrobe, I have to admit I felt much better. The crew brought me breakfast and Steve brought me Denise Jones! My first miracle of the race! Denise is well known for treating blisters and she agreed to treat mine and tape my feet. I rested while Denise worked her magic: first draining the blisters, and then applying 2nd Skin and tape. An hour later I was ready to go; my feet tender and still wrapped in sandals, Steve and I started the climb up Father Crowley's.

Steve had completed Badwater a few years earlier and I think walking up Father Crowley's brought back good memories for him. Several steep switchbacks loomed ahead as we turned every corner; there didn't appear to be any end in sight. The day was slightly cooler, only reaching about 120 degrees. There was cloud cover throughout the day, so that helped to ease the burning effects of the sun on my skin. I am not sure at what point it started, but a tight knot developed in my lower back. I was very worried as there was still so much more climbing to do.

After I had just told Steve that it was getting tighter, a car came by, a window rolled down, and a very pretty girl declared herself a Massage Therapist and asked if anyone needed a massage? My second miracle! Debbie the Massage Therapist was there to crew for another runner and as she was making her way back along the course looking for her runner she was offering massages along the way. She swiftly set up the massage table and after a quick two-minute massage I was up and on my way, feeling so much better. As I resumed my progress up Father Crowley's, I had to give my head a shake and ask "Was that a mirage?"

The climb continued on all day. I was very fortunate to have Steve at my side, doling out encouragement the entire way. I was tired and my feet hurt, but when I got to the top of Father Crowley's and turned around and saw the endless miles behind me, I realized then and there I would finish. I hadn't come this far not to run, walk or perhaps trudge on to the end.

By the time we got to Darwin it was nearly 5 p.m. on Wednesday afternoon; I had completed 90 painfully slow miles. The crew suggested a short break and we tried again to see if I could squeeze into any of the numerous pairs of running shoes in our vehicles. Everyone in the crew brought out all their shoes, but none of them seemed to fit. Then I remembered a pair of size 10 shoes I had thrown in "just in case;" they were still in the box, as they had been two sizes too big at the start of the race, but our thought was perhaps now they would fit! Eric tried to put them on my feet. My blistered feet screamed out in pain and I said this isn't going to work. I eyed my sandals again and the crew all looked at each other. They knew if I continued at our current pace I was not going to make the 48-hour cutoff for the buckle. They didn't say anything to me at the time, and I had no idea we were even that close to making the cutoff. You see, I actually couldn't think about much at all... except putting one foot in front of the other.

Steve was talking about having to find a shoe I could run in. I was thinking "who's running?" *I could barely walk!*

Eric started to cut the toe out of the pair of size 10's. I was protesting they were brand new shoes and never worn, but Eric continued with the knife. I tried them on again. I could walk gingerly in them and after a few minutes the pain dulled enough that I started to run very slowly. I was off again.

The crew was elated, as they hadn't seen me run much since Tuesday morning. I can only imagine how exhausting my slow progress had been for them. When I say I can only imagine, that is because they all stayed so positive, and even at the absolute lowest points we found something to laugh about; keeping things light helped me to cope.

We stopped at the 100 mile mark for a photo: *my first 100 miles ever!*

I was excited to be running again. I don't think it hit me that I had already traveled 100 miles and that my body was tired, so although I was thrilled with my new-found ability to run again, it wasn't long before it became a struggle and I really had to focus on each and every step. The reality of how many miles I had left hit me just after that 100 mile mark: there were still 35 miles to go, and 12 of them straight up Mount Whitney!

I assumed a routine of run four minutes, walk one minute. I kept this pattern up quite consistently all the way to Lone Pine. It was a long second night and I have to admit I was starting to see things that weren't there. I was running and the crew wanted to keep it that way. Areef and John took turns running with me. At times I know I became irritable: the lights marking Lone Pine were visible for what seemed like an eternity, but as with the previous night, we never seemed to get any closer. Occasionally stones from the side of the road would get in my open-toed running shoes, which would require Eric to assist me with removing them. Eric thus became known as "the shoe guy."

For hours I focused intently on the white line on the road: it kept me steady. I felt panicky if I lost sight of it, as it would give me the impression I was going to fall off the road. If I lost sight of the white line, I would end up on the side of road getting those small stones in my shoes. At one point I had my headphones on and I was listening to music. I slipped off the road onto the shoulder and looked at Areef saying "the stones." He simply smiled and nodded his head. I was getting really irritated with him and pointing to my shoes, and he finally understood. He was thinking I was saying that I was listening to the Rolling Stones; we had a good laugh about that. During the second night of no sleep for me and very little rest for the crew, just about anything could make us laugh... or cry. I was getting pretty frayed.

Finally we arrived at the check-in at Lone Pine. I was so focused on getting to Lone Pine I had forgotten about the time cutoff. All of sudden I realized I had no idea how long it had taken me to get there. I asked Steve if he thought I was going to make it in time for a buckle. He looked at his watch and said "it's possible." I didn't know then he was actually thinking he had his doubts; thank goodness he didn't tell me the actual time, as I think I would have given up on the time goal.

I knew I had the climb up Mount Whitney ahead of me. It was dark and I could see the steep ascent that lay ahead. I just walked as fast as I could possibly go. I was now focused on not wasting any time in hopes of finishing under the 48-hour mark. The crew took turns walking with me; Eric and Lanny did most of the hills with me. Amazingly we passed many runners on the climb, and that spurred me on. I had thrown in a pair of cross country ski polls and I thought I could use some steadying, so someone eventually found them in one of the vans.

That really helped as I was exhausted. I got into a good rhythm and made pretty good time to the top. As we got close to the finish, our emotions soared: it was the most incredible feeling for all of us to hold hands and run the last few yards and break through the tape as one.

We were there.

I had covered 135 miles in the hottest conditions ever and would live to tell about it... it was a proud moment. I looked at my crew and was so thankful to have such good and kind friends. They had been with me every step of the way.

I will always be grateful they shared this experience with me.

2003 Finishing Time – 45:23:46
Twenty-second Place

© Thinkstock/iStockphoto/Fluid Illusion

CHAPTER TWELVE – MARSHALL ULRICH

From Marshall's 2003 Badwater Application:

Age: 52
Brighton, Colorado

Previous Badwater Racing Experience:

- *10 Badwater finishes (15 total crossings of Death Valley)*
- *Record holder – running across Death Valley from Badwater to the top of Mount Whitney covering 146 miles in over*
- *120 degree heat in 33 hours 54 minutes*
- *Former record holder – four-time winner of the Badwater 146 desert race*
- *Record – 10-time finisher of Badwater 146 desert race*
- *Record holder – 133 mile south to north summer crossing of Death Valley Monument (28:01)*
- *Record holder – and only person to finish a self-contained, unaided, solo run pulling a 220-pound cart 146 miles from Badwater to the top of Mount Whitney (77:46)*
- *Record holder – first to complete Badwater double, triple and quad (584 miles from Badwater to the top of Mount Whitney and back again – twice – over 10 days*

THE DESERT FOX *By Scott Ludwig*

With ten finishes on his resume – four of which were overall victories, including three straight from 1991 to 1993 – it would have been easy for him to dismiss the 2003 Badwater Ultramarathon as "just another race." But that, you see, is not indicative of the spirit of Marshall Ulrich; one that exists to perpetuate the sport of running and prove to people they can do more than they ever dreamed of doing.

Marshall has spent the better part of the last two decades pushing himself to the very edge of physical and mental exhaustion, serving as living proof that there are still countless boundaries limits that remain to be explored.

In its original form, the Badwater Ultramarathon was 146 miles long, finishing at the summit of Mount Whitney. However, as the area beyond the Whitney Portals (134.4 miles, the current finish line) is a national wilderness area, the race was not allowed to extend to the very top of the mountain. As a tribute to the original format of the race, each year Marshall obtains a permit which allows him to continue to the peak of the mountain once he crosses the finish line; sometimes right after he finishes the race, sometimes after a rest of several hours, and once in a while after enjoying a "night off" and returning the next morning.

But that, by no means, is where Marshall's commitment to pushing himself to his limits ends.

In 1996, Marshall added the Furnace Creek 508, a 508-mile bicycle race through Death Valley to his resume, finishing in 38 hours and 31 minutes becoming the first person to complete both races in one season. After adding in his Badwater time of 33:01, he set the record for the Death Valley Cup with a cumulative time of 71 hours and 32 minutes.

In 1999, just running Badwater wasn't enough for Marshall. Before the official race but still in July (as all record attempts in Death Valley must be completed in either July or August), he did the first (and still *only*) Death Valley SOLO (unaided and completely self-contained) crossing on the original Badwater course in 77 hours and 46 minutes. Marshall covered the 146 miles by pulling a 220 pound cart carrying all the water, food and miscellaneous supplies he needed to not only finish, but to survive. Just a couple of weeks later Marshall ran the Badwater course in 35:52, finishing in sixth place. Naturally, he went to the summit of Mount Whitney afterwards.

Then, to top off his adventures in the desert, in 2001 Marshall completed the Death Valley Quad, which is exactly what it sounds like. Marshall completed the original Badwater course of 146 miles (Badwater to the summit of Mount Whitney and back two times) an amazing four times in 253 hours (10 days and 13 hours)! In fact, for the third crossing he actually competed in the official Badwater Ultramarathon, which he finished in 54:59 and 44th place (after which he climbed to the summit and then ran back to Badwater one more time to complete his journey of 584 miles). So you see, it would have been very easy for Marshall to dismiss the 2003 Badwater Ultramarathon as just another race. Especially when you consider that not only was it going to be his 11th Badwater; it was also going to be his 16th crossing of Death Valley. But this year Badwater was different. Marshall had ventured into mountaineering in 2002 and began his quest to complete not only Badwater but to reach the summits of the seven highest mountains in the world. He called the quest "Journey 2 Extremes."

At the end of June 2003 Marshall traveled to Africa where he conquered Mount Kilimanjaro, which precluded him from having done any running for the five weeks leading up to Badwater, as running on the mountain, or out in the Serengeti where runners could be considered prey is not very prudent. Not only that, he hadn't done any heat training (his normal pre-Badwater regimen consisted of sauna workouts in the six weeks prior to the race – up to 75 minutes with a few breaks with the temperature at "a couple of hundred degrees"). He was, however, very acclimated to the *cold*. Unfortunately, Death Valley is one of the *hottest* places on earth.

So in 2003 Marshall set his sights on taking it easy. He started the race at a nice, steady pace with his good friend Bob Haugh. However, Haugh had to drop out of the race with a medical problem at Stovepipe Wells, so Marshall continued on with his support crew and crew chief, wife Heather. Marshall eventually met up with Badwater rookie Mike Karch, who was having difficulty in his initial attempt in Death Valley. With Marshall's support, Karch was able to successfully complete the race in a buckle-earning 47 hours and 19 minutes (Note: Marshall, who started the race two hours later than Karch, finished in 45:30).

Although the days of winning Badwater – and finishing in times almost 20 hours faster than his 2003 time – are behind him, Marshall says he enjoys his runs across Death Valley and now sets his sights on taking it easy and maybe "helping someone along the way." That's not to say, however that at 61 years of age he's ready to rest on his laurels anytime soon.

In fact, quite the contrary. Marshall began mountaineering at the age of 51 and in less than three years reached all Seven Summits (Everest, Aconcagua, Denali, Kilimanjaro, Elbrus, Vinson and Koscuisko) – all on his first attempt! Marshall is the personification of enjoying diversity – and his firm belief that you shouldn't stop when you reach the age of 50.

Marshall's ventures in the sport of adventure racing – which he took up to show people that they didn't have to feel like they had to be trapped in one sport and should "think outside the box and try something new" – are legendary. He is one of three people *in the world* to have competed in all nine Eco Challenge adventure races.

Marshall Ulrich: Ultra runner. Mountaineer. Adventure racer.

Although his exploits and adventures in Death Valley echo throughout the desert, Marshall Ulrich says he still fills out the official Badwater Ultramarathon application every year as he doesn't expect any special consideration.
Marshall Ulrich: Gracious. Humble.

The history of the Badwater Ultramarathon wouldn't be as rich without the accomplishments of Al Arnold, Ben Jones, Pam Reed...

and Marshall Ulrich, the Desert Fox.

2003 Finishing Time – 45:30:04
Twenty-fourth Place

CHAPTER THIRTEEN – RUBEN CANTU

From Ruben's 2003 Badwater Application:

Age: 60
Santee, California

My Weirdest Experience:

In the 2000 Badwater race I had hallucinations in the Panamint Valley around 2:00 a.m. I saw Quonset huts and tanks and other visions. In the Alabama Hills I saw many different kinds of small animals, like baby elephants and hippos.

A RUNNER'S HIGH *By Ruben Cantu*

I am returning to Death Valley to run my fourth Badwater Ultramarathon.

Badwater is a grueling 135-mile race across one of the hottest places on earth. My work associates, friends and family all question my sanity each year, but afterwards are happy and proud I was successful in completing the run. Unless you have been there as a runner, crewmember or race staff, it is understandable why we are so judged and misunderstood. I have been fortunate enough to have the right crew, God's blessings and the fortitude to finish each of the last three years. I have three buckles in my closet.

This year I am 60 years old so I plan to raise the bar and run a Badwater double. That is an out and back for a total of 292 miles including the summit of Mount Whitney. I want to be the first person 60 or over to run a Badwater double. My crew is set with Mike Devlin, my best friend and running partner. Mike crewed for me on my initial Badwater in 2000 and knows me and my running ability better than anybody else. He supports and encourages me like no other. He has been my training partner from the time I decided to run Badwater. Also joining my crew is another very good friend, H.E. West. H.E. is an experienced Badwater crewmember as he crewed for me in 2000 and 2001.

H.E. initially crewed for my Badwater idol, Marshall Ulrich, around 1990 when Marshall set the record for the fastest run from Badwater to the summit of Mount Whitney; a total of 146 miles. The racecourse has since been changed to the current finish at the Mount Whitney Portal and 135 miles.

I also have another returnee and friend Kristen and her friend Bram (Badwater rookie crewmember). With Mike will be Jeanne, his fiancée, also a Badwater rookie crewmember. So I am set with another outstanding crew. This being my fourth Badwater I think I am ready for a double.

The Race

The race started on time and all looked well off of the line with only Kristen and Bram crewing as the remaining crew was not expected to arrive until later in the race. Mike and Jeanne were due to join us later in the first day with H.E. West joining us the next morning. Mike and H.E. had prior business commitments. This normally works out OK as they augment our ice supply when they arrive and are well rested and not fried from the first day's sun.

The Badwater race has a staggered start composed of three waves: 6:00 a.m., 8:00 a.m. and 10:00 a.m. We were in the first wave at 6:00 a.m. To ease the psychologically long-distance pain I break down the race into intermediate milestones or goals. My first goal is Furnace Creek, just 17 miles but a very critical 17 miles as it sets the tone for the entire race. My goal is to get there in approximately three and a half hours. (I play a game where I "store time" for later. By that I mean that my goal is 45 hours to the finish.

That requires a 20-minute per mile average pace for 45 hours). Therefore if I run the first 17 miles in 3.5 hours, I will store approximately two hours.

We reached Furnace Creek pretty much on time and looking good. The temperature was very normal compared to my three previous starts: around 100 degrees at 6:00 a.m., then gradually rising as the sun breaks through. When we reached Furnace Creek it was a comfortable 115 to 120 degrees. At this time we did not expect anything different than in the recent past. However, the road to Stovepipe had something in store for me; extreme heat. It turned out to be the hottest year in current history, somewhere in the neighborhood of 133 degrees.

Stovepipe is about a marathon away from Furnace Creek. This for me is the toughest and most challenging part of the race. But crazy as it may seem, it is also my favorite. This is where you separate yourself from the rest. If I can make it from Furnace Creek to Stovepipe in decent shape I feel I should be able to complete the race.

Too Hot, I Quit

This year presented the hottest environment of any of the four Badwaters with which I have been involved. The rumored air temperature (not official) was 133 degrees when we were around mile 36 on the course. (This figure came from another runner's crew vehicle thermometer.) The reflective temperature was somewhere in the 170's (again not official). The sun was so hot that at one time after I finished drinking a soft drink in an aluminum can and was carrying it to hand over to the crew, the can got so hot in my hand that I had to drop it. In my experience, the hot sun made this the most challenging race, requiring the runners to dig deeper and push harder than ever before. At one point, right around the area of the beautiful sand dunes I was forced inside the support vehicle to cool my head. I sat in front of the air conditioning vent breathing in the cool air. For the first time I felt like saying the dreaded words "I quit." But the crew would not allow me. It was also at this point that I sent my pacer into the support vehicle as I felt it was too dangerous for a person not properly trained or acclimated to extreme heat to continue running.

We limped into Stovepipe and spent a couple of hours cooling down while my crew replenished our ice supply and rearranged the support food and drinks. (I usually go through 500 pounds or more of ice during the race.) As we expected Mike and Jeanne to arrive anytime, we needed to prepare to change support vehicles and give the current crew some badly needed rest. This was also the best time to contact my wife Carol back home to give her an update on our progress since there is no cell phone service in Death Valley. A kind word from her does a lot for my psyche. We have finally climbed out of the Badwater basin at 282 feet below sea level and reached sea level at Stovepipe

Now for the third milestone: Townes Pass. A mere 17 miles but they feel like they are straight up. We must now climb from sea level to almost 5,000 feet in 17 miles. The bad thing about going up towards the summit of Townes Pass is not just the distance, the oppressive heat and the steepness of the uphill climb, but all of that is compounded by the hot winds that whip around the hills blowing like a hair dryer. The good thing about climbing towards Townes Pass is that for every 1,000 feet of climb the temperature drops about five degrees. However, I am starting to experience heartburn and upset stomach regardless of what I drink or eat. This is a problem I have come to experience in every Badwater Race, and it is a problem that I have not been able to develop a good solution for yet.

Once we struggled up and got to the top of Townes Pass I took a half hour break. By then the temperature had dropped to about 85 degrees and it felt so cool that I had to use a blanket while I lay down and tried to get some rest. As happy as I felt having reached that milestone, I was also very disappointed that Mike had not shown up yet and was also worried that something may have happened because Mike is very dependable. That is not good because the last thing you need during Badwater is having to worry about your crew.

Up and over to milestone four, Panamint Springs, at approximately 72 miles on the course and about 3,500 feet down from Townes Pass. This section, although mostly down hill, is not easy by any means because by now my quads are worn, my legs are wasted and my feet are hurting. Panamint Springs is normally my third scheduled rest stop. I usually plan another half hour break in Panamint Springs. I struggle as necessary to get there because I want to check in at the Time Station. This allows my family and friends at home to check on and track my progress on the live webcast of the race.

My body may have been wasted and my legs ready to explode but I felt strong and determined to go on. This is when we made contact with Mike and Jeanne and knew they were on the way. What I enjoy about this part of the race is that my Badwater pace puts me near Panamint Springs in the dark of night or early morning. I enjoy seeing the long line of blinking lights from the runners" vests and their support vehicles on the way down to the Panamint Valley then up to Panamint Springs. It is a scene like no other.

The heartburn had become unbearable and a major problem. I needed to eat and MUST hydrate but everything I consumed caused me great indigestion. Nothing seemed to work. Even my favorite Gatorade was torturous to my stomach. While feeling down and trying to rest at Panamint Springs, my fellow runner and great friend Chris Frost caught up to me (he was in the 10:00 a.m. wave). Seeing me in such pathetic shape he offered me his magic stomach potion: ginger. Another fellow runner, I believe it was Lisa Smith-Batchen, gave me some of her magic juice: Baby Pedialite. I don't know which one or if it was the combination of both, but it proved to be the right stuff. I just know I was able to eat and hydrate enough to continue.

Mike and Jeanne

Another thing that motivated me was the arrival of Mike and Jeanne. It was like giving me a shot of adrenaline that I needed for milestone five, Father Crowley Lookout Point. We left Panamint Springs feeling great and ready to attack the next upgrade. The road going up to Father Crowley is narrow, winding and unrelenting. Add to that the start of another hot and humid day (due to the light rain we got while resting in Panamint Springs) and you have a climb that is absolutely no fun at all. However, the scenery visible during the climb is awesome if you are able, and take the time, to enjoy it. I made it up to Father Crowley and took a quick break and drank some Coke and ate some watermelon and went on with Mike and Jeanne pacing me.

The next milestone for me is the Darwin Turn-Off. A spot in the race so close to hell I don't know how those brave volunteers who man it can do it. It is literally in the middle of nowhere with no protection from the hot blowing wind. Getting there requires following a long undulating road where you can see where you are going but can't seem to get there. But on the positive side it is a break from all the climbing during the previous 20-plus hours. Once we got to Darwin Turn-Off I felt comfortable that we would not just finish but we would also buckle. The weather was not too hot but it was still a little humid. This section is where we leave Death Valley. A minor milestone, but good for the psyche.

After Darwin I aim my thoughts to the mile 100 sign just up the road. Not an interim goal but important to me as our total mileage covered hits triple digits. Also I start to "smell the barn" as we now clearly see Mount Whitney and are getting closer to the finish. Not an easy trek but within reach. From here I know I can finish in belt-buckle time but it becomes more of a death march. This year I am not able to run during this section but feel good.

Lone Pine

The great town of Keeler and the dry Owens Lake bed are up next on my agenda. If there is a boring part of Badwater, this is the place. It is a flat dry area where you not only see Mount Whitney but you can also see the lights of Lone Pine. This was the only place where we experienced some really bad sand storms. The wind blows the sand perpendicular to the road and really blasts your left side. However, if the winds are not bad and you are lucky enough to go through Keeler early in the afternoon, you will see some of the locals sitting out in their lawn chairs watching the "crazy Badwater runners" go by. I was lucky and enjoyed their presence and interest in our race. Comments were made that perhaps this is one of the most exciting things that happens in Keeler all year. It is a small place.

Lone Pine is my final milestone before the finish. The road to get there has some long, straight and flat sections but by now the weather has cooled down quite a bit. So all I have to be concerned with is getting there. One good thing I look forward to in Lone Pine is seeing my good friend and great supporter Don Meyer. As we approach the time station at Badwater Headquarters at the Dow Villa Hotel in Lone Pine, Don recognizes me and gets me a thunderous welcome (he does that for every runner). It is good to get this far. Now the last stretch to the finish.

Home At Last, Home At Last

The road up to the end of the race is 13 miles in which we climb another 5,000 feet. I am quite wasted but have the resolve to continue. At one point about three miles from the finish I asked for a five-minute break. I sat in the cab of the crew vehicle and actually slept for about four or five minutes. Jeanne had been walking up with me and said she did not expect I would get much rest or sleep in five minutes. But when I returned to the road she was surprised how much better I felt and how much faster I resumed our trod up the mountain.

I was able to finish in a very good (for me) time. My finish time was 45:54:01. I was so elated to have beaten the course again that when Race Director Chris Kostman asked me how I felt, I kiddingly asked for next year's race application. The Badwater Race is obviously doable but it takes a team of very dedicated people for support. It is a team effort where all of the members are critical parts. My 2003 team was just that. It is said that if a crewmember is not busy doing something to support the runner for three minutes, he/she is not doing his/her job properly. I had a great crew without whom I could not have accomplished what we did.

Double Next Time

I started this story talking about doing a Badwater double. That entails running from the Badwater Basin to the summit of Mount Whitney and a return trip to the Badwater Basin, a total of 292 miles, commonly referred to as a "Badwater 300." I had wanted to be the first person age 60 or over to accomplish that feat; however, I will have to leave that for somebody else or come back some other day. We had Mount Whitney overnight passes, which are required, but I think the Mount Whitney Gods were not on my side.

On the day we had planned to attempt the summit, the weather on top was not conducive for amateur Alpinists like us. Lightning is very common at the summit and by all the reports we heard and by watching the clouds over the mountain; going to the top was not advisable. Well... having gone through the hottest Badwater Race in history and the mountain not wanting us on it, I decided to cancel any plans for a double and be happy with another Badwater Buckle. My crew did not object to that so I figured it was the right decision.

2003 Finishing Time – 45:54:01
Twenty-fifth Place

CHAPTER FOURTEEN – BONNIE BUSCH

From Bonnie's 2003 Badwater Application:

Age: 45
Bettendorf, Iowa

Previous Badwater Crewing Experience:

2002 Crewmember and pacer for Jason Hodde.

Ran/walked approximately 15 miles during the race period.

Learned: Be prepared for the unexpected, things can happen very quickly; patience is required; things don't always get worse; and a little luck always helps.

TEAM EFFORT *By Bonnie Busch*

Death Valley, July 2002

The rental SUV cruised comfortably down the two-lane blacktop, passing a scattering of pedestrians that were making their pilgrimage to a far away finish line. Often nearby would be a parked caravan of gypsy crew that would attempt to satisfy the ghostly pedestrian's physical and emotional needs. We had been part of that scenery until our runner carefully and deliberately declared did not finish (DNF) status. Now that we were simply part of the motoring public, we watched and wondered what it would take to finish this race. From participant to spectator, instead of focusing on our runner's needs we were free to observe, question and ponder the possibilities.

It was the third week in July 2002 and we were meandering through Death Valley. Four of us had come together to crew a friend on his second attempt at finishing this race. Jay Hodde was the runner and the crew was made up of his friends from the middle of the United States. Jay as well as his friends Corey Linkel and Simon Bollin were from Indiana, a mutual friend Nikki Seger from Illinois and me from Iowa. Other than Jay's previous attempt with Corey crewing, none of us had seen this scenery, had never run/walked this distance on a road only course, and had never experienced the heat of Death Valley in July for a run from Badwater to the trail head on Mount Whitney, some 135 miles away.

We would wave and hoot as we came upon a runner moving slowly down the road. Stopping to visit the crews gave us a chance to see and hear how they were handling themselves and their runner, giving away some of our unneeded supplies almost in trade for the information and the opportunity to observe. We were very excited to simply be part of this any way we could. There was passion to try this again. We discussed the possibilities out loud. Out of the five of us, two were not runners, another declared that their upcoming work schedule would simply not allow the time to train and one didn't think their running resume was current enough. They would crew if I could get in as the runner. We could test our theories and learn.

My Turn: One More Try

I thought about our pact every day between that July day and the next January, the latter being the formal application period for the next race. A trip to the post office was required to weigh a stack of documentation and send my race application with next day delivery. In those eleven ounces of paper was a record of nearly every ultra I had done since 1988. The race officials demanded the application process to be taken seriously. If we were going to be denied I wanted to know everything had been done, no excuses. We had to get back to this race.

Every day I would anxiously scan the mail delivery. This would go on for weeks, and then one day a simple envelope appeared with hints on its exterior it was from the race. I jettisoned it back into the stack and stepped back from the kitchen table. My mind was racing. Was it big enough to welcome us to the race and provide instruction or was it small enough to say thanks but no thanks? It was small. Aimlessly I wandered around the house, then sheepishly went back to the kitchen and retrieved fate from the stack. With sounds of a car in the driveway, I shoved it into my computer bag like a guilty love letter. It stayed there until I could no longer resist its demand to be opened. We were in, Badwater 2003! Take a deep breath. Oh no, now what?!?! A quick E-mail to the crew and then I tried to figure out how to tell my family.

Jay, Corey and Nikki were all onboard for the task of crewing; I just needed to find one more person to share our journey with. I didn't think my husband would be a good match for the job and he confirmed with a one-word answer: "No." The same response came from several friends; evidently this wasn't everybody's idea of a dream vacation. This could be resolved later, so while snow blanketed the Midwest, I focused on training and planning – logistics, reservations, food, fluids, clothing, and so many details.

Run, run, run was the first step of my training plan. Assess, adjust, and run some more was the second step. Looking to strike a balance between load and recovery, I laid out a calendar and tried to identify goals for each week. A variety of races with increased mileage would be sprinkled in to add longer tests and keep my interest focused. It did not take long before fear and doubt became a constant companion. Fear of disappointing the team, fear of failure, fear of injury, fear of investing time and money without return, fear of the heat, fear of what I had not thought about – these fears kept me focused, moving and thinking.

The basic logistical plan was written the year before: collect crew in Las Vegas, pick up two vehicles, stock both with coolers, ice and food – basically everything to be self-sufficient for roughly three days, head to Badwater and hope for the best. Reservations were made, permits acquired, shopping lists made, another crewmember, Tammy Vinar agreed to come - each task made this dream more real; we were indeed headed back to Badwater to try again.

The recommendation to attend a heat training camp seemed like a great idea. A small group was planning to meet at Furnace Creek over Memorial Day weekend and over the fourth of July for several long days of running. Memorial Day was the perfect time to test preparations and still have time to make adjustments. It would be hot, but not nearly as hot as it would be during the race two months later.

Training Camp

Training camp day one – run/walk thirty miles. Things didn't work out very well. Temperatures were hotter than normal and my plans unraveled quickly. By dinner on the first night, I looked and felt like a hollowed out shell of a bug. Chewing one mouthful of food required more energy and concentration than what I could muster; I just stared at the plate of food. What little I could reach to my mouth with a fork and push around in my mouth had no flavor. Other participants that had come for the same training offered words of encouragement and bad jokes to humor me. I would acknowledge the sounds but I didn't understand the words. Brushing my teeth was nearly too demanding. Completely numb, lifeless and without thought, I was too exhausted to hurt. Attempts at sleep were not rewarding. I lay on the bed at Stovepipe Wells and listened to the sounds outside – a few cars coming or going, muffled voices and the wind. This was a disaster. *How would I tell the crew that our plans would have to be scrapped?*

Training camp day two – walk. With barely more energy than I had the night before, I headed back out to the road for more. Running wasn't even a consideration. With despair and self-pity, I walked. My brain was foggy and sluggish. I wasn't thinking; I was just barely *being*. Within a couple of miles, my silence was broken by the company of Ben Jones and another trainee. They had light steps compared to my heavy plodding. They considered the extra heat a real bonus. They offered conversation and friendship. We walked, they talked and somewhere over the next four hours and thirteen miles they changed my outlook. I had indeed gotten what I came for - assessment of my training, first-hand knowledge of the course and supply options, and a demonstration of how my body would react. Within the time it takes to fly from Las Vegas back to Iowa, I relived the journey from hopelessness to hope. The comments that Ben Jones and others had made several nights earlier at dinner in Stovepipe Wells finally surfaced into my conscious thought. The material I had been reading, all the people I had talked to and a flood of memories from a year earlier came rushing at me like color to a black and white picture. I hoped I could put these puzzle pieces together fast.

So little precious time remained to rethink the whole plan. Not eight ounces of fluid per mile; make it sixteen every mile. More sauna time with more drinking and weighing. Mix the fluids stronger to account for the dilution of lots of ice. Don't scrimp on the ice; ice in the bottle first, and then top it off with fluids. Rest early and often. There is no such thing as too slow. Keep the skin covered; breathe in through your nose. Use iced towels and bandanas. Deal with issues early. Use time and energy wisely. Control what you can, accept what you cannot. You cannot finish if you quit – physically or mentally.

Preparation

Despite the approaching Midwest summer, I continued to wear winter clothes when I ran – tights, long sleeves, jacket, hat and sometimes gloves. My running friends were getting scarce. I almost got use to being soaking wet from perspiration – either on the run or in the sauna. Instead of adding more running miles, I added long walks to my training activities. We would be walking those long climbs out of the desert valley and I intended to use a run/walk strategy on the rest of the course. My first training walks were just a few miles, but eventually they would be up to 15 or 20 miles each. Oddly enough, the walking also conditioned me to accept scenery at a very slow pace – something that had never occurred to me in the context of Badwater – patience. My training now consisted of:

- 65 miles of running a week, longest runs usually 20-25 miles

- 25 miles of walking a week, longest walks usually 10-15 miles

- 4 times a week in the sauna, usually between 120-165 degrees, longest sauna time usually 90 minutes.

The month of May would be the biggest for training with two races, one of over 100 miles on a track and another of 50 miles on trail, plus the two days of heat training camp in Death Valley.

The original goal from the conversation in 2002 was to finish Badwater within the 60-hour time limit. We liked the idea of paying tribute to the pioneers of this event, so we added a summit of Mount Whitney as a second goal. I added one more goal - to finish the Bix 7 mile road race at the end of the week, a hometown race.

The Bix 7 race was the reason I started running in 1982 and it served as motivation to keep running all those years since. This was the one race I had done every year – it was run with people I considered my friends. They taught me to run, they helped me run, they organized and sustained a running community, and they were a group I wanted to be considered part of. On a number of occasions I would cut a vacation short just to come back and run Bix. I ran it injured, and I ran tired. I ran it for a "fast" time and ran it for fun. This time I just wanted to run it.

In the weeks leading up to our flights, I started to fill an extra bedroom with all the stuff I would be taking to the race: A slightly modified pair of white Cool-Max yoga pants and a long sleeve technical shirt would be my attempt at keeping sun off my skin and trying to stay cool. I updated the pants to have a loose elastic cuff at each ankle and a small thin pocket to hold a small tube of lip balm.

The pants were a reluctant compromise; I preferred to run in shorts, but after all these months of discovery and study, it was clear that exposed skin allowed faster evaporation of precious fluids. I spent months learning to run and breathe through my nose instead of my mouth so wearing pants didn't seem so hard. My mother crafted a hood from a hand towel that would be iced and hopefully keep me cool in the worst heat. It had a Velcro closure to hold it on close to my head in case the winds got strong. Over the Fourth of July weekend I would do my final preparations: haircut, new white underwear and an extra pair of shoes one size larger.

Goal #1

Tammy and I flew into Las Vegas well after dark. After several cycles at the luggage carousel we concluded one of my bags was missing. A similar looking bag was the last remaining luggage from our flight. We had wasted enough time looking for something that wasn't there so we filled out the luggage claim form with a promise the bag would be on the next flight and promptly delivered to our hotel.

Skeptical, we took what we had and headed for the car rental agency. After a long slow wait in line, I approached the counter only to discover I had taken us to the wrong rental agency! Back on the shuttle to the airport, another shuttle to a different rental agency and finally we could pick out an SUV for ourselves. Tammy wasn't happy with me when I vetoed her selections – no sunroof, no black paint, no leather seats – yes, the plain-Jane tan one would be the one. It was late when our flight landed and now it was very late. Tammy drove while I tried to read a map by the light of the glove box. I chalked up a couple of missed exits to the continued sprawl of Las Vegas, but soon it was clear we were not where we thought we were. Turn around, go back and try again. And again and again, as we were directionally challenged in the dark and unfamiliar surroundings.

After seeing all four corners of Las Vegas, we were finally at our hotel. Excited we both jumped out of the SUV and promptly ran into the glass front door. It was locked! Tammy started surveying the building for what she referred to as a doorbell; I thought she was insanely tired until her search turned up a small round button that indeed was a doorbell. A desk attendant snapped to attention from his slumber to usher us in. After a scripted apology and the usual paperwork and exchange of credit cards and room keys, Tammy and I were already lights half out, ready for our quiet room. We had taken two steps toward bliss when the attendant taunted that an airline had tried to drop off a missing piece of luggage; however because we had not yet checked in he could not accept it, the airline took it back to the airport. It had been a very long night and I opened my mouth to make some pretty stupid comments. Barely a breath separated the rant and necessary apology. I backed away from the counter knowing I needed to get a grip on myself before morning, which was now only a couple of hours away.

Daylight came earlier than it should have. Indeed my bag had arrived and we found Corey who was enjoying time with a portion of his family that had changed their RV vacation plans to come through Las Vegas when we were there. The six of them made a fine distraction for our upcoming commitment and I felt so relaxed around them. We spent our day shopping, getting things organized and talking through the events that were about to happen. Nikki would arrive on a late night flight and we would reluctantly bid farewell to Corey's family. We were ready to leave Las Vegas. Jay would be coming in on a flight after we left the next day. He would pick up a second rental and then drive out to meet us in Death Valley. It was likely that I wouldn't see him until the first crew exchange during the race. We collected ourselves and left Las Vegas in the morning.

As the desert rolled out before us, we renewed our friendship and the crew got to know each other. The non-stop talking ended quietly as we drove up to Dante's view. It was fun to watch Tammy's reaction to the scenery, the same that the rest of us had experienced the year before, gasping over the beauty and strangeness. Laughing that it didn't seem that hot, we leaned over the ridge and felt the updraft from the valley below; a blast of furnace air sucked the life out of us. We scampered back into the air conditioning and sped towards Furnace Creek. The orientation for Tammy then shifted into a full-blown cram session for everybody. At the visitor's station, we stayed just long enough to get park permits and handle the mandatory runner check in; then back on the road headed towards Stovepipe Wells to get our hotel rooms. We went into a virtual replay of the year before: unloading supplies and organizing the more immediate "need now" things separate from the "need later" items. Some things would go back in the SUV in the morning; the rest would stay in the hotel room for retrieval later. Put signs on the SUV, talk through our plans and try to relax.

Several times we would make the 25-mile trip between Furnace Creek and Stovepipe Wells and each time I marveled at how far it actually was – and that was at 55 miles per hour with the air conditioning on. On our trip back to Furnace Creek for the mandatory runner/crew meeting we talked about the heat. Reasoning that it was the same for everybody and we could do nothing to change it, we agreed to manage ourselves and not discuss the heat. Quiet moments went by when the silence was broken by one of the crew who declared simply "It is f@$!ing hot!" The addition of the universal adjective pretty much shored up the statement and for the rest of the trip the phrase would be used to shift momentum. The statement was a serious assessment with a request to keep things in perspective. We laughed every time the phrase was uttered.

This crew would be my lifeline over the next few days. They would be my entertainment, my conscious thought and my safety net. They knew the objectives: Safety, fun and three goals. I knew I needed to try to do whatever they suggested. Collectively, they had some of the best background one could assemble. They were unique individuals and each brought something to the table. I trusted them. We were as ready as we could be.

Race Day

Time to execute. Nikki, Tammy and I drove to the start of the race under a dark sky happy the sun was not radiating. Yet, anyway. We were earlier than we needed to be. I munched on cereal while the other two tried to figure out was wrong – *no coffee!* The SUV was turned around and we went back to Furnace Creek for coffee. Despite our coffee stop we were still early. A hint of light was now intruding into the dark valley that stretched out ahead of us. The prior year's experience told us that by the time our race started it would be good light; the high cliffs bordering the valley to the east would prevent direct sunlight for several hours, something we should enjoy. We idled as other vehicles pulled up and out poured crews and runners. It was fairly hard to distinguish crew from runner: both tended to be lean, weathered, with lots of protection and loose light-colored clothing. A few nervous smiles for the cameras, the Star Spangled Banner and the 6:00 a.m. starters were set adrift down the road.

Our plan was for the crew vehicle to meet the runner every mile – a constant opportunity for a cold bottle, snacks, and sunscreen and to fix whatever needed fixing and share information with the crew. Quickly we fell into a rhythm and stayed with it hoping we could do it another one hundred thirty-four more times. New iced fluids every time, salt supplement every thirty minutes, food every so often, get the bathroom scale out every hour to weigh. Nikki and Tammy had the bottle ready every time; my job was to bring it back empty.

At the start, runners and crew were a bit bunched up providing chaos, safety concerns and entertainment. Every mile spread the population wider. The fresh blacktop cut through the washed out scenery. Crews and runners were more colorful than the backdrop of sand, salt and sky. Many were trying to take advantage of the shade and comparatively lower temperatures. I watched them, their crews, and my crew. In these early hours, the crews were clearly very busy - preparing bottles with fresh ice and then fluids, putting food in baggies, hunting for supplement pills, filling bandanas with ice, and squeezing out sunscreen for a quick application. All the work necessary for a quick and efficient delivery when the runner arrived. I tried to emulate the efficiency while providing good feedback on how I felt and what I was thinking but none of it was clever or funny. Nikki and Tammy absorbed my comments and would scurry back to the vehicle to do it again in another mile. They carefully wrote comments in a logbook; it would be our diary. Some stops included a bathroom scale to track our weights. I tried to remind them to do for themselves all the things they were doing for me; I knew I needed them more than they needed me.

We approached civilization at Furnace Creek, our first milestone. Comfortable and well hydrated, we had no complaints. Time for a crew change. It was a happy, simple exchange – at least from my perspective. Nikki and Tammy had delivered me in good shape and very near to a time we had thought would be reasonable for a conservative start. Now it seemed that Nikki would take a hard earned break as Corey, Jay and Tammy stayed on the road. The crew had worked out their own plan for supply replenishment and rest. Not that I didn't care about their plans, I did. It was their plan, and theirs to manage. It was one less thing for me to be concerned about and without knowing all the details; I wouldn't worry when they made needed adjustments. I took note of my condition so that I had something to compare to when I saw Nikki again. This was the first opportunity runners could have a pacer and I enjoyed a couple of miles with company.

Making the sweeping left turn now heading west for the first time on the road, this was progress. This is where the road had become so unforgiving for Jay the year before. The wide shoulders were littered with crew vehicles and the wavy dots of runners/walkers were spread out on the landscape. The wind that had been gently pushing us all morning was now a notable cross wind-stacking sand along the shoulder in shadows to any obstruction. We were barely moving. I felt guilty as I accepted another cold bottle and iced towel. The towel made for a nice hood with the Velcro closure that the wind would tug at constantly. It was big enough to have almost another three inches past my nose on both sides of my face and it surprised me to discover that the depth gave me slightly colder and moister air to breathe. The crew didn't have it so good. I asked for my tape player so that I could spare them from also having to accompany me. It was f@$!ing hot.

Although just a mile, it was forever between stops. The wind, the sun, and the heat were relentless. I walked and tried to drink the bottle the crew left with me. I drank half of it as soon as they handed it to me – that's when it was the coldest. Then I would sip as I walked. If I sipped too slowly it would be too hot to drink and I wouldn't touch it. The fluid no longer had any flavor no matter what it was. The only difference I could detect was its temperature or consistency. One of my beverage choices was thicker than the rest and was getting hard to choke down. My walk had slowed and then slowed again; I don't know if it was fast enough to even call it a walk. It was slow and deliberate, like the walk you do in line at a funeral visitation. My eyelids operated in slow motion, drawing down and up ever so slowly over what felt like sandpaper, I tried to blink as little as possible and kept my eyes barely open. Because the crew moved approximately every mile, I decided we must have still been making some progress. One more mile, one more bottle.

Heat distorted objects into wavy figures and was melting my mind. I so enjoyed the periodic company of a pacer and yet I also enjoyed the time alone because I kept thinking it gave the crew a bit of a break. I was still wearing my white pants and white long sleeve shirt with a wet iced towel draped over my head. Despite the water dripping down from my head, my shoes and socks were not getting wet from it. The passages in my nose were dry and crusty, bleeding lightly from time to time.

I gave the crew so much to make fun of yet they resisted. Walking along the very edge of the road, I noticed a car pulling off the road and parking a few lengths in front of me. Out jumped mom, dad and a couple of kids. They ran towards me at full speed and surrounded me. Perhaps out of the staggering race participants, I was the one who looked inviting enough to stop and talk to? I expected the obvious question and then anticipated their amazement as I answered. What I got was "Would you take our picture?" as they pointed at a road sign I had just passed. They pleaded for me to hurry because it was hot. They grouped together and I obliged with a couple of snaps of their camera. They ran back to me, retrieved their camera and then yelled back a thank you as they climbed back into the car. Off they went. Quite an entertaining little break for me and it put some perspective on my day. For a short period of time, I almost forgot it was f@$!ing hot.

Up next was Stovepipe Wells; finally we could almost see it from here. I had spent all day trying not to think about it; I had fought to stay in the moment, not to worry or wonder what would be. Taking care of the here and now might give us a future on this road. When we took the left turn on the road, it was just too hard not to think about it. What had been a cross wind turned into a stiff head wind that seemed to get stronger with each step. The sand was still drifting. I needed to hang on until Stovepipe Wells, where we would take an extended break – a shower and some time in the shade were just what I needed. I imagined the crew would be giddy about the idea of getting in the hotel pool. Perhaps, me too.

The crew crossed the road to deliver yet another fresh bottle and left Jay to walk with me. Jay was chatting happily but that's all I could comprehend. He continued to talk while my fuzzy brain slurred his words and tried to figure out what was happening. I would look at Jay and see his lips moving; the sound would reach my ears but I couldn't put meaning to it. Abruptly I interrupted Jay declaring it was time to go to Stovepipe Wells. Yes, now. Jay waved at the rest of the crew and we hurried across the road to the parked vehicle. They stabbed our race numbered stake into the soft sand where we would need to return to and we were off. I had barely sat down on the seats and we were rolling along at highway speed. Something smelled awful; how could the crew put up with whatever was causing it? I think they laughed at me and suggested the cause of the smell was typically running or walking along side the road. I don't think I got their point before we got to the hotel. It was roughly 4:00 p.m. and it was f@$!ing hot.

We rolled up to one of our reserved hotel rooms. I was ushered into a room where I would sink into the bathtub after removing only my shoes. I turned the water on and just let it run all over me. The water seemed to heighten the nasty smell that had taken me all day to collect. I enjoyed the water longer than normal and eventually emerged from the bathroom with some of my brain function returned and pruney fingers. Tammy took my wet clothes and offered to wash them out; no doubt they would dry before I needed them again. I floated over to a bed and let it absorb me. I faced the inevitable questions: why was I here and what happened? I carefully told my short story: I was hot.

They didn't seem surprised but apparently expected something far more dramatic. Lying quietly, sleep escaped me. Nikki brought food back to the hotel room and we ate. This was the first time that we were all together, and we laughed at ourselves and each other. The stories were great. It took quite a while before I felt guilty for being there; maybe it was time to get back out on the road. I hinted at leaving and the group tore into action. I thought we were ready again. The hotel room door opened up to blinding sun and same oppressive air. What reserves I thought had been revived in the last two hours was gone immediately.

We drove back to our stake with naïve optimism and resumed the march. Running was out of the question; Nikki joined me for the walk. An hour and a few miles later we came into the official checkpoint at Stovepipe Wells. It wasn't quite the feeling of achievement I had hoped for. I marked the occasion with an ice cream sandwich from the convenience store as I lay on a bench outside their door. I grew up eating these frozen treats and I couldn't help but enjoy the memories flooding my mind. After it went down (much too) quickly, the crew requested some action: either we head down the road or go to the hotel room and really try to cool down. Again they were correct; I took the right turn out of the convenience store, heading for Townes Pass.

Maybe I had eaten too much during the hotel room break, maybe I wasn't drinking enough, and maybe I was just simply hot. I walked. And walked. A habit of coming over to the SUV every mile developed quickly. Sit in the lime green folding Barbie chair, feet up on the bumper, chew on ice. The sun wasn't setting as fast as my energy. I didn't feel good. We didn't need to discuss it; the crew knew. I was having trouble complying with their simple requests, but they kept trying. They listened and reacted swiftly. On one stop, I commented about my scratchy dry eyes and they produced eye drops. With one drop, I yowled. It became blindingly obvious we should always keep the eye drops in the cooler! They made a note of that and I left without doing the other eye.

The heat was really getting to all of us. On the low, nearly flat part of the road to Townes Pass I could see our crew vehicle parked deep on the right shoulder, by now a very familiar sight except that I did not see the crew milling about the back of the SUV but instead found them sitting in the SUV which was not running. All the windows were rolled up tight. The wind was blowing straight out of the south and was relentless. Tammy had already burned her legs from the hot breeze, while Nikki stayed covered head to toe. Now they were tucked in the SUV; I had to laugh. This was a crazy race with crazy circumstances; good to know the crew was crazy, too.

At one stop at the back of the SUV, Nikki declared that if I was going to sit there then I should make better use of the time – eat. She handed me a cup of yogurt and told me not to give it back until it was empty. Of course I tried, but needed a little help from the rest of the crew to honor her request. When the spoon finally reached the bottom of the cup, I got complimented and was handed a diet cola. As soon as the beverage hit my tongue, uneasiness consumed me. I leaned over the arm rail on the chair and emptied my stomach. One of the crewmembers backed away and the other two came closer. We examined the exposed contents; this might be another clue as to what wasn't working. I left with an iced bottle and a pacer this time. We walked some more. Oddly the incident left me optimistic; perhaps this was exactly what I needed.

Nope, things weren't working. I still felt lousy and had reached the absolute end of my energy. Now staggering with sleep in the dim light, again I came over to the SUV. No chair necessary, no trip back to the hotel; just some sleep here on the shoulder in the rocks and prickly scrub. The quick-thinking crew dislodged an ice chest from the SUV and I crawled into the opening. Sleep swallowed me. The crew woke me up after 25 minutes; it seemed like three. I sat up and hung my legs over the tailgate. This wasn't going to work, so I lay back down.

After what seemed like minutes later, I woke up slowly. It was dark and I could hear snoring. Where was I? A voice in the darkness asked if I was ready. I slid to the opening by my feet and jumped to the ground and said yes. That second nap seemed to make a world of difference. Now that I was awake again, I noticed I didn't feel so good, but not awful, and it was still f@$!ing hot. Chewing on ice chips, we clawed through the darkness. The dots of the red taillights of other crews outlined the route that seemingly had no end.

Finally we were at the top of Townes Pass. I emptied my stomach again and again, thinking this could be a new beginning. Early light slowly started to invade the night and I was finally starting to feel a little bit better. After a few more miles, the burritos that Tammy made looked good. Feeling a need to get across Panamint Valley before the sun could do damage, I picked up a pacer and we ran. We were flying down this steep downhill with a full view of the valley at Panamint. It seemed like I had to stop to pee several times every mile. Now that it was light I thought it might be important to see what color it was – dark yellow with a slightly red tint. The crew absorbed this information and instructed me to slow down just a bit and eat. After more burritos and a sampler from our assorted groceries, we worked through those until we got to the checkpoint at Panamint, the halfway point. We had avoided the heat in the valley and prepared for the climb out. Things were good. The crew was great.

Climbing out of the valley, I ate cereal out of a small plastic bag and listened to the overpowering morning silence. A very light rain began to fall. After several snake turns of the road I began to hear voices fading in and out. The dialog of the crew Jay and Nikki drifted down to me from their carefully chosen spot along the winding road. I couldn't hear the exact words, just the tone and laughter as the conversation passed from one voice to the other. Their laughter was the most important thing to me this morning. A stronger endorsement could not be had – it didn't matter what the topic was. I was convinced they couldn't be that happy if we were headed for failure. I trusted them. So that I wouldn't invade their private conversation I asked for my tape player again. Listening to blue grass music, I ate cereal and climbed; this was great.

CHAPTER FOURTEEN – BONNIE BUSCH

The climb up from Panamint seemed much longer than what I thought it should have been. We had a lot of road behind us and yet so much in front of us. The short views and tight turns made it hard on the crew, but I enjoyed the constant change in the morning light. Finally Father Crowley's point; it was here I assumed the course took a downward roll all the way to Lone Pine and we would pick up speed. Quickly disappointed, it became clear I remembered nothing of this road, especially the length. My mood soured. The population on the road had dwindled to only us and one other runner with a crewmember on a bicycle. They annoyed me. My efforts to get away from them were stymied by my own snail's pace. What earlier had seemed like a comfortable, efficient rhythm was now just monotonous. Eat, drink, run, walk, stop. Eat, drink, run, walk, stop. Where is Darwin?

The day before, I had soaked up the 360-degree wide views that I slowly moved through. I was memorizing everything from jagged mountain ridge to the way the sand drifted with the wind; the way the air smelled when it had passed through scrub little bushes. Today it seemed like all I could see of the landscape was the white line on the left edge of the road. Anything that touched my tongue either had no flavor or a slightly annoying metallic taste. I changed shoes, but they didn't even feel like mine so I changed again and again. I couldn't think of anything to think about.

The crew kept a running conversation that I periodically interrupted with my stop. I made no contribution but would leave with a snippet of their thoughts and would mull over that for the next mile. I didn't have anything to complain about but I wanted to anyway. Although I tried to be either positive or silent, I don't think I was successful. The crew was on top of their game: They had everything, they were organized, and they were in control, just as they had been since we touched down in Las Vegas. The crew kept moving the SUV so I followed them. A tent appeared in the middle of nowhere; either I was losing my mind or this was the checkpoint at the Darwin turn off. We welcomed another person to our conversation and probably enjoyed it a little longer then I should have.

I had no idea how far we had come, nor how far remained. I knew the mileage up to Stovepipe Wells, but hadn't studied anything beyond that, nor had I crewed this section before when one gets a real good chance to enjoy the scenery. The crew had the race mileage, but in the time between stops I decided not to bother them by asking. What difference would it have made? We were here and moving; what else did I need to know? This decision momentarily seemed to free my mind and lift my attitude. Both were also much improved thanks to the coaxing by the crew to consume more calories and run a little. This was a good place to be.

Tammy and I had been chatting as we ran along the empty road. Nikki and our crew vehicle were somewhere out of sight up ahead or still behind us; we had done this so many times, I lost track. A car pulled into a small lane on the side of the road. A woman got out and started towards us. She produced two ice cream bars and became our best friend. Tammy offered to save hers to share with Nikki, but as the chocolate started to melt down her wrist and arm she realized there would be no saving it. The cold, smooth, mild chocolate went down quickly. What an angel; her visit might need to be our little secret.

Nikki and I crested a small hill together that opened up a gentle valley in front of us. One of only a handful of cars that was on the road silently came towards us. As it neared we could hear it's motor and then the quick fade after it passed. *Boom!* A thunderous noise was on us. Alarmed I glanced over my shoulder to Nikki. She freaked out and was doing a high-stepping prance, yet her screams could not be heard over the deafening volume of the explosion. A military jet had snuck up behind us from the opposite side of the hill and was over top of us just after the car had passed. Close enough to see the bolts on its sleek body; the jet was now scurrying away. Nikki was still screaming as the noise disappeared as fast as it had come. We had been hearing them on and off throughout the morning – just never this close. Along with serious goose bumps, my blood was really pumping now!

The girls and I continued to snake our way through the landscape and came upon a couple of other participants and their crew. This time I looked forward to the extra company. We exchanged some encouraging words but never engaged in a real conversation because each of our reinforced habits was a little out of synchronization. Multiple times I would pass John Radich only to be overtaken by him later. Mile after mile this would continue; mile after mile I would creep close enough to read "Set a good example" on the back of his shirt. The phrase settled into my thoughts and stayed there. As John and his crew decided to enjoy chairs along the side of the road, I wondered if he knew of the gift he had given me.

Another runner that had been on our heels for hours finally was close enough for a few short exchanges – names, "how you doing" and such pleasantries at first. Once it was established we had started two hours before they had, the dialog became friendlier. Before they faded back, they predicted we would finish within buckle time. Evidently I hadn't read that part of the race packet all that closely and had to ask what that meant. Runners would qualify for a buckle if they finished the race within 48 hours. We had been doing some running during this ever-so-slight downhill section so we entertained the idea of running more.

Clouds formed over by the mountain range on the left and slowly they started towards us across Owen's Valley. The falling moisture created short rainbows and lots of changing color to the sky. They inched towards us and made us ponder the pros and cons of getting wet. Finally the rain made it over to the road we traveled. Big drops of rain hit our faces and bare arms, but hardly made a difference to the dry pavement. What a crazy place this was.

The sun started to set for the second time during the race and despite looking at Lone Pine for much of the day, we seemed to be no closer. The crew kept me pointed in the right direction and fed me warm pizza. It was nirvana. It was crunchy and gooey; mild rich cheese with a bit of a kick in the sauce. I walked and enjoyed this exotic treat. About the time I was wondering if the crew had more, my point of view changed abruptly. I was nauseous and dreaded what I had consumed. The crew didn't offer and I didn't ask for more.

The crew was working extra hard now. They listened to my endless whining and either tried to address the origin or distracted me from focusing on it. They had been trading time on the road for a little break to restock supplies, pick up ice, and when it worked out, get a little hotel time for a shower and short nap. It all depended on what we needed out on the road and how far they had to travel to get back to civilization. They had to be as weary as I was to face a second night on the road. The flashing lights we wore played tricks on my tired eyes; they blurred and confused the darkening scenery. I had been hearing a barking dog and as we got closer to a small clump of houses; the sound became more and more agitated. For the first time in two days I didn't feel safe. Maybe there were multiple dogs, nothing a white picket fence that outlined the yard would contain. I desperately hurried down the road. Corey crossed the road to bring me a fresh bottle of fluid and some encouraging words. I begged him to stay with me. He wasn't prepared to run or walk with me; he seemed confused, but he didn't hesitate when I started to explain about the dogs. At this point I couldn't possibly outrun them, nor really defend myself with a flashlight and water bottle. With two of us, maybe they wouldn't attack. We needed to hurry out of this situation. It took several miles before the menacing bark faded away. There really were no houses, no white picket fence, and certainly no dogs. Calmly, Corey tried to talk me out of my hallucination and when that didn't work he did convince me the danger had passed. Lucky for us.

The flashing red lights of a radio tower were getting no closer. And now the road suddenly had become overcrowded with other crew vehicles. This was about as unsettling as the dogs. Too much traffic pulling off on an undefined shoulder, then quickly back on the road once the runner had passed by; in some cases multiple vehicles for a single runner. The taillights were blinding and the blinking lights worn by people were not enough. I had to pick up the pace and get out of this. I focused on the blinking tower and ran. The road took an odd turn to the left and I was no longer facing the tower. "What's this?" I demanded of the crew. In their infinite patience, they pointed out the lights of Lone Pine I had completely overlooked. I was crushed. A couple of miles with a crewmember helped me put my head back on. I ran to get away from the cars, so why couldn't I run to Lone Pine? The act of trying changed my perspective.

Now that we were finally under the streetlights of Lone Pine, anything seemed possible again. Although I had worn a watch since the beginning of the race, I had never looked at it, nor did we talk much about the time or the mileage. But being in Lone Pine was significant. The SUV went to the hotel to pick up our off-shift team member, so we would all be together for the final push up Mount Whitney. I left the last race check-in where the volunteer noted that it was midnight. Taking the left at the streetlight, we had just six hours to get to the finish line for a belt buckle. I had driven this section multiple times the year before and knew this would be a 13-mile walk. We started marching. I was eating candy and anything that offered quick energy or caffeine. I was bouncing between falling asleep and a sugar/adrenaline high. I marched with the energy of the crew. They rotated at each stop. We laughed, we sang, we listened to the tiny rocks falling along the cutouts. We looked back on the events that had unfolded since we had left Las Vegas. I was recording all of this in my mind for later reflection. I couldn't digest it now, however; I needed to march. The switchbacks were getting steeper, the air cooler and the sweet, clean smell of pine swallowed us. The twinkling lights of Lone Pine and the vehicle lights of the race caravan outlined where we had come from. A big left hand switchback was the last big milestone. The crew was electrified. I panicked, now that the end was near. I did not want it to end, this great, great dream.

At Last!

46:04:26! Goal #1 completed. It was just after four o'clock in the morning and the dark of night was giving way to a new day. A few official photos were taken and I was almost speechless. Too amazed and shocked to believe we had actually done what we had set out to do, I watched the crewmembers dancing. Before the start, I had reasoned that we had a 50/50 chance of finishing. What I had failed to take into account was the crew – their skill, experience, perseverance, creativity, attitude and incredible will. This was going to take some time to digest--lots of time.

Goal #2

With one goal accomplished, we started to shift our focus to the next. We needed to clean out the crew vehicle, get organized for our Mount Whitney hike and get some much needed rest. I hoped for sleep, but it came only in short segments. Our schedule allowed us to get to the race's awards ceremony and enjoy a hot meal. As we found our way to a table, I couldn't help but notice how many people knew the crewmembers. They exchanged handshakes and hugs as old friends do. How did they know so many people? It was here I discovered they not only had been helping me over the last couple of days, they had also been helping anybody they could! As we sat in the crowded gym, they shared that they had run across one crew without any ice so they gave them some of ours. They had come across a runner whose only crew was one guy after the rest of the crew had succumbed to the heat; they gave him several supplies and some warm, gooey, fresh pizza they had just picked up. Several more crews got ice, sodium tablets, etc. They shrugged off all the races they had saved or improved. These four reaffirmed their hero status with me.

Jay said his good-byes and he started the long drive back to Las Vegas. Instead of heading off to bed, the rest of us took the SUV back up the portal road. With flashlights and packs, the four remaining team members started up the trail at Mount Whitney portal. As we trudged forward on the dark trail, we reminisced about the events of the last few days, telling each other things we already knew or missed while we were off doing some needed chore. It may have been here I learned the guys had not been feeling real good in the heat, so the girls spent more time crewing during the daylight hours. It also might have been here I learned that we had been getting low on ice so when Jay came out to crew the first night they sent him instead to Lone Pine – about 80 miles one way to get ice. I only had to make forward progress while they had endured the same conditions and the multipliers of stress and worry.

Corey had us singing on the trail once he taught us the lyrics. Eventually, the chatter and singing slowed, as did our speed on the trail. The trail was reasonably easy to follow except for open high-traffic areas. The temperature was coming down as we were climbing up. After the campground, we started on the rocky switchbacks. The rain down in the valley earlier in the day had also found the trail that had become a waterfall in many areas and now being above the tree line we were catching significant wind. Corey was not feeling well, we were slowing, we all had cold feet and Nikki in her running scandals likely got the worst of that. Silently we trudged on.

While resting at one of the switchbacks we dared to have the conversation about whether we should continue. Nikki stated the absolutes and the obvious: Corey had to go back down fast, he couldn't go alone, and some of our flashlights were starting to fail in the cold. She requested input. My heart wanted to go on, but my head was confused. I desperately wanted us to stay together for the trip up, but Nikki was right: it was not an option. Tammy declared she would support whatever decision Nikki and I arrived at. Corey offered no input. Nikki shined a flashlight in my face and asked me what I was going to do. Timidly I speculated that Tammy and I could continue, offering if we were within 20 minutes of the needle we could then be on the back side of the mountain, potentially out of the wind and wet trail. Nikki wasn't real happy or surprised with my thoughts, but she conceded to the plan and handed us her best flashlight. If we couldn't get to the backside of this mountain in 20 minutes we were going to turn around and come back down. We checked our watches and parted company; Nikki and Corey down, Tammy and I up.

Shortly Tammy and I noticed the wet trail was finally dry and shortly after that we crossed over the needle to the backside of Mount Whitney. Our increased speed allowed us to stay reasonably warm. I checked my watch and we agreed there was no reason to turn around now. An hour later, I took a stab at guessing our summit arrival time. It seemed that if we kept up our current pace we might make the summit in... total darkness!?!

Slowing our pace slightly, we found ourselves coming across the mountaintop in silent darkness. We signed in at the hut before stepping inside to get out of the wind. We managed a few clothing adjustments in the dark enclosure and ate a snack before emerging into the earliest light of the day. The day was waking up before us. We had yet another magical day on our hands.

Between the two of us, we could have appropriately clothed one person for this hike: Tammy had on shorts, a T-shirt, a hooded jacket and a baseball hat. I had on Lycra tights, two shirts, a nylon jacket and a headband. We shared a pair of gloves, had one working headlamp that was Nikki's and one dim flashlight left. We were cold and we were happy. We snapped a few photos and then headed down before the full sun could greet us. Tammy was stunned by the scenery we quickly moved through. She had gotten all this way in the dark and would now be seeing if for the first time. She would now quit asking me why we had to do this climb.

After a couple of hours, we started seeing other hikers on their way up. We exchanged greetings and conditions ahead. We kept on moving as we needed to get back to Lone Pine before noon in order to get back to Las Vegas in time for our flights. Although the trip down was far less taxing, we were indeed tiring in the warmer air. It seemed to be taking too long. We wondered how Corey was feeling, how long it took Nikki and him to make it back, and if they were comfortable – especially after we found the keys to the vehicle in Tammy's pocket – oops.

We moved from a landscape of high mountain tops to fields of rocks, then into some trees and bushes, then into grasses and blooming flowers. Hurry through the water, hurry down the switchbacks, into the evergreen trees and sneak a glance at the valley views, the sun was in full force now. We came down to the trailhead just as the food that Nikki and Corey had ordered from the store was ready. That may have been the best hamburger and fries I have ever had. We piled back into the SUV and raced back to Lone Pine to see if we could still get a shower in our hotel room. Goal #2 completed.

A fast shower and we were again on the Badwater route in reverse headed back to Las Vegas. Every turn stirred a memory that caused each of us to reflect on the same events from our individual perspectives. The ride through the desert ended as the outskirts of civilization reappeared.

Tammy and I boarded our flight on time, Corey had some time to kill, and Nikki planned to do some gambling. This overnight flight would get Tammy and me into Chicago by morning. Nestling into my seat on the plane, I thought that sleep would come easy. It did not. I could not stop replaying the events and scenery, seemingly even reliving some of the smallest details. I fidgeted in my seat, unable to get comfortable. I took my shoes off and started scratching an insatiable itch. Bumps started to break out on my forefoot, then up my ankle and then crept half way up my shin – both lower legs were consumed by this out break. The woman next to me gave me a look in the dim light that simply said "Stop it!" I tried but was unsuccessful. This torture would continue until the excitement of landing in Chicago took over. We were almost home.

With the wait between our flights, I picked out a spot on the floor next to our boarding gate and arranged our luggage. Tammy was aghast as I explained I intended to sleep there on the floor. Surely the commotion of people boarding would wake us up on time for our flight; it seemed like a good plan to me. Tammy vowed not to fall asleep because this was not only unsafe but also potentially flawed. I woke up about an hour later. I was using the luggage as a pillow and Tammy was using me as a pillow. She was totally out and it took some effort to wake her up.

Goal #3

The 45-minute flight home left just enough time to wake up with a little breakfast and some coffee. I had been revising that third goal – we would be starting the Bix 7 race after most people had finished. We could save time by not driving to the start of the race but instead starting at the halfway point and run to the finish. My husband collected the two of us and our luggage at the airport. We pinned on race numbers and Tammy directed him to drive to the start of the race – nothing halfway now. We started a watch as we exited the car. The streets that had been filled earlier with thousands of runners were empty now; the only evidence of a race was the wet spots on the pavement where the aid stations had been. It was Midwest hot, not f@$!ing hot; only a few spectator parties were still going strong, and many of them joked with us as we made our way along the deserted streets. We had left Las Vegas in our running clothes and full water bottles that we enjoyed now.

Coming down the last hill, we took a 90-degree turn to the finish. Where was it? The finish line area had been completely dismantled – and there were no officials around. We slowed our pace and toasted our accomplishment with water bottles. We walked a short block to the post race party and bumped into one race official that we both knew. I begged him to take our race number tags so that we would be recognized as official finishers. With the official clocks stopped quite some time ago, he questioned how we could get an official time. I showed him my watch that now read one hour and seven minutes, but suggested he could simply use the official start time to calculate a finish – the time wasn't important to me. Tammy refused to turn in her race number tag; she didn't want to be associated with that kind of time for a seven mile run. Goal #3 three completed.

Reflecting

It was a week like no other before or since. Months of preparation, planning and worry and joy had come to this. During the Badwater race, we had used 45 bags of ice and 10 rolls of film; I had lost about five pounds of weight, consumed about 60 ounces of fluid each hour and had less than an hour of sleep. The crew helped me patch up some hot spots on my feet before they turned into anything worse, and we didn't spend much time working on or worrying about them. Some swelling in my feet and lower legs seemed to be eased with all the activity immediately following the race. Everything did not go as we might have planned, but maybe it was better that way; it did work out and it worked well.

Home again with about six hours of sleep for the week, all my dirty laundry and a head full of details I had yet to arrange into an orderly memory. All of the crew should be safely home by now too. For some reason all the choices, circumstances and events in each of our independent lives aligned for us to come together for this one week. It was a magical experience with magical people in a magical place. I am so fortunate I was able to experience it with these people, and I dream of doing something similar again. And again. After a couple of days of trying to put my thoughts in an E-mail to the crew and another E-mail to the race officials, volunteers and other participants and crew, I gave into my lack of skills to truly convey my thoughts. While it was woefully inadequate, all I could I write was "Thank you! Thank you!"

Team #45

* Bonnie Busch
  Badwater finisher 2003, 2007; 28 consecutive Bix 7 finishes; multiple Badwater crew assignments
* Jay Hodde
  Badwater finisher 2007; multiple Badwater crew and staff assignments
* Nikki Seger
  Badwater finisher 2005, 2007; multiple Badwater crew assignments
* Corey Linkel
  Ran his first ultra, Chicago Lakefront 50K 2005; multiple Badwater crew and staff assignments
* Tammy Vinar, 1960-2005; rest in peace
  Runner, race walker, ultra runner, co-worker, gardener, friend, teacher, mother, inspiration.

I was reluctant to believe Tammy's diagnosis of pancreatic cancer barely a year after we had watched the sunrise on Mount Whitney. She brought grace and passion to everything she did as long as she could. Our Badwater team sent a potted cactus to her funeral in August 2005.

It was a f@$!ing hot day.

2003 Finishing Time – 46:04:26
Twenty-eighth Place

© Thinkstock/iStockphoto/Fluid Illusion

CHAPTER FIFTEEN – MIKE KARCH

From Mike's 2003 Badwater Application:

Age: 34
Arroyo Hondo, New Mexico

The Charity that I will represent and raise funds for is:

I personally participated in both the Pentagon and World Trade Center Search and Rescue efforts between 9/11 and 9/15/01. I set up one of the first medical MASH units at Ground Zero – "Ground Zero MASH West" on the night of 9/11. What I saw was devastating and will stay with me for the rest of my life. The New York Fire Department will always hold a special place for me; it will be the charity I support at Badwater.

A Lesson in Life *By Mike Karch*

I trained for Badwater for seven months. There are many theories on how best to train for Badwater, but I focused primarily in three areas: heat, altitude and psychological toughness. All of my running during this time was at altitude. I quit my swimming regimen altogether as it was creating too much upper (dead) body weight; besides, the water temperature was too cool. I began running in a dry sauna with shorts and a T-shirt at 120 degrees three months before the race. Initially I lasted less than 10 minutes and got sick easily, but over time I trained upwards of two hours a day wearing four layers of underclothing – sometimes wearing a fifth layer consisting of my whitewater kayak rubberized dry top and pants. As you might imagine this was incredibly boring, so I began to visualize the course and all possible scenarios I might encounter in Death Valley during the race: wind storms, sand storms, elevation changes, mental depression, mental (runner's?) highs and pure physical pain.

I also visualized the finish – over and over again to the point where I had every step memorized. I did this so I would be prepared to deal with all of these scenarios *before* race day; I didn't want any surprises. To combat boredom, I practiced addition and subtraction problems, citing integers both forwards and backwards, and calculating multiplication tables in my head – all in an attempt to distract myself from the heat. It's so easy to panic in the heat I was going to face, so my focus was on remaining calm and not wasting any extra energy by pushing through the inevitable panic.

I drank as much as 40 and 50 ounces of fluids per hour, an amount I felt would keep me going in the extreme heat of Death Valley in July. Prior to my training, I had been consuming 20 ounces per hour. Additionally, I went on a seven-week carbohydrate-free diet in order to better simulate race conditions. It's estimated that a person will burn 20,000 calories per day in this race, and since I figured it would take me two days to complete Badwater, it would be virtually impossible for me to consume 40,000 calories while running – even if I was running for almost 135 miles. That would mean that my body would tap into its protein and fat reserves. This diet helped me to become highly efficient at tapping into them prior to the event.

My crew consisted of my fantastic wife Kim Escuder, MD and Nicole Shweiri, MD, our family doctor from Long Beach, California and a very close friend or ours. I have to say first and foremost they were both incredible. Badwater is a team effort and small mistakes can snowball into huge disasters, so obviously they have to be avoided if at all possible. Kim and Nicole worked like crazy – virtually nonstop the entire race. They monitored and charted my fluid intake, urine output, caloric intake, sodium and calcium intake, core temperature, body weight and mental status each and every hour without fail. They also submerged me in a 90-second ice bath every 15 minutes for over 100 miles to bring my core temperature down. They drove every mile of the course – stopping every mile along the way. I know in my heart that Badwater was every bit as taxing on them as it was on me.

I was assigned an 8:00 a.m. start time and by the time I started the temperature was already in excess of 105 degrees. My plan was to begin extremely conservative (slow!). No whooping it up for the cameras or television crews. I focused on staying calm, taking in fluids, conserving energy and maintaining my focus. I never let myself think of the distance in front of me and simply concentrated on completing one... mile... at... a... time, making each mile as efficient and productive as possible without making any mistakes. Miles 17 through 42 are considered the "Death Zone" as temperatures are known to soar to 130 degrees ambient and 200 degrees radiant off the pavement. Most runners who fail to complete Badwater drop out during this portion of the race. I was told if I could just make it to mile 42 where the course begins to climb out of the heat my chances of finishing would be greatly enhanced. My goal was to go slow and reach mile 42 in 12 hours at precisely 8:00 p.m. My feet were scalding hot and the soles of my shoes were literally melting off. Despite being dunked in an ice bath every 15 minutes, I would be completely dry within four minutes and therefore would bake for the next 11 minutes before my next bath. The hot air felt like it was cooking me from the inside out with every breath I took. I stuck to my target of consuming 40 to 50 ounces of fluid every hour and supplementing it with sodium, calcium, Gu (every hour) and Boost energy drink (every two hours). It's impossible to describe the heat, but if you were to stand in front of a hot blow dryer or blast furnace for 12 straight hours you might be in the ballpark. Runners began dropping out during this section of the race, but fortunately my crew kept me going and I reached mile 42 in 19:59:38 – 22 seconds off of my projection.

This is where it all began to fall apart. I had convinced myself that when the sun went down it would magically get cooler. Actually it became hotter as a gradient was created between the hot pavement and cool sky that led to incredible hot wind gusts bouncing off the pavement and into the runner's face. Kim and Nicole went to a motel to rest (at my request, because I thought it was going to cool down and I wanted them to get some rest). I learned later that 40% of the medical emergencies during the race were for crewmembers, not racers. During their absence I thought I could "borrow" fluids from other runners and crews. At mile 42 the course follows a steep (between six and nine degrees) incline for 19 miles. I ran out of water in 15 minutes, and the teams ahead of me kept going while the teams behind me turned back –since their runners were dropping out on the incline.

I was alone and quickly became confused. I lay down on the side of the road and suddenly I had my first hallucination: A bird-like creature flapped around my left shoulder and landed on it. It was Goofy (the Disney character) dressed in a devils outfit. He started stabbing me on the shoulder with his trident (it actually hurt like hell) yelling in my ear for me to quit. I tried to swat at him but he kept on doing it. I got on my knees and begged him to stop, but he wouldn't. I tried to get up and run from him and the next thing I knew, Nicole was there. All in all, I had been out of water for 80 minutes. Nicole put me in the ice bath for 15 minutes but my core temperature would not go down. We decided to "stake out" and return to the motel. (In this race, a runner has the option of placing a stake in the ground, leave the course and return later to start where they had "staked out.") All three of us took a 90-minute nap, showered, ate and returned to the course two hours later. It was well-needed rest for all of us and quite possibly the best decision we made.

After the climb the course drops back down to sea level (and 120 degree heat) and then climbs up 5,000 feet to Crowley Summit. I was feeling very good at this point and ran most of the hill. I kept telling myself that as soon as I saw Mount Whitney, I knew I would finish. I finally saw the Promised Land around 80 miles – it was still 55 miles away. At this point I ate a bowl of soup and drank a cup of coffee and started charging down the hill while pointing and yelling at Mount Whitney that soon – very soon I would be standing on top of it. I was every bit the crazed maniac you can imagine in your mind's eye.

This is also where I had my second hallucination. Essentially my head had become a pulsating 3-D box and inside the box were hundreds of three-dimensional cubes. Each cube was either positive or negative. The positives represented my wife, my crew, my training, and my desire to finish while the negatives represented my blisters, my ankle pain, my calf and hip pain, and my desire to stop and lie down. The negative cubes were multiplying faster than the positive cubes. I had the ability to grab a broom and sweep and the negatives out before they multiplied; all I had to do was sweep and keep the box positive. Pretty wild stuff (I'm still the crazed maniac from the previous paragraph, you see). Actually the hallucination was paying off, as I kept repeating to myself "just keep the box positive" – perhaps a million times or more and each time the pain would go away and I would pick up the pace. "Keep the box positive" became my mantra.

About 50 miles from the finish I caught up to Marshall Ulrich. Marshall is widely known in the Human Achievement World. He has run Badwater more than anyone else – 11 times. He is also the only person to run the "Badwater Quad:" Badwater to Whitney, Whitney to Badwater, Badwater to Whitney and Whitney to Badwater all in a row (10 days). He is the only person to complete the Badwater Solo, pulling a 220-pound cart of water, food and ice across the desert. He is a nine-year Eco-Challenge Team member; has run across the United States; has run the Continental Divide Trail; completed the Leadville 100 Mile Trail Run in less than 24 hours allowing enough time to drive to the start and run the Pike's Peak Marathon the next morning –you get the idea: the man is a giant. Anyway, I was fortunate enough to run the last 50 miles with Marshall and we totally hit it off. His goal in life it to do something that no other human being has done at least once a year, every year. I felt extremely lucky to be in his presence and really learned from him. He is a huge inspiration and a great leader; a completely unassuming person who is completely supportive of others. He wastes no energy but yet every thought is 100% positive, driven and motivated.

Marshall did the math and decided that if we pushed the pace, I could finish in less than 48 hours – the coveted goal of most Badwater participants. Marshall started at 10:00 a.m. (two hours after me) and essentially had the 48-goal in the bag. I however decided to go for it and picked up the pace. The major obstacle to finishing is the last 13 miles, which offers the exhausted runner a 19% grade that is virtually impossible to run and usually takes plus or minus five hours to cover. Many runners routinely drop out during this section even though they can count the remaining miles on two – and occasionally one hand. Marshall's plan was to cover the remaining 13 miles in less than four hours. To me, the plan sounded a bit psychotic. But in this race... well, we had to go for it. After all, I really couldn't say no to Marshall Ulrich.

We arrived at Lone Pine (mile 122) at 3:30 a.m. My target for reaching the finish was 7:59 a.m., which would mean a finish in under 48 hours. At Marshall's recommendation, I grabbed my ski/hiking poles from Kim and we took off. It was by far the most grueling finish of any ultra I have ever encountered. By the end I couldn't feel my legs or arms and had developed a huge blister on the sole of my foot that I didn't even know was there. Marshall dropped off the pace a bit with three miles remaining (remember, he was two hours ahead of me as he started at 10:00 a.m., not 8:00 a.m. like me). I persevered and reached the portals of Mount Whitney (the finish!) in three hours and 49 minutes, absolutely exhausted.

The current version of Badwater officially ends after 135 miles. Originally the race went to the top of Mount Whitney, a total distance from Badwater of 146 miles and reaching an elevation of 14,496 feet, the highest peak in the contiguous United States. However, due to national park regulations that don't allow races on park property, the race was cut back to 135 miles several years back. The unofficial race to the very top, however, is still on and is done under "gentleman's rule" the next day after the post-race awards ceremony. As long as a runner drops all race-identifying material (such as a race number), they are free to go at any time but no one really starts until 6:00 a.m. the following morning.

After patching up my blisters and hobbling into my sandals (my regular shoes wouldn't fit due to the excessive swelling of my feet), Kim drove me to the trailhead at 6:00 a.m. and I began climbing. I completed the 11-mile solo with a small pack and poles and reached the top in six hours and 10 minutes. It was snowing heavily when I finally arrived to a round of applause from 20 hikers who were already there – and knew I had finished Badwater the day before. As you might imagine it was a hugely emotional moment. The climb down was extremely tricky as my quads were shot and the snow made the rocks very slippery. Despite using very good gear, I was freezing and decided to try and run to generate some body heat. I now wished I were back in Death Valley again wearing my turban hat. I ran the last five miles and when I got to the finish I found myself wanting it not to end. So I kept running for another mile while promising myself I would be back next year.

One cannot put into words what it's like to train for and run this event with a group of extraordinary people. It is extremely humbling but motivating at the same time. Even though a large number of the runners did not finish the 2003 edition of Badwater, the positive energy I encountered on the course is hard to explain. These are normal, everyday people – cabdrivers, writers, teachers, businessmen, doctors, laborers, amputees, cancer victims, mothers, fathers and grandparents – who come to Badwater for one reason or another. One thing we all have in common is we have learned how to tap into a source of energy and mental focus that the vast majority of the population doesn't even know exists. They simply "keep the box positive" at all times; they don't focus on small negatives because they know the negatives in life tend to multiply quickly and become overwhelming. This race is different than other modern athletic events. Racers are more humble when they finish than when they began: The desert has a strange way of doing this to a person. There is no money, there is no fame. Most participants are laughed at or called freaks by the general population. Finishers receive a medal and a T-shirt and if they finish in less than 48 hours, a belt buckle. Essentially, Badwater has nothing to do with winning or losing. It has everything to do with each person battling themselves, nature and their perceived limitations. To watch someone explore and expand their limits right before your eyes is truly a powerful moment. This race is a great lesson on life.

2003 Finishing Time – 47:19:09
Thirtieth Place

CHAPTER SIXTEEN – ANDY VELAZCO

From Andy's 2003 Badwater Application:

Age: 55
Jonesboro, Georgia

Why I want a slot on the start line of the 2003 Badwater Ultramarathon:

Mike Smith and our 2002 Badwater crew are all members of the 50 State Marathon Club. We decided during Badwater that we all would try to finish the run. We all plan to return as runners and crew until all of us have had the chance to run it. Badwater has been a mental goal in the back of my mind for many years. It was an experience to see it as a crewman; now I want to experience Badwater as a runner.

A FRIENDSHIP FORGED IN HELL *By Andy Velazco*

In March of 2003 I received my letter of acceptance into the Badwater Ultramarathon. The Badwater race was (and still is) an experience that has forever defined my life as a runner; however, that letter was just one more step of my journey. The following describes the experience...

Believing You Can

In the fall of 2001, I was a runner trying to run a marathon in the Fifty States – all fifty States. I had gone to Tulsa, Oklahoma to run its marathon and "get the State." At the time, I was running one marathon a month and trying to go to different States. The Tulsa Marathon was the annual meeting of the Fifty States Club. At the pasta dinner I sat with a group of runners so we could talk about races done and future races to do. I soon realized that I was a "runner baby," and all my fellow diners at the table were very, very experienced runners. They were ultra runners. They had run 50 milers, 100 milers, and even 24-hour races. They had jobs and families, but they still had succeeded at long events. Seemingly by fate, I met Mike Brooks, Tom Detore, Allan Holtz, Mike Smith, and Walter Prescott.

Mike Smith mentioned that he had applied for a Badwater number, and I said I had just read Rich Benyo's book about his Death Valley crossings and was enthralled by it. Someday I wanted the experience too. I remember this moment well because that weekend I did my first double marathon.

We were running the Tulsa Marathon on Saturday; however the ultra runners told me that I could run again on Sunday (to do a double) and that I could run farther than 26 miles (which was as far as I had ever gone). They had plans to run the Gobbler Grind Marathon in Kansas City 200 miles or so away on Sunday. I called the Kansas Race Director and was able to get a number. So on Saturday afternoon after the Tulsa Marathon, I followed them to Kansas. On Sunday, during the race Mike told me he had been accepted into Badwater and asked if I would be part of his crew. I accepted, and suddenly I was Badwater bound. Soon after, I finished my first double marathon (4:05 and 4:35) and nothing in my body had broken.

Mike Smith had selected Mike Brooks, Walter Prescott, Bob Wehr and me as his crew. They encouraged me to run with them at The Olander Park 24-hour a month later. They told me to walk and eat a little every mile. We ran and walked together all day. I was amazed when I reached 93 miles in 22 hours –my first ultra.

BADWATER 2002 - Mike Smith

The planning for Mike's run was exhausting. He talked to other experienced runners, and planned our supplies and training. Mike had a great run; it was difficult, but he toughed it out and finished in 45:12:10.

During Badwater 2002, we all decided that we would each run it, and we would all come back and crew for each other. I did about 90 miles as pacer for Mike, and finished the Vermont 100 mile a week later. The group agreed that 2003 the following year – was to be my Badwater year.

Badwater 2003 - The Hot Year

After my experience in 2002, I knew what to expect. I knew the amount of training needed to complete the run and how difficult it would be. I was concerned about my capacity to do well for my team, and to test myself against the course. Badwater is the most difficult ultra race on the planet.

Alec Velazco: It's hard to believe it's been over seven years ago since the hottest summer of my life. My 15th summer started out like most before it; another lackadaisical school year and three months of professional teenaged couch-shaping projected for my rear-end. Although something on the home front was not normal... nor had it been for about four months. Frequently my siblings and I would be woken up to the sound of footsteps pounding above us at 2 or 3 a.m. Sometimes dad would start running on the treadmill before I went to bed and I often would venture upstairs and ask him how much longer he would was going to be. I remember my shock when he would inevitably reply, "Oh, maybe four or five more hours – we'll see." To most his behavior would seem outrageous and borderline psychotic. If you are going to run for six hours on a treadmill –which is already masochistic in its own right – why do it during the night? It's not like my father only did this on weekends either. Monday, Tuesday, Wednesday... having to go to work at 6 a.m. made no difference as to whether or not he would train through the night. On the other hand, being up all night with his training never made him late for work either. Then there was the "sweatbox" my father came up with. At the time he drove a Mini Cooper S, and I feel sorry for the person he sold it to: He would drive it to and from work across hot and humid Atlanta with the heater turned on full blast. Now, engineers spend considerable time and effort making air conditioning systems ¬– which actually work these days – and my father couldn't have cared less. He lined the car with towels to absorb his stench, using his daily commutes as a virtual sauna.

A day after my acceptance letter arrived, I had my team: Mike Smith, Mike Brooks, and Walter Prescott were all returning as pacers, and Jeff Titus as driver. My son Alec was coming to help as a crew person. I was grateful of the time each of them were giving to me away from their families and jobs, and placing themselves in an inhospitable terrain in the most undesirable conditions imaginable.

Mike Smith: One of the downsides to running in Badwater in 2002 was the debt I ended up owing crewmembers, that for reasons still unclear to me, decided they too would like to experience the race first hand. This led to crewing for Andy Velazco in 2003, Mike Brooks in 2004, and Carl Hunt in 2005.

Mike Brooks: This would be my second year of crewing and pacing at Badwater. Last year I crewed and paced for Mike Smith and this year it would be for Andy Velazco. Last year we were all new to Badwater but Mike did a great job organizing things so 2002 went pretty smooth. Mike would be "crew chief" this year making sure everything went as smooth as possible during the race.

Walter Prescott: This was going to be my year of decision at Badwater. Did I want to enter the "world's toughest footrace" for myself, or was I even capable of finishing such a grueling task of running 135 miles covering three mountain ranges in the desert during the hottest time of the year? I certainly got a taste of the Death Valley experience last year as a member of the crew for Mike Smith. It was one of the best times of my running career! But I was the driver of the crew vehicle for Mike, whereas this July I would experience crewing from a pacers point of view for my friend, Andy Velazco. I was looking forward to doing some running in the desert to help with my decision.

I was overwhelmed by the planning and logistics, but I had help on the crew book from Mike's run. He is a meticulous planner, and the previous year had written a complex detailed book with all the information needed before, during, and after the run.

Mike Smith: In addition to myself, Andy had recruited veteran Badwater crewmembers Mike Brooks and Walt Prescott. The two rookies were Andy's brother-in-law Jeff and his son Alec. A cautionary note for prospective Badwater runners: asking family members to crew for you is typically frowned upon, as they have a difficult time distancing themselves from the variety of miseries the race can deliver upon its participants. Luckily for Andy, Jeff and Alec seemed like they could care less about the degree of pain and suffering Andy was experiencing. Crew dynamics are always a challenge. I have been told I can be a bit anal in my preparation and execution of crewing responsibilities. I admit I have a routine for setting up the crew vehicle and administering aid that may be a bit inflexible at times... OK, I like it my way. Having admitted that, I think we worked out our responsibilities and set about preparing for the race.

Jeff Titus: I was meeting an excited Andy at the Las Vegas Airport with his huge grin (the only other time I saw him smile that big was when he got his Testarossa!). I was surprised at my lack of discomfort in the dry heat. Lots of laughter at that night's dinner after saying I was going outside to cool off. We shared funny stories of other crazy runs, the hunt for necessary supplies, and the barren drive to Death Valley, only dotted by casino signs and Joshua trees. It was really neat to see the historic Furnace Creek Inn where Andy had arranged for us to lodge. Getting to know the course the following day was tough.

Alec Velazco: The first day of our Badwater vacation started unlike any other as soon as we arrived in Nevada. After two cookies and checking into the Doubletree Hotel, the assembled crewmembers all went straight to Wal-Mart to begin preparing for what seemed like Armageddon. Prior to the trip, my father had engineered his running supply list to account for not only himself, but each crewmember as well. Twenty-five gallons of water, chips, crackers, deli meat, bread, four coolers, toilet paper... the list goes on and on. We bought so much water that I thought a more appropriate name for "Badwater" might be "Nowater." Had there been an army surplus store nearby, we probably would have bought MRE rations as well.

We arrived at the Furnace Creek Ranch – our hotel in Death Valley. For the rookies Alec and Jeff, our arrival was an experience akin to walking in and slowly toasting in an oven. There is no way to describe the heat. Words like massive, oppressive and intense do not do it justice. The best analogy is to open a hot oven and place your face in front of it.

Alec Velazco: After loading the backs of two Ford Expeditions, we set off for Badwater. There are a few things you have to experience for yourself before you take someone's word for it seriously. By the time we reached Badwater, I wished I had believed my father when he said how hot it was; I wouldn't have been there if I had! Badwater, California is hotter than anywhere you should ever willingly go. Take my hypocritical word for it! The heat is immense and saturates your face like an oven the moment you open a door or window. There is no escaping the heat anywhere near Badwater. I was amazed how cool they kept the hotel rooms, or at least how cool I thought the hotel rooms were once stepping inside from the desert heat. After about an hour I realized that even indoors, the air conditioning could only achieve a cool 80 degrees. Nevertheless, I have a new respect for any and all air conditioning systems. Especially the ones that have to perform in the desert.

The Ranch hotel was full so we were relocated to the Furnace Creek Inn. The Inn only opens at the desert's peak season, which begs the question: is there a Peak Season? As far as I could tell, we were the only ones there and had the swimming pool to ourselves.

Mike Smith: Typical of every year, runners and crew coordinated arrivals into Las Vegas a couple of days early and rented the crew car of choice, a Ford Expedition, as well as a second chase vehicle for shuttling crewmembers and supplies. I'm sure we made the obligatory supply run to Sam's, sparing none of Andy's expense. The variety and allotment of food may have changed a bit from year to year while crewing and running, but it seems like we were always donating enough at the end to feed the homeless in Lone Pine for several months to come. Then off to Furnace Creek, hopefully with the air conditioning turned off in the car to speed our acclimation to the impending HEAT.

Crew Run

We decided during our first year to do a trial run of our equipment and team. On the day before, the crew runs from the Badwater start to Furnace Creek Ranch (17 miles) and the runner drives the truck. This year Mike Brooks, Walter, and Alec ran it. I was proud that Alec ran well and all our arrangements seemed to work great.

Mike Smith: I remember the trial run with the vehicle and crew on the stretch of road from Badwater to Furnace Creek. We typically do this to square away any loose ends in the crew vehicle and continue the crews" acclimation. The runner for that year typically rides along (absolutely no walking or running at this point) or stays back at the hotel conserving energy.

Walter Prescott: This year's team included veteran runners Mike Brooks from Maine, Mike Smith from Indiana, myself from New Hampshire. Alec Velazco, Andy's 16 year-old-son and Jeff Titus, Andy's brother-in-law from Florida. To prepare ourselves for this week in the desert, we had done a lot of heat conditioning (scheduling runs during the hottest part of the day, running in the sauna at the health club, etc.) even though we were members of the crew, and not the participant. The year before had taught us that we had to come prepared to be baked in the sun. So on the morning before this year's race, a couple of us started running at Badwater, at the lowest elevation in the Western Hemisphere and ran/walked the 17 miles up to Furnace Creek to try to condition ourselves for the coming days. It was incredibly hot (about 125 degrees) but there were no problems with the heat. I wore the same sun precautions suit from last year, and kept well hydrated as we took turns spraying each other with water to keep cool.

Race Day

Mike Smith: Driving out to the start, passing the 6:00 a.m. starters along the way always gets the blood pumping. You arrive early enough to secure a parking spot and take the required pre-race photos. Then the fun begins! As a runner, I felt a great deal of relief once the race started. There is an incredible amount of preparation, both physically and logistically that you go through for this event. It's nice to know when it is no longer in your hands. You will simply get from point A to B; it's someone else's job to take care of you and all the associated challenges in between. As a runner, all you have to do for 134 miles is survive air temperatures up to 130 degrees, road temperatures probably closer to 200 degrees, winds that feel like they are originating from a blast furnace, sand storms, sunburn, never-ending mountain climbs, pounding road descents, dehydration, blisters, hallucinations, and the occasional moment of self-doubt... piece of cake!

I was in the 8 a.m. starting wave. The moment the race started, my fears literally melted away. I just had to trust my crew and only worry about moving forward. The whole crew saw me off and then they split into two teams.

The A Team – Mike Brooks, Jeff Titus, and Alec – went to Furnace Creek to eat breakfast, pack the suitcases, and load the crew truck. The B Team – Mike Smith and Walter Prescott – stayed with me. Pacers are allowed after the Furnace Creek check point at mile 17. I was weighed then and had my first and last foot check. I never get blisters, and I never take my shoes off during an ultra until the race is done.

Walter Prescott: It was an early morning for us on race day with all the final preparations. Jeff, Alec and I were the "A-Team." Jeff drove the car and Alec got the drinks and food ready, and I mostly paced/ran with Andy. Mike and Mike were the "B-team, with Mike Smith (the "bad Mike") driving and Mike Brooks (the "good Mike') pacing. We had 4 to 6 hour shifts for each team. Temperatures got up to 133 degrees on the first day, which was a lot hotter than last year, and it took its toll on the runners.

Alex Velazco: It was nice having two crew vehicles so that one crew could sleep while the other was tending the sheep. I have been to the start of enough races to know the start of Badwater is by far the worst to attend. It is simple, actually: The start is naturally the furthest point from the finish, which logistically is the worst place to begin. By the time I saw my father on race day, he was already 17 miles into the run. Standing amongst the other teams and crews watching them take in their runners and sending them off, I found it comical how almost all of them asked how their runners were feeling. At 17 miles of a 135-mile race, you do not want to hear if your runner is feeling bad. In their defense, I started finding it hard to come up with things to ask my father while he was running that was not gong to annoy him. So it is 133 degrees out – uh, are you hot?

I left towards the Stove Pipe station 23 miles away. This is the section of the course that is the most difficult as we have to run it in the afternoon heat, after the ground and road has had time to heat and bake. The hot air rises along the valley walls, hitting the upper atmosphere, then turns down coming towards the valley floor – a perfect geological convection oven. As the air churns and churns, the valley gets hotter and hotter. Mike Brooks was the pacer. The crew was doing six-hour shifts.

Mike Brooks: Andy picked a tough year to do the race with the temperature reaching 133 degrees in the shade, one degree below the all-time record. It was so hot you could not touch any metal without letting go quickly. Andy had trained for the heat but this was extreme. We had two crews and two vehicles, which made our jobs fairly easy. One crew would rest while the other crew stayed with Andy. I started pacing Andy at Furnace Creek and stayed with him from noon until 4:00 p.m. on the first day. Andy was feeling good despite it being well over 133 degrees in the sun.

While we were moving along Team B had checked out of our hotel and moved into our hotel room at Stovepipe. They had eaten at the hotel restaurant and procured more ice. Later I found out that the hotel ran out of ice.

Jeff Titus: Alec and I worked four hours on, and four hours off together, which was pretty cool because I really hadn't spent much time with him beforehand. We talked about his plans for college and our opinions on different types of cars. To break the monotony we had a wind-breaking contest and believe me, you did NOT want to be in our Expedition! It was a mad dash on our off time to reload supplies get food and perhaps some rest.

Alec Velazco: Mile by mile we drove along the course, stopped, and waited. Many might think the waiting was boring. On the contrary: it was the best part of the trip. Badwater is one of the most beautiful places I have ever been to. The desert, canyons, cacti, colors, and the peacefulness of the whole oasis were amazing. Often we stopped in the middle of nowhere and I enjoyed trying to listen to rocks I flung into the desert. Nowhere else can you hear so clearly. I believe my experience at Badwater directly resulted in my choice to live and go to school in Colorado, where I can enjoy the outdoors and easily go places that are away from the cities, politics and media.

The section before getting to the Sand Dunes was the most difficult. The afternoon sun was tremendous, and this area was the hottest and the worst. I was drinking 20 ounces of fluid every mile, taking a salt capsule every 15 minutes, and trying to eat some solid food. The hot air hitting the ground was bouncing up and cooking my legs. I felt like I was roasting alive. Finally I had to put on my long desert pants, since I could not stand the superheated air inside my shorts that was scorching my legs. I was literally cooking. A wet towel on my shoulders would dry up in five minutes, and my sprayed-soaked shirt only stayed damp for a minute or so.

I wanted to quit. But my crew was also suffering, and I did not want to let them down.

The crew drives one mile and stops to wait for the runner. There is no air conditioning allowed because we are trying to keep the truck from overheating. While the crew waits, they prepare the next bottle, keep the log (fluid, calories, and inventory), and drink, eat and take salt. While they do that the pacer is running with a water-mister to keep the runner's shirt wet, trying to get an idea what the runner needs and passing it ahead to the truck.

Alec Velazco: The two crews my father assembled alternated and continued to provide him assistance throughout the rest of the day and into the night. The two vehicles kept in contact using walkie-talkies that were an enormous benefit, as cell phone companies haven't exactly marked the desert as a place to improve coverage yet. We radioed his position and condition at regular intervals, noting whether or not the other vehicle needed to bring anything extra for the next shift.

Mike Smith: As challenging as this race is for the participant, crewing is no vacation in Death Valley. Race Director Chris Kostman always cautions us every year about the number of crewmembers that succumb to the heat, sometimes taking their runner out of the race with them. While we had no serious crew incidents that year, I think it can be a "learning experience" for all each year. You never quite know how it's going to go with your runner until you spend a few hours out there in the heat. As time goes on, you learn how to support their fluid, nutrition, psychological and other various needs. Accept the fact that at some point, there is absolutely nothing more you can do for them but drive off down the road another mile and hope they survive to see you once again.

Mike Smith: Then there are the incredible moments when they are completing milestones like reaching Furnace Creek, Stovepipe Wells, Town Pass, Panamint, Lone Pine, and the final climb up Whitney. Personally, I've never experienced much downtime while crewing. You are constantly prepping for your runner and maybe the pacer's arrival. At each stop keeping runners cool during the day with water spray bottles or ice, providing a variety of fluid and food alternatives, monitoring his weight, and watching electrolyte consumption are just some of the challenges that face you at each stop.

Alec Velazco: By mid-afternoon the first day, I began to have my doubts as to whether my father would complete the run. The heat began to visually drain my father and I really began worrying how many brain cells he was destroying. At one point I thought he had finally killed enough: around mile 40 or so, each time he reached the crew vehicle I could see in his eyes his own doubt that he would not make it to the finish. Every time he left for the next mile, I figured that would be the one where he would throw in the towel and be done with this madness. But every mile he continued on. I will always remember the determination and dedication he displayed that day. As much as I knew he did not want to let himself down, I knew he cared more about not letting his crew down. It is a daunting task to tackle Badwater. Not only does the runner have to actually run the race, but the runner must also call upon friends, family and people with literally nothing better to do to come and assist them in their desert adventure. Many take days off from work or sacrifice valuable time to come and support their runner. It takes weeks and months of planning to put together a proper Badwater race team. To let them down by not even making it half way is a burden my father luckily will never have to face. That first day will always be a motivational tool for me throughout life.

So I kept on moving.

Finally I saw Stovepipe and ran – straight into the hotel's swimming pool. The water was hot, but being immersed in liquid was the most wonderful feeling. I ate a plate of spaghetti (Walter's dinner), changed back into shorts, and left quickly going up the hill.

Walter Prescott: Despite the fierce heat Andy started off really strong and kept a fast pace for the first leg of the race. By the time we were allowed to start pacing him after Furnace Creek, he was pushing himself way too fast during the hottest time of the day. I actually had a hard time keeping up with him when I joined him near the sand dunes outside of Stovepipe Wells at mile 32, and kept telling him to slow it down so he wouldn't burn himself out too soon. Already there were a number of runners that had dropped because of the record heat. When we arrived at the rest stop at Stovepipe Wells Hotel, we both jumped in the pool, clothes and all, to cool off in the tepid water. We quickly ate our dinner, while Dr. Andy fixed the blisters of another runner.

Jeff Titus: Alec and I went ahead to the next stop to rest, wait for Andy and order dinner. When Andy arrived he wasn't too hungry, and then promptly ate two plates of food – one of them mine! I, always trying to find the fun in every situation, thought "I sure am glad you're not hungry" after he had finished both plates of sandwiches and spaghetti and meatballs. And they weren't small plates, either! I wasn't hungry because I had been snacking along the road, and ended up being the only one on the team who actually gained weight during our adventure.

To Towne Pass

It was getting dark. We had survived the hot desert and I was going uphill. The climb to Towne Pass at 5,000 feet is 18 miles long. The temperature dropped down to about 100, but now we had a head wind. Walter caught up to me and slowly we moved up, passing runners and crews, but still being passed ourselves. The moon was out and we kept moving with our headlights illuminating the way. All we could see were red dots (car tail lights) ahead and up from us, and the sound of voices brought by the night wind.

Mike Brooks: My next time pacing Andy it "cooled down" to 94 degrees at 2:00 a.m. at an elevation of 3,000 feet. I stayed with Andy from 10:00 p.m. to 4:00 a.m. and we walked 99% of the time, as this was all uphill towards Town's Pass

We reached Towne Pass. Chris Kostman and his roaming motorcycle were there. We stopped for a photo and starting running downhill towards Owen's Lake and Panamint.
Mike Brooks: After leaving Andy, I went back to Stovepipe where I slept for several hours. With two crews and being well organized crewing and pacing was easy, especially with the heat training we had all done.

I had a five-minute breakfast at Panamint: an egg burrito. "Good Mike" and I kept on.

Father Crowley Pass

The second climb is from Panamint to Father Crowley's Pass comprising a winding ascent over 15 miles. Mike Brooks was pacing and keeping me entertained. We saw several fighter jets flying low – *very* low – and doing attack runs along the dry valley floor. It was a welcomed distraction.

Mike Brooks: *While I was crewing I fell into a deep sleep and was dreaming that a freight train was coming towards me at a rapid pace. Startled I woke up to a low flying jet several hundred feet overhead! That was about the most exciting part of crewing for me.*

We reached the top and there was a lady with a massage table next to the road. She was giving massages to the runners. I got a five-minute treatment that was great. It was free; I would have paid a lot for it.

Walter Prescott: *I was definitely enjoying my duties as a pacer, either running to get Andy's water bottles, his trekking poles, or his night-lights and flashers. I sprayed him with water, got cold towels for his head, and generally did anything he needed to be done. But mostly I provided company, moral support and kept him on pace and out of harms way. We did a lot of alternating running and walking. Toward the end we were running for two minutes and walking for two minutes. Sometimes I would try to read his temperament and would trick Andy by telling him that two minutes had passed when it was actually more or less. During some of the brutal mountain climbs I tried to get him moving a little more steadily since he was taking WAY too many breaks. But then again, Andy was the one climbing all of the 13,000 feet of cumulative vertical ascent, and I was able to look forward to a break at the end of my six-hour shift!*

Mike Brooks: *Crewing gives you a chance to talk to other crews and see the other runners which helps make the race more enjoyable. I started pacing again at 10:45 a.m. – 14 hours and 45 minutes into the race. We were around mile 76 and Andy was still moving well, in good spirits and taking short breaks. It was break time for me at 5:30 p.m. and I headed off to Lone Pine for some sleep and food. I was back pacing at 11:30 p.m. and Andy was suffering from muscle spasms in his back and was leaning severely to the left side. I walked next to him on his left side to keep him from going off the road. He looked like an old ship listing to the port side getting ready to sink. Andy was hallucinating some. He thought he had an inner ear problem and that was why he was having a problem keeping his balance.*

We reached the boundary of the National Park and moved on towards the next checkpoint at Darwin's Turn Off. I was having difficulty running in a straight line – always going left.

Alec Velazco: *Once the heat of the first day was over, my father's condition improved and the crewmembers' job became repetitive. The second day of Badwater is a blur to me. I remember some odd-looking cacti and rock formations, but it was mostly just a long day spent in the desert driving one mile at a time. Ironically I bet I remember more from that day then my father does. After being awake and running for over 24 hours, he became a zombie. Somewhere along the second day he became a crooked zombie, developing a slight lean to one side. Remarkably, that tilted zombie continued moping along one mile at a time for the entire 135 miles.*

Jeff Titus: In the early morning of the second day, Andy was exiting the second mountain range with a slight tilt. We called him over and he said he was having problems with his back. We iced and massaged the aching muscles and that seemed to help him. He later told us he thought the pacer who was running in front of him was crooked – not realizing he was the one who was not upright. This was just about the time he said he started seeing things, but we had been told this was normal. Weird! The good news was that he kept going; the bad news was it slowed him down a lot.

Team B had driven to Lone Pine and checked onto our hotel and rested. The whole crew got together and had a celebration as we passed the 100-mile mark on the road.

Finally in the haze of the afternoon we saw the Sierra Nevada's and Mount Whitney in the distance. As the night set, we saw the lights of Keeler and Lone Pine. As I was following Walter I realized that he was leaning. Initially I thought I had suffered a stroke, that my vision was impaired, and that I was hallucinating. Looking at him, closing one eye, then the next, finally I realized that I was the problem. I had been experiencing back pain for a while and the result was that I was leaning far to the side while running. I had several hallucinations, which I found entertaining as they let time pass more quickly. The best was the Space City (the stars in the clear night connected by streaks of light).

Jeff Titus: The deathly silence of the desert at night was eerie. A time or two a scorpion would appear on the road in front of us and that – at this point – was an interesting sight.

Walter Prescott: Sometimes we talked a lot, but as the race progressed we just kept moving forward without much chatter. Andy would quite often wander out into the road and I would keep him in check. We tried to follow the white line, but he kept falling off the edge toward the end of the race. Both of us experienced some hallucinations during the last night when we were really exhausted. Andy saw a face in front of him and he felt a bat on his shoulder. When we focused on the far away lights (just like those "magic eye" posters where you can see 3-D items in the picture by staring almost cross-eyed at a spot on the poster) we saw all sorts of things. The white line at the side of the road was whipping up and down like a whip for me. The clouds and sky came to life with giant creatures. Andy saw a non-existent building and we both saw a flying pig. I saw a shark in the sky, and a giant spacecraft, like the one in the movie "Independence Day." The most frightening experience for me was when I heard a very loud growl, sort of like a wolf or coyote, just off the side of the road in the brambles. So I started to sing very loudly "One hundred bottles of beer on the wall" and Andy thought it was funny.

The blinking lights slowly got larger. Finally, we reached Lone Pine.

Lone Pine – The Whitney Portals

Mike Smith: *One of the challenges I remember for the crew during Andy's race was working with him to overcome a tendency he had to lean to one side as he made the final climb up Whitney. I'm sure there is a medical reason for this phenomenon, but despite our best efforts we couldn't seem to get him vertical. Initially, he even thought he might even be the butt of a bad joke practiced by his dedicated crew. Questioning us about why we were leaning to one side while attending to him. Now I can admit it was pretty funny to see someone bent at the hip to one side at nearly a right angle while trying to progress in a straight line up a mountain. I'm convinced that posture cost Andy quite a bit of time and added distance as he tried to right himself. What would a race be though without these kind of moments? I dare say less memorable...*

The ascent to the Portals of Mount Whitney was difficult. I was tired. I could not stand food. I remember Mike Smith trying to reason with me about eating while I steadfastly refused. I think I had a tantrum. The sun came up, and with five miles to go and seeing the switchbacks remaining was demoralizing. Two runners passed me by. My back was so tired that I was looking at the ground and getting my direction from Mike Brooks' shoes.

Walter Prescott: *By the time we made the turn at Lone Pine (mile 122) and started the ascent up Mount Whitney to the Portals, Andy was suffering badly because of his back. He had bent over to the left so much that he would tend to walk in that direction. We had to stop all the time and I thought he was going to fall over. He actually did fall off the pavement several times, and became a bit frustrated. But Andy was a real trooper and powered through the pain. When he crossed the finish line with his crew at hand, it was a really sweet moment for all of us. We had shared in the frustrations of more than two days of miserable heat and brutal climbs, and we were now overcome with relief and joy of Andy's success at running the race under extremely difficult conditions. The entire team was incredibly proud of Andy's accomplishment!*

Mike Brooks: *I was back pacing Andy an hour later and he was hurting even more. The crew told me he had turned angry and grouchy, which is not like Andy. I guess that is why they wanted me to pace again. He was bent over at the waist, the top part of his body parallel to the ground, barely able to move. I placed a trekking pole in his hands with the other end in mine. This was to guide him up the mountain because he was bent over so far he could not see where he was going. Andy's mood was grim. He no longer cared about buckling; all he wanted to do was finish the race. Andy was persistent, moving along at a snails pace but going as fast as he could.*

Finally, the finish line. We crossed the line together, and I finally sat down.

Mike Brooks: *At 8:54 a.m. Andy crossed the finish line and managed to smile now that it was all over. Our job as crew and pacers was over; Andy made it, finishing one tough race despite the pain and hours without sleep. It was a great feeling for all of us that Andy finished. Two things Andy said after the race that I will never forget are: "I might have quit but I did not want to let you guys down" and "you did things my wife would not even do for me." The second one I wonder exactly what he was talking* about; I hope it wasn't some kind of sexual hallucination!! In celebration of Andy's finish we all ate giant pancakes near the finish line and rested up before enjoying some of the best Mexican food I have ever had back in Lone Pine. It was a great experience crewing and pacing for close friends Andy and Mike. If they ever go back to Badwater I hope I can help out.

Walter Prescott: The Badwater Ultra was a tremendous amount of fun with a really great bunch of guys, and the memories will remain with me forever. Our team had come back to the desert for two years now, and everybody wanted Mike Brooks and me to continue the streak and to do the race together the next year. (It turned out that "Good Mike" did bring us all back to Badwater in 2004). When totaled, I had run about 80 miles of the course this year while pacing Andy. So I had answered my own questions about knowing if I was capable of finishing the race. But I also discovered I felt a greater sense of accomplishment knowing I was a part of someone else's success. Maybe someday it will be my turn, but for now I'm content with knowing I could do it if I wanted, and that I achieved great things with my team.

Jeff Titus: Andy limped on towards the finish line. All of us crossed the finish line together, hands raised in jubilation, all of us proud to be a part of Andy's achievement! I would like to thank Andy once again for giving me the honor of being able to witness this incredible moment in our family's history. I am in awe of his sheer doggedness, his amazing mental strength, and his stubborn perseverance – bordering on insanity – to get us to the finish line.

Alec Velazco: A funny thing about Badwater is the finish is not really the finish. Sure, that's where the runners finally stop running, but if it were 135 miles – or even 134, it would make no difference to the runner. The race is however long it takes for the runner to mentally commit to finishing. For my father, I think he finished Badwater somewhere around mile 50 on the first day when he decided he could not let his crew – or himself down. Each time he decided not to quit and to keep going, just one more mile...

Mike Smith: In closing, I'm going to include some random moments and thoughts about the race, just to give prospective participants and crewmembers some things to consider:

1. Learn to lie to your runner, or maybe just don't share all of the truth with him or her. Do they really need to know you have managed to run out of ice and it's another two hours to the next store that has any?

2. Keep your crew car windows rolled down, keys in the ignition, and don't dare turn the air conditioner on. We were lucky enough to only lock ourselves out of our crew vehicle once – right after Andy had finished the race.

3. Consider the crew dynamics and pair up people accordingly. Things are challenging enough without the crewmembers attempting to kill each other.

4. Have theme music. My personal favorite is turning the volume up on "Cool Water" by the Sons of Pioneers as you are passing runners in their trek across the Valley.

5. *Don't take it personally. Your runner and your fellow crewmembers may get a bit testy at times. It will get better...*

6. *Offer your runner a variety of food. He may be convinced that secret mixture in his bottle is all he will need, but at some point he's going to welcome the variety.*

7. *Remember your runner is really brain dead at times. You have to remember when he took that last electrolyte pill, finished that last bottle of water, or remind him that two more Ibuprofen one mile after he took the last two is not the recommended dosage.*

8. *No amount of positive reinforcement or reasoning with your runner is going to work at times. Stop talking, get him on his feet, fold up the chair, put it in the car, and drive to the next stop. Don't look in the rearview mirror...*

9. *If you are lucky enough to be at the Portals in the morning, order one of those really big pancakes they fix. Even if you can't eat it, it's worth seeing.*

10. *If you are crewing, try climbing Mt. Whitney afterwards. Then you have gone from the lowest to the highest point in the lower 48 in one week!*

2003 Finishing Time – 48:54:12
Thirty-second Place

© Thinkstock/iStockphoto/Fluid Illusion

CHAPTER SEVENTEEN – LISA SMITH-BATCHEN

From Lisa's 2003 Badwater Application:

Age: 42
Victor, Idaho

Why I Run Ultras:

I love to challenge my mind, body and spirit. The people you meet along the way and the beauty of each course. I also raise money for a wonderful organization that takes care of children: The Religious Teachers Filippini.

SUMMER SCHOOL *By Scott Ludwig*

Lisa Smith-Batchen is known for her ability to run exceptionally long distances. In 2003 when she crossed Badwater's finish line it marked her sixth successful completion of the toughest race on the planet.

But if Lisa had her choice in the matter, she would rather be known for her ability to *train others* to run exceptionally long distances. In fact over the years she has coached, encouraged and motivated over 50 runners to run Badwater... and all of them have reached the finish line at the portals of Mount Whitney. And their coach, trainer, mentor, inspiration and guiding light couldn't be prouder.

Lisa's early ventures into Death Valley proved to be very successful. In fact she was the women's champion in both 1997 and 1998, recording a personal best finish of 37 hours and one minute in the former (Lisa made her Badwater debut in 1995, finishing as the second woman less than an hour behind the women's winner). She modestly states that "Badwater is not very difficult for most ultrarunners, but what makes it difficult are the elements." Other than aching teeth, burning nostrils, the intense heat radiating off of the asphalt and the occasional wind and/or sand storms, "the course is pretty runnable."

The 2003 Badwater Ultramarathon stands out in her running career because there was more suffering during the race; not only by the runners but by the crewmembers as well.

Lisa attributes her success as a coach on her experience as an ultrarunner and that she has "made every mistake there is to make." She in turn is able to develop a program tailored to the individual runner, focusing on capitalizing on their individual strengths and strengthening their individual weaknesses. Plus, she makes it a point to "pass along the magic that works for her." Lisa realizes "no two runners are alike," so she develops specific nutrition, training and conditioning programs for each of her students. When asked which of her students she is most proud of, she quickly replied "all of them."

As Lisa openly admits, she's made her fair share of mistakes. In fact, one of the worst of her career was during the 1999 Badwater Ultramarathon which was featured in the documentary film *Running on the Sun*. Lisa was having a pretty good run when suddenly – with only eight miles remaining in the race she was rushed to a hospital. It was there doctors discovered one of Lisa's crewmembers, a former trainer for a football team, had rubbed DMSO all over her legs. After the medical staff treated her, they told her that if the DMSO had been rubbed on her torso she would have died, as the chemical, a known solvent would have been absorbed into her body – which would make for a dangerous combination with the addition of dirt, sand and perspiration. Somehow Lisa was able to return to the course and finish the race in an unofficial time of 48:24 (during her hospital stay, Lisa endured an IV to replenish her fluids: according to Badwater rules, if you receive an IV during the race you are disqualified), which makes the 1999 Badwater Ultramarathon one of her "proudest races ever."

Following her ordeal, it took a while for a full recovery as Lisa suffered through the experience of losing all of her toenail beds, seeing the lymph nodes in her groin area grow to the size of golf balls, and a few other maladies which won't be mentioned here as a favor to the squeamish.

Through her experiences – both the successful ones and the ones that (for the sake of sounding positive) "presented opportunities for improvement," Lisa has learned the following tips work well when faced with running 135 miles across the combination of a blazing desert and a mountainous terrain:

* Keep your body cooled down by placing ice under your hat, in your groin area and on your wrists and neck (basically anywhere there is a major artery!)

* Slow down during the hottest part(s) of the day(s).

* Choose a strong crew – humans could not survive without on this course without a crew!

* Know how to manage your body: when to slow down, when to pick up the pace and when to take a catnap (hint: *when you can't keep your eyes open!*) knowing that the rest will pay dividends later in the race.

As Lisa rapidly is approaching Badwater finish number ten, she is setting her sights on retiring from competitive running and spending time with her children, ages six and nine. After all, she says: "It's their turn."

But don't expect Lisa to stop teaching anytime soon. In the "summer school" that is the Badwater Ultramarathon, the professor emeritus is still alive and well.

2003 Finishing Time – 52:11:39
Thirty-third Place

© Thinkstock/iStockphoto/Fluid Illusion

CHAPTER EIGHTEEN — NANCY SHURA-DERVIN

From Nancy's 2003 Badwater Application:

Age: 53
Northridge, California

Why I Run Ultras:

It needs no explaining to those who understand and it could never be explained to those who don't. But it's probably related to a severe chemical imbalance in my brain, but my love Larry says that I'm the person he would most want to take into battle with him, so it must be a good thing!

"MORE ULTRA… LESS LADY" *By Nancy Shura-Dervin*

There is nothing "lady-like" about ultra-running, my personal motto being "I don't do it for the glory… I do it for the *gory!*" Ultrarunning has often been compared to childbirth in the sense that with both you surrender to the forces of nature, and in the process toss aside your modesty. With this thought, I wanted my Badwater crew to be made up of my UltraLadies Sandy Gitmed, Saundra Whitehead, Michele Vela and Wendy Young (yes, I believe in midwives over obstetricians), plus my darling Larry Dervin (who was never in the delivery room with me) and my daughter Heather Shura (who was in the delivery room with me, but doesn't remember). A late arrival to our crew was Mike Stephens, an accomplished 100-mile runner and emergency room nurse who should be able to handle the "gory!'

On the morning of the "big day" Heather said something to calm my nerves: "Mommy, it's scary!" Being Mommy, I consoled her, "Don't think of it as 135 miles… just break it into little goals… we're just going to Furnace Creek and then to Scotty's Castle turnoff… then Stovepipe Wells." I suddenly felt in control and ready to go!

So here is my Badwater story, goal-by-goal:

Training: The first goal was to balance training for a high-profile race such as Badwater while maintaining a full-time career, family relationships, UltraLadies" Coaching, and my responsibilities as race director for June's Valley Crest Half Marathon. Fortunately no one particular area suffered too much: The Valley Crest race was a huge success; the UltraLadies ran smoothly; I didn't get fired from my research position at USC and most importantly my family and friends still speak to me! Because of time constraints, the theme for my Badwater training was "moderation." I always kept my total weekly mileage below 75, with no single run exceeding 35 miles.

Heat Training: I did a significant amount of heat training. About eight weeks before Badwater I began driving home from work each day with the windows rolled up and the heater blasting through the vents. I covered my car seat with towels and wore sweats. When I would step out of my car an hour later, the sweat was dripping on the pavement as I walked from my car to strip down in the garage. I also spent 45 minutes in a 180-degree sauna Monday through Friday each week. The diluted salt concentration of my sweat was quite noticeable after just a couple of weeks. I believe in simulating race conditions so I went to both official training weekends in Death Valley (DV), plus my crew and I went to DV two additional weekends during June. I would typically start my desert training runs at 10:00 or 11:00 a.m.; late enough to benefit from the maximum high temperatures. Once, when the temperature only (*did I just write "only?"*) reached 108 degrees, I jogged through DV wearing my black, long-sleeve, fleece pullover and knitted cap. What a sight I must have been! The hours I spent training in DV were invaluable to me in helping to work through problems I might encounter during the race. On some of the runs I experienced prostration, headache, vomiting, and one particular time I developed debilitating heat cramps of the skeletal muscles of my torso and neck so much that my ear was pulled down to my shoulder. Needless to say, I left the course that day and went straight to bed! My heat training mantra became "the more I suffer now, the less I'll suffer later." After a lot of trial and error, all of my heat-related problems were finally left back at the training runs. My crew and I had learned the fine balance between pace, cooling, to say, I left the course that day and went straight to bed! My heat training mantra became "the more I suffer now, the less I'll suffer later." After a lot of trial and error, all of my heat-related problems were finally left back at the training runs. My crew and I had learned the fine balance between pace, cooling, hydration, electrolytes and calories... another goal accomplished.

Pre-Race Jitters: Being a medical research nurse means I am neurotic about details and I approached my Badwater race prep with the same dedication, leaving no stone unturned. By the time I made my last drive out to DV, I knew I had done everything possible to prepare for the expected as well as the unexpected. During the pre-race festivities, I needed to keep my psyche relaxed so as not to use up unnecessary energy. Humor really helps me relax, so my crew and I marched into the pre-race meeting wearing our Team UltraLadies' "More Ultra... Less Lady" yellow T-shirts and of course I wore my "big nose glasses" that have been with me through all my 100-milers! Even though one finds herself at the premier ultra event in the world... it pays not to take oneself too seriously!

Middle of the Pack: I was happy with my 8:00 a.m. starting time... middle of the pack... hopefully I would finish close to that! I liked the fact I could sleep until a normal time, eat breakfast, etc. I will admit to feeling a few "butterflies" on the drive out to Badwater. Before long I was standing on the runner's side of the start banner, posed for some photos, took a few deep breaths, and I would soon have nothing to think about except getting to Furnace Creek in good condition. I always wondered what a person's last thoughts are while hearing the countdown. My last thought? *"Here goes nothing!"*

Badwater to Furnace Creek (miles 0-17): The first stage of the race was my settling in period, getting my body working in the 100-plus degree heat, adjusting to my liquid diet of multi-flavored Gatorades, Chocolate Slim-Fast, Club Soda and ORS (oral rehydration salts). Over the next 52-hours, I would consume nearly one bottle an hour of each of the first three beverages plus one liter of ORS over four hours. My first crew (Larry, Heather and Mike) settled into spraying me, replacing iced bandanas, weighing me, and monitoring my urine output while doing the same for each other to keep in good condition to continue supporting me. By 10:00 a.m. the temperature had risen to 119 degrees. We reached Furnace Creek at 12:45 p.m.; just a few minutes after being passed by Pam Reed, who I understand did quite well in the race. A short rest in the shade and we were off to pursue our next goal... Scotty's Castle turnoff.

Furnace Creek to Scotty's Castle Turn Off (miles 17-35): This is where the heat really fired up. Several reports had the temperatures at 130 degrees. Some leg cramping at mile 28 cautioned us to increase my sodium and potassium, which corrected the problem. At 5:00 p.m. around mile 29, we changed crews and on came my UltraLadies Wendy, Saundra, and Michele. Admittedly, this stressed me a little as it altered the routine during a time when I was feeling tired, sore, and vulnerable, but I stayed deep into my techno music and before long the new crew had it all together. Although I managed to avoid blisters on the training runs, it was here I began to feel them forming on the bottom of both heels and pinky toes, so I changed into my Asics DS Trainers and did some major insole trimming to get me to Stovepipe Wells. I wanted any "down time" fixing my feet to coincidentally occur in an air-conditioned room! The liquid diet was holding me along with saltine crackers and me continuously nursing my ORS solution. The turn at Scotty's Castle was eventful in that I knew I only had about seven miles to reach my next goal!

Scotty's Castle Turn-Off to Stovepipe Wells (miles 35-42): During this section my crew suspected that I needed more calories and began to feed me little squares of a peanut butter and jelly sandwich. I had almost no pacing before mile 35, as I was content to stay in my techno zone and wanted to keep my crewmembers as fresh as possible. My friend Greg Minter (who I crewed for in 2001) stopped by to pace a little bit with me on the way to Stovepipe. A light show was visible in the northwest sky and the hot wind blew so hard at times that Greg had to hold onto my shirt to keep me from blowing off the road. Coming into Stovepipe was a great feeling. I just wanted a cool shower and to get my feet fixed.

Stovepipe Wells to Townes Pass Summit (miles 42-59): After a 90-minute break to shower, repair blisters, re-tape feet and drink chicken broth, I was back on the road. Mike, in his first ever attempt at blister treatment/taping, did a great job! It was well worth the time spent, as we did not need to tend to blisters again during the remaining 93 miles! Marching up the lower half of the climb to Townes Summit was a grind for me. The air was hot and the sets of red lights ahead of me seemed to be ascending straight up, as though on an escalator. Around 1:20 a.m. I felt sleepy and was allowed a 15-minute nap sitting up in the driver's seat of the van. At 2:00 a.m. another crew change occurred and I was back with Larry, Heather and Mike. As Larry paced me up the mountain it began to sprinkle, and we enjoyed the cool 88-degrees and a magnificent blanket of stars. At 6:30 a.m. (55 miles) I laid on a tarp on the ground and slept soundly for 30 minutes. This would be the last time I would sleep for the remainder of the race. I reached the summit at 7:57 a.m., 24 hours into the race. Another goal accomplished!

Townes Pass Summit to Panamint Springs (mile 59-72): I was warned this was a long stretch so I took it slow, covering the 13-miles in just under six hours. I wanted to run some of the downhills but was extremely intent on just conserving energy. During this time I was visited by a couple of runners who had dropped from the race. Norm Haines met me just as I began the descent into Panamint. Ben Jones drove slowly past, leaning out of his window to talk. The appearance of these disappointed athletes increased my caution, causing me to slow down, probably more than I needed to. I mentally envisioned all of us as little ducks in the shooting gallery, moving along the white line... and pop... down goes another one! The break at Panamint was longer than expected partly because it was timed with a crew change and partly because I was enjoying the air-conditioned trailer I shared with the famous Scott Weber. At 1:45 p.m. we began our climb up the second mountain!

Panamint to Father Crowley's Point (mile 71-80): The first few miles leaving Panamint were uncomfortably hot, but I began to rally as the temperature cooled. Michele, Saundra and Wendy got me up the mountain, each one pacing me in two-mile stretches. At Father Crowley's Point I did some creative shoe cutting and had my dead feet rubbed back to life, beginning a routine that would be repeated often in the hours to follow. It was probably here that I transitioned into my "robot mode" and began my "Lamaze breathing" and stopped asking stupid questions like "Where am I?" or "Didn't I just take a salt tablet?" At 4:26 p.m. – 32 hours and 26 minutes into the run, I passed into new territory, where every minute spent on my feet was a new personal record.

Father Crowley's Point to Darwin turnoff (mile 80-90): The 10-mile stretch to Darwin turnoff was exciting for me. Darwin was a major goal to reach because it was the beginning of some long downhills as well as the beginning of the second night. The dark clouds ahead brought lightning, headwinds and rain blowing in my face. A bright spot here were visits from Rick Nawrocki and Denise Jones, who both smiled from ear-to-ear for me! Darkness fell early and we put on our reflectors and lights. I was looking forward to the second night knowing that funny things can happen to "your brain during Badwater." Eventually the time did come when the little bushes by the roadside morphed into strange shapes and seemed to turn and face me as I passed by but I showed them who was boss by stating out loud "I know you're not real!"

Darwin turnoff to Second Sunrise (mile 90-117): This was a great part of the race for me. The girls added Hammer Gel and Coke to my diet, a couple of caffeine pills, and I was good to go! I felt cooler and quite refreshed by the downhill sections. My legs felt good enough to run but my feet felt like hell. I had intense foot throbbing that was temporarily relieved by really vigorous foot scratching/rubbing. I bargained with my crew that I would run the downhills in exchange for five-minute foot scratches to be performed every three miles. My feet would feel quite good for a mile and a half after each scratching. We covered miles 90-110 in about five hours, passing several runners/crews along the way. 2:00 a.m. was crew-change time and seeing Larry and Heather again was a big boost to me. Entering the Owens Valley in the dark allows you to see the twinkling lights of the crew vans on the mountain, snaking up the switchbacks to the portal and the finish line. Larry paced me through much of this section and as he and I walked quietly together in the pre-dawn darkness, I finally began to allow myself to think about the finish line just 20 miles away.

Sunrise to Lone Pine Checkpoint (mile 117-122): The march into Lone Pine was rewarded with a short rest in a lounge chair and some nibbles on McDonald's scrambled eggs and of course... another foot scratching ! Some of Louise's crew came over to say hello and knowing that Louise finished the race about 12 hours earlier I commented "Aren't you glad you didn't crew for me?" Mike had to leave for work so we hugged good-bye and my two crews became one for the final push to the last goal... the Whitney Portals and the finish line of the Badwater 135-Mile Ultra Marathon!

Lone Pine Checkpoint to Mount Whitney Portal (mile 122-134.9): I had 12 hours in the bank to complete the 13-mile climb... no sweat! But for the first time in the race, I nearly lost it in those early uphill miles. I felt incredibly hot, sweaty, dizzy and very sleepy. My heart seemed to pound out of my chest with every step. Larry called to me to pick up the pace after reporting I had just completed a blistering 40-minute mile! I was trying to calculate the time versus mileage in my head, but all I could remember was that I had fewer miles remaining than fingers on my hands, and I was not going to throw it all in the toilet! With Larry, Saundra, Heather and Michele taking turns pacing for one-mile intervals, we picked up the pace. With about four miles remaining I saw a familiar face, Craig Chambers by the side of the road and asked him to walk with me. Craig took me the rest of the way up the mountain, giving my crew a much-needed rest. Craig was telling me I was strong and that the last mile would be wonderful. Craig's smile in the photographs more than make up for the lack of mine. The portal road climb probably required the most from me yet my split of 5:13 for this section of the course was actually quite good. After more than 50 hours of creeping along this "comfortable road," changing clothes, peeing, and pooping in public view, every ounce of modesty was gone. I had morphed into some kind of wild animal grunting up the mountain, which is how I must have sounded. I had such a feeling of urgency knowing I would make it, but at the same time fearing I wouldn't. My wonderful crew kept appearing around corners, smiling at me and just like a woman about to give birth, I wondered out loud "What the hell is everybody smiling about?"

The Finish Line (mile 135): Finally as rain began to fall, my team in their yellow UltraLadies' shirts came out to greet me. Larry, Heather, Sandy, Michele, Wendy, Saundra, Mike (actually a hand-made, stuffed dummy, filling in for the real Mike), Craig and I all crossed the finish line; holding hands, as it was meant to be. To run 100-miles and have your crew meet you here and there is one thing, but to complete this incredible journey, where your accomplishment and perhaps your very life is in the hands of your entire crew is quite another thing. And just as each mile was shared, so the finish should be!

Post Script: I made a wonderful recovery after Badwater. I attribute my physical condition to the special care given to me by my exceptional crew. Words cannot express the gratitude and love I feel for them: My beloved Larry Dervin, who believed in me more than I believed in myself; my daughter Heather Shura, who completely gave herself over to helping me (even though she herself has yet to become a runner); my selfless friend Sandy Gitmed, who was the backbone of our crew, performing all the ice runs, hotel arrangements and feeding the crew; my special UltraLadies' friends Wendy Young, Saundra Whitehead, Michele Vela and Mike Stephens (UltraLadies' Man), who spent time away from work, family and friends to be a part of this incredible journey. I thank you all, and I hope to return the favor some day!

My friend Craig Chambers lost his battle with melanoma in the summer of 2008. He is missed.

2003 Finishing Time – 52:35:36
Thirty-fourth Place

© Thinkstock/iStockphoto/Photo Illusion

CHAPTER NINETEEN – BILL LADIEU

From Bill's 2003 Badwater Application:

Age: 53
Harrisburg, Pennsylvania

Why I Run Ultras:

Personal satisfaction… and I really do enjoy running.

BADWATER, A GOOD COMFORTABLE ROAD *By Bill LaDieu*

When I decided to run Badwater my loving wife Marilyn was not very enthusiastic about it. She was concerned about the extreme conditions, but excited with the possibility of seeing Death Valley. Marilyn's brother Dave was much more enthusiastic over the whole idea and offered to crew for me, assuming I was accepted into the race. So with the makings of crew I began in earnest to plan for the 2003 edition of the race. To finish out my crew Dave recruited his son Scott and we lined up good friend Stan Clarkson who seemed to be genuinely interested in the event once he heard about it.

My first major training run was the Virginia Happy Trails Fat Ass 50K in December 2002. I rode down to the race with my training partner, Randy Dietz. As runners are wont to do we spent our time together talking about our plans for the coming year. I told Randy I was going to do Badwater. Randy thought that was really neat, but thought I was a little bit crazy as he reminded me the run is all on the road and my feet would probably hurt quite a bit, considering my plantar fasciitis and all. I admit I hadn't considered that possibility, but figured since my feet hurt most of the time anyway, could it be much worse at Badwater? At the Fat Ass we had great Badwater Training conditions: mud, hills and lots of water. I figured if I could survive this run, a little trot through the desert with a crew at your beck and call couldn't be that tough!

My training went really well. Randy and I did multiple long runs in the Pennsylvania Mountains. A typical run would be to get up at some ungodly hour of the morning, drive to a remote trail head, run all day on wet rocky trails at the lightning quick speed of 3-4 miles per hour and conclude the run by quaffing a couple of beers. With this strict training regime plus numerous sessions of baking in the sauna at 150+ degrees prior to leaving for Death Valley, I felt I was ready for the race.

The plan was to travel to Las Vegas where we would purchase most of our supplies. I had decided to run in shorts and a T-shirt, foregoing the haz-mat style sun protection suit that many runners prefer; I just couldn't bring myself to do it.

A major issue for this run was to make sure we had enough ice for the race before arriving in Death Valley. To accomplish this we filled a 120-quart cooler with 100 pounds of ice and layered 35 pounds of dry ice on top to keep it frozen. This worked very well, the ice lasting intact throughout the first day.

My crew, consisting of Marilyn, Dave, Scott Wilbur and Stan Clarkson and I arrived at Furnace Creek Ranch on Monday just in time for registration and the prerace briefing. I had my first opportunity to experience the desert heat in person (it was in the low 120's) and was it ever hot, especially with the heat radiating up from the pavement. Race registration and the pre-race briefing was a protracted affair lasting about three hours in a hot auditorium. With conditions being so tough during registration I figured that the race would be piece of cake. At least we would be outside where there would be a breeze.

I was assigned the 8:00 a.m. start time. After a good night's sleep we all filed down to breakfast at 6:00 a.m. for the buffet, graciously set up early for the runners by the folks at Furnace Creek. After getting ourselves more or less organized, we traveled to the start at Badwater for the obligatory pictures and runner check-in. The race started promptly at 8:00 a.m. on a Tuesday, and we sauntered off toward Furnace Creek (mile 17.4).

My crew met me every mile or so to replenish my fluids, electrolytes and to make sure I was eating. I really enjoyed this section of the run, as I was able to visit with the other runners and just cruise along.

After Furnace Creek the race began to get interesting as we were now in the heat of the day. It became very tough to maintain anything resembling a run. I was relegated to walking after about 35 miles or so. During this section I spent some time with Barbara Elia, a Badwater veteran. She told me to make sure that I took a swim at Stovepipe Wells to cool down and regroup before heading up to Towne Pass.

As I was on the edge, I considered this to be good advice. At the sand dunes just outside of Stovepipe Wells, I got sick and emptied the entire contents of my stomach. I am not sure if I was sick because of what I was eating or the heat and hot wind, which had come up that afternoon (it was reported that the temperature that first afternoon reached 130+ degrees).

After vomiting I felt better, but had no energy as I stumbled into Stovepipe Wells (mile 42.7) where we all jumped in the pool to cool off. Fortunately, I was cognizant enough to take off my shoes and socks. We spent about 30 minutes swimming and getting our act together before venturing into the dark up the mountain to Towne Pass.

While all this was going on my wife Marilyn was having trouble with the heat. Dave told her to get off the course to cool down. She spent some time in the air conditioning at the Stovepipe Wells store before Stan drove her ahead to Panamint Springs where we had reserved a room to rest. I didn't see her again until the next morning when I arrived there.

The climb up Towne Pass (5,000 vertical feet in 17 miles) was interesting to say the least. It was hot and very dark, which coupled with the fact that I didn't feel particularly well made for a long night. The climb went something like this: walk a couple of miles; get into the car to whine about how slow and bad I was feeling; finally eat and drink. I was in "Poor Little Ole Me" mode in a big way. Dave, Scott and Stan were great during this section in that they kept me hydrated, fed and didn't pay attention to my moaning and groaning. In retrospect, I was pretty pitiful. With the rising of the sun I started to feel better, especially after drinking several bottles of half Coke and half water.

I reached Towne Pass (mile 58.7) early on Wednesday morning feeling somewhat peeked as I had pushed rather hard for the previous four or five miles. After some down time to get myself back together I got up feeling rather good and started the long down hill into Panamint Valley.

The downhill into Panamint Valley was probably the highlight of the race for me. I felt great, the views were spectacular and all I wanted to do was run. I cruised down the mountain at a good steady clip just enjoying myself. I was higher then a kite; life couldn't have been better. Dave came riding by in my crew car and hung his head out the window to comment: "Are you f%^#$^ nuts!"I guess he couldn't rationalize why I could feel so bad one minute and so great the next. As it turned out the bad patch at the top of Towne Pass was my last for the race.

I arrived in Panamint Springs (mile 72.3) around 10:00 a.m. I was tired, but otherwise feeling well. I took a short nap on a real bed to get off my feet, reenergizing myself for the second half of the race to the finish line at the Mount Whitney Portals.

Leaving Panamint Springs I started the climb towards the Father Crowley Turnout. It was overcast but turned bright and sunny shortly thereafter. I ended up doing most of the climb in the heat of the day, which really took the stuffing out of me. During the climb you could clearly see your position in the race with respect to the other runners while maneuvering through the switchbacks leading up to the pass. Coming up behind me was Marshall Ulrich, who finally caught me at Father Crowley's Turnout (mile 80.2). I walked with Marshall and his wife Heather for a mile or so. It was great to get some perspective on the race from one of the legends during our short time together.

After Father Crowley the wheels started to come off. My ITB started to tighten up which made it difficult to run. Even walking was becoming uncomfortable. Recognizing that I couldn't maintain a pace fast enough to earn a buckle for a sub-48 hour finish, I shut it down and elected to enjoy myself, simply aiming for a respectable finish and not worrying about speed.

I arrived at the Darwin Turnoff (mile 90.1) around 6:00 p.m. just in time to experience a late afternoon desert shower.

To illustrate how "loopy" one can get during a run like this, I was talking strategy (as if I had one at this point) with Dave and Scott at the turnoff. We were standing out next to the time check when I decided I needed to pee, which I did without hesitation. Neither Dave or Scott noticed that I was peeing until Scott remarked: "Uncle Bill you are pissing on my foot!" to which I replied much to my surprise "Sorry" and continued peeing, although I did shift slightly to the left just missing Dave's foot. I was the butt of many jokes as this story was retold countless times over the next couple of days.

Shortly after Darwin Turnoff Marilyn and Stan rejoined us. They had gone onto Lone Pine to pick up ice and other miscellaneous supplies. While in Lone Pine Marilyn and Stan decided to pick up sub sandwiches for everyone except me! As I was coming down the road I saw both crew cars together and everyone eating a delicious looking sub. Marilyn offered me a bite, which I graciously accepted. I could have eaten the whole thing but didn't want to eat her supper. After eating supper my crew stayed together for the next couple of hours while I leapfrogged positions with Ken Eielson of Colorado. The highlight of this section was the ice cream bars that Ben Jones' crew gave us while on their way to Lone Pine. With the coming of darkness Dave and Stan went to Lone Pine to sleep while I was crewed by Marilyn and Scott.

My ITB had really tightened up and I was having a lot of trouble making forward progress. Scott suggested I get into the chair so he could stretch my ITB and hip flexors. After that he stretched my legs every two miles or so, which worked great on the right leg, although the left leg remained very sore. With the coming darkness we lost all perspective of where we were on the course; it was just flat and dark. I had trouble gauging my pace and staying focused, which coupled with my sore left leg made for a very long night. I found that I could run somewhat more comfortably than I could walk, however I didn't have the energy to run so I just shuffled along as best I could.

I reached Keeler (mile 107.8) around 1:45 a.m. (it is now Thursday) where Stan and Dave came back from their break to relieve Marilyn and Scott. They were with me for the rest of the night on the run (walk???) into Lone Pine.

Both Dave and Stan walked with me for the next several hours to keep me company. While on the way into Lone Pine we could see the lights of runner's crew vehicles as they made their way up the Portal Road off in the distance. This was discouraging, as I knew that I had several more hours before I too would be climbing. Dave and I got into a big discussion of how far it was to Lone Pine. I was really focused on Lone Pine because I knew once we were there the end would be in sight. Since we really didn't know how far it was we sent Stan to clock the distance to the Dow Villa Hotel. Stan took off in the crew car and left Dave and me walking toward Lone Pine. By this time I was becoming irritable and very impatient. I had it in my head that I had four miles to go; however when Stan arrived he reported that the distance was closer to seven miles, which really sent me into a tizzy. I took off running, as I had no intention of spending the next two to three hours on this long straight road. I ran most of the way to the Highway 190/395 intersection (mile 120.3). I had had enough fun for the past two days and was anxious to get the whole thing over with.

I reached the Dow Villa (mile 122.3) around 7:30 a.m. Dave and I chased Scott out of bed and I went into the bathroom in an attempt to wash off a tube of SPF 50 Sun Block, which was on my hands and arms after being religiously applied by my crew throughout the race. I felt like a grease ball. After washing up, I bolted out of the Dow Villa heading for the Portal Road; only I didn't know where it was. Dave and Stan were getting a cup of coffee and noticed me going up the wrong road. Dave took off after me and finally got me headed in the right direction. Needless to say I was somewhat irritated at this point and in no mood for jokes.

With my full crew intact we headed up the Portal Road though the Alabama Hills to the Mount Whitney Portal and the finish. This portion of the race went very well for me. I had plenty of energy and was able to climb at a good pace despite my sore left leg. I enjoyed walking with my crew and the spectacular views as I progressed up the mountain. I finished the race at 12:49 p.m. for a total elapsed time of 52:49:18.

All in all a very satisfying and memorable experience; even if I did pee on Scott's foot.

2003 Finishing Time – 52:49:18
Thirty-fifth Place

© Imago sportfotodienst/Norbert Schmidt

CHAPTER TWENTY – JOE PRUSAITIS

From Joe's 2003 Badwater Application:

Age: 48
Austin, Texas

Why I Run Ultras:

The finest people in the world run these things. I enjoy seeing strange and wonderful places, and I'm good at it. I love to run long.

SAND SPIRITS AND SCORPIONS *By Joe Prusaitis*

At first glace, it seems a bit foolish to run 135 miles across Death Valley in July. But if I go for adventure, an education, and some answers, what then? No doubt, it will be exciting. I will certainly know more when I'm done. But really all I want to know is: "Can I do it?"

My wife Joyce and I land in Las Vegas and escape quickly into the Amargosa Desert. We turn off the highway at an old run-down gas station that might be all there is to Lathrop Wells. With Devil's Hole on one side and the Funeral Mountains on the other, we enter California and then Death Valley. The road ripples ever so slightly downward, snaking through the desert while the heat visibly radiates off her back. I know the desert has a life of its own, but the only things moving are the dancing heat waves. There are no trees, the brush sparse and scattered. We drop below sea level as we enter Twenty Mule Team Canyon and arrive by noon at Furnace Creek Ranch, our home for the next two days. The large thermometer out front reads 120.

As we step out of the car, the heat slams us. The air is hot and the wind even hotter. My body soaks up the heat and begins to dry out fast. I need to feel something cool on my body so I head straight to our room for the shower. I can't seem to figure out which knob is cold. Hot water comes out of both. One of them finally cools down to warm.

With no relief in the shower, we crank up the air conditioner and sit in front of the vent. Joyce looks at me with a questioning look that I can't answer. *This is gonna be a bitch!* I try to sleep but can't get comfortable, a headache developing. I give up and go for an early dinner. They bring us a pitcher of water before we ask: same as they do for everybody else.

We were expecting Rich Benyo by now, but flash floods from last night's rare desert storm have washed out the road on Towne Pass. They reopened the pass, but his truck broke down. Finally arriving after dark, we meet his wife and brother for the first time. Rich wrote the book *Death Valley 300*. He ran from Badwater to Mount Whitney... and back. Three. Hundred. Miles. His wife Rhonda has also done "the Double" as did Rich's brother Drew. Joyce has paced and crewed in dozens of 100 milers and knows me better than I do. I could not have a better crew.

An early breakfast is followed by a logistics meeting about food, fluids, electrolytes, clothing, shoes, crews, vehicles, shifts, and so on. And not just for me. The whole team will be out there in the heat. Rich and Drew on one crew, Joyce and Rhonda the other. I've made advance reservations at hotels in three of the four towns on our route, and there's a limited supply of ice in each of them. Our car is the shuttle for ice, as well as hot meals and sleep. The truck will stay on the road with me. Rich is our field general. This is his team and he's in charge. He's been here before and knows what the desert will do to you. I on the other hand am just the runner.

My decreasing mental capacity only allows for me to answer questions concerning pee flow, what color it is and how I feel about it. They'll suggest to me what I should do and if I don't agree, then they'll find a more subtle way to do it anyway. This should become easier and easier.

To the visitor's center for race check-in at noon, I pick up my number and let them know I'm here. Short and sweet, we're back at the ranch for lunch before 1 p.m. Everyone is required attend the 3-p.m. briefing, so the room is packed: runners, crews, medical, media, and race organizers. It's a bit long and a bit hot, but this is Badwater and it seems to fit. Driving slowly back the short distance to the ranch, Joyce and I see a coyote walk out of the desert and cross our path. In no hurry, he glances at us and continues across. This is a good omen... I think!

Rich brought along his white desert jammies for me to use. The hat has a long brim and a wrap around veil to protect my neck and face. The shirt has an open collar and sleeves that extend past my hands. They've made many trips across the desert. I'm honored to wear them. The gang's busy all evening, Rhonda slicing watermelon and cantaloupe, while Rich and Drew organize the equipment. The boys are soaking wet from hauling heavy ice coolers and boxes. The girls will nurse my feet, so they inspect and discuss their current condition while I lie about and watch TV. Joyce can't sleep and sits up to watch an action movie, and I can't sleep either because I've been just lying about. Eventually the show ends and we fall asleep.

The field of 73 starts in three separate waves, with the fastest going last. The 6 a.m. group is going out as we drive in. The fast group begins at 10 a.m., while our group goes at 8 a.m. Badwater Basin is a shallow pool of saltwater 282 feet below sea level hiding in the shadow of 5,000-foot Dante's View. It's very comfortable; until we start running, that is. The mountain shadow stays with us for a while, but the sharp edge of it is clearly visible in the distance. Daydreaming, my thoughts drift until suddenly I'm blinded by brightness. The feeling is startling! Moving from shadow to sunlight, I'm slammed back to reality. The air temperature catapults past 110 and continues to climb. The wind coming off the black asphalt burns. I attempt to run off road, but it's more work than I care for. Waiting at each mile, Rich asks a few questions and studies me, gauging my status. The crew assisting me every mile seems a bit much for now, but I enjoy the fresh cold drink, and the ice-cold bottle feels good in my hands. I can't possibly drink the whole thing before I see them again. Running easy, controlled, keeping my head and hands covered, I drink at regular intervals. Before long, my stomach gets a hard lump that feels bloated and rides up under my ribs. Coming into Furnace Creek at high noon, it's taken four hours to go 17 miles.

They've created an oasis in the shade of date palms. Stripped to shorts and laying on a cot, the girls wash me down with ice-cold rags. One of Rich's many tricks is the scum bucket: rags in ice cold water. After a short rest, the girls check my feet while I eat. The only hot spots are leftovers from last week's Hardrock100 Mile Run: two small toes on the right and the pinky on the left. Rhonda patches them with care and Elasticon. Rich suggests the long white desert pants now, because it's getting hotter. An hour later and revitalized, they send me back out on the course.

The girls have gone ahead to check in at the Stovepipe Wells Motel. It's another 25 miles and still below sea level. The boys take the day shift, serving fresh fountain drinks with sides of watermelon, cantaloupe, and grapes. The service is very good. Despite the hot wind blowing very hard, Drew holds a large beach umbrella to block the sun while Rich serves food and drinks. They do this a couple times, but stop when they decide I'm stopping way too often. I suspect they think I won't stop as often if I'm not quite so comfortable. At 6 p.m. Rich tells me its 130 degrees and the hottest Badwater on record. He asks how I feel and seems impressed I can still create sentences. As the sun slowly approaches the horizon, the sky lights up, and the air begins to cool. A gentle slope dips down into the valley prior to Stovepipe Wells. The team is in serious discussion and doesn't see me coming. Must be shift change. The girls are back and have dinner, so I sit down to pasta with chicken while they patch my feet, both heel and sole. None of the roadies are working, so I try the trail shoes. They're all I have left. Next move will be to cut parts of the shoe off.

The wind has been there all along, but doesn't dominate until after dark. The calm evening turns ugly and miserable with sand blowing about. Faces in the flying sand chase each other across the road and through my light's beam. And under them, scorpions roam the road. I know the sand spirits are my mind's playful eye, but the scorpions are real. I tell Joyce about them and wonder if she thinks I'm starting to hallucinate. I turn the flashing light I wear straight up so I can be seen but not blinded by the dark space between the strobes. The wind shoves me about until I'm exhausted by the time I arrive in Stovepipe Wells at 42 miles. It's 10:30 p.m. and I need some sleep, so they take me to the room where the boys are asleep and put me to bed also. At midnight, Joyce and I leave quietly, so as not to wake the others. Thankfully, the wind has died, and although it's not as hot as it was, it sure isn't cool either.

Joyce and I leapfrog with Mark Cockbain and Scott Weber and their crews. Partners in pain, we share ice, watermelon and a word when one of us passes the other. 18 miles of steady uphill to 5,000 foot Towns Pass. The sun rises on us long before we summit. Rich and Rhonda arrive in the morning, sending Joyce to get some sleep. A natural funnel leads out of the mountains directly to this spot where the flash floods came through and washed out the road. Smashed into the asphalt on a blind turn is a very large scorpion.

My mind wanders: first light, early morning, seeing things more crisp and clear than usual. My eyes are hyper-focused, surreal, while my reactions are hyper-slow, everything in slow motion. My body is asleep, my mind dreaming. This must be the time of every morning when I fall into my best dream state, because I'm there! Paying no notice to my pains or the cars going by at high speed, I float uphill very quickly.

The road rolls across the narrow summit and turns decidedly downward. My momentum builds as the road tilts more steeply. My walk becomes a jog, then a run. My body is confused, sending contradicting signals to my brain: I feel great, this hurts, my stomach aches, the wind feels awesome, and so on. But everything's overruled by my need to keep my feet under me. Anyway, I'm moving fast for a change. I buzz by a few amazed people who likely think I'm insane for sprinting off this mountain. Rich goes ahead two miles because I'm running so well and there aren't many places to pull over. For eight miles of steep descent, I stop for refills only. As the slope flattens out and goes straight across the dry salt flat to Panamint Springs, I lose my momentum. The cool morning is gone, the downhill is gone, and so is my water. I can see for miles and watch the truck go farther and farther away. Reduced to a walk, I'm done, but he doesn't know. I yell at him to stop, but he can't hear me. Jets roar overhead, pounding the air with supersonic sounds, while I silently melt down. I study them sitting on the tailgate while they study me walking in. It was only two miles ago that they last saw me looking fresh and full of life. The miserable wretch that walks in surprises them. I sit down behind the truck and lay my head on the tailgate. Rich: "You're going too far." "OK," he says, "I'll back off." Trashed, I drag the last few miles into Panamint Springs by noon. At 72 miles, we're half way!

Again, I strip down and lay in the shade. Unlike the last time, there's much less shade and I'm far from comfortable. Left to myself for a bit and then taken to a room in the hotel, Rich says I have an hour. I need to sleep so I can handle the next long climb. It's a swamp-cooled room, but there's no chance of sleep. A very noisy runner and crew move into the next room. Even though I'm lying in a comfortable bed, I feel as if I'm still out there on the road moving. The girls bring me a grilled cheese sandwich. They cut and tape my blisters while I eat. They're worried about my progress. With half the time gone, I'm only half way. I need to pick up my pace to make the 60-hour cutoff. If I go any slower I'm done. If I stay the same, I'm on the edge. I have to go faster to create some sort of comfort zone. There where only nine people behind me when I came into Panamint. Most of them are ahead of me now. I'm either last or near to it.

Rich walks me back to the road, explaining the situation. It's time for me to go faster and I have to quit sitting every time I come in. I have a long stiff climb directly in front of me and the road is canted such that I have to walk up against the guardrail for a level surface. I finally have some cloud cover and feel pretty good out of the direct sunlight, so I establish a good pace and keep it going. After going through a few water handoffs, I surprise the boys by sitting in a ditch to rest my feet while I finish my Ensure. It makes no sense to me to stand up while I'm not moving. I feel really good charging the switchbacks and start to build some momentum. Rich teases me about my new high speed pace, a 15-minute mile. I surprise them in a quick series of turns, tossing my bottle into the cab as I go by. Drew has to run me down on his bare feet to hand me a refill. A different world waits on top at 4,000 feet Father Crowley Point. It's cooler now, with rain clouds above a gentle rolling road. The boys go ahead to collect our rooms at Lone Pine, and the girls are back for night shift. Dark clouds yield a spot of rain here and there, and finally I get lucky, attracting a good downpour. It's the one and only time I run past the truck and need nothing at all. I don't wish to stop while I'm wet for fear of my body temperature spiraling downward. It turns into a beautiful evening and a colorful sunset. I pass by some Joshua Trees that create some interesting silhouettes in the setting sun. They look like anything but trees.

After dark, Joyce joins me on the road. She wants to run for a bit and share the road experience with me. After so many hours of being left to myself, it's nice to have her for company. It's too dark for me to tell if the road is flat or hilly. Joyce tells me it's downhill, but Rich led me to believe it would be a steep downhill. I'm going easy, waiting for the last big downhill, but Joyce says this is it. We discuss it for minutes before I reason out she just drove this road during the day and should know. I'm finally convinced I misunderstood Rich and this is the hill. Once reasoned out, I feel obligated to run again. We pass Darwin after 9 p.m. at the 90-mile point. The rolling downhills continue and I'm still running well. Bats start buzzing us. Just one at a time, but one is near us for more than a few miles.

I feel good for a while but slowly, my feet really start to hurt. A little at first, then more and more, until I slow to a hobble. I have to get off my feet, so Rhonda gets the chair out every time I come in. I ask Rhonda if she can cook some hot broth or chicken soup. She needs some time to figure it out, so she drives ahead; about two miles this time. It's the best meal I've had in days. I slurp down the whole pot. She also checks my feet and discovers a couple large blisters. A repair job and a few painkillers have me running well again. My pace picks back up quickly. In the darkness the road seems to go on forever. All we can see are the occasional scorpion and the bats that buzz our heads. I ask for more hot soup and when I get to the truck, Rhonda has a surprise for me. I sit in front of the tailgate, which she has covered with a towel. She pulls the towel away to display a row of soup cans. "Your choice," she says with a smile. It's hilarious, but I'm very serious about my selection. I slurp another full pot of broth at the next stop, and continue on in wonderful spirits. I have no idea where we are until we pass Keeler at 110 miles, just 12 miles from Lone Pine. Joyce stops me to see a rather large scorpion, translucent under her green light and very much alive. Now she's checking the ground and air every time we stop to pee.

The boys are back at 4 a.m. Rhonda heads to bed in Lone Pine but Joyce wants to stays on the road with me. She intends to run with me to the finish. Mark is back also. We drift back and forth with one another, visiting his crew and him. The thought of the sun rising on another flat salt bottom starts me running again. To the amazement of Rich and Drew, I push the last five miles into Lone Pine very hard. Mark starts running too and stays just behind me. The Inyo Mountains rise straight up out of the desert east of us and keep the sun off our backs even after the sun has risen. Free sunlight without the cost of the heat. The sun finally rises above the mountain's horizon just as we enter Lone Pine at mile 122. Rich thinks I need some rest before the final push to Whitney Portal so they roll me into our hotel room and put me to bed at 7:30 a.m. on Thursday. They give me an hour and then once again the girls cut and patch my feet prior to sending me out the door.

The Lone Pine checkpoint is one block past our hotel. I pass by at 9:15 a.m. I take note of Mount Whitney as I wait at the traffic light to cross the road, my last turn. This road ends at the portal. With only 13 miles to the finish, I now know for certain I will finish, and so does my crew. Not that we ever got heavy-handed or overly serious, but now the mood is all jokes and laughter. A lightness in my stride and it seems more bounce in the crew as well. It has been a long haul and the whole team has a feeling of accomplishment. We have been successful. What we did worked. I questioned them many times, but rarely ever challenged what they suggested. I am after all only the runner: dumb from sleep deprivation, extreme heat, and way too many miles.

Joyce remains by my side as we power hike up through the Alabama Hills. The landscape is phenomenal. All the rocks are smooth and round, stacked one on top of another in unusual patterns. It's all very pristine and comfortable. A noisy bubbling brook cascades next to the road. It's still quite hot and the backs of my legs appear to be burnt up, so Joyce covers them with sunscreen. I down an entire bottle of water before we climb the first mile. Joyce goes ahead to get more for each of us but it's steep enough to keep her from going much faster than me. I'm feeling pretty strong for my third day. My feet are so numb I no longer feel any discomfort. The steepness of the slope becomes easier as we reach the long straightaway and I can now see the switchbacks a few miles ahead. A large, dark cloud mass hangs over Whitney and her neighbors. I'll be in their shade once I reach the base, and maybe even some rain.

At the start of the switchbacks, I stop for my last sit down after climbing the first steep step. I drink my last Ensure and start my Diet Coke. I leave behind my hat and my water bottle for the last three very steep miles. Joyce and I charge the uphill, slowly pick up speed, and start to pass others as we surge on up. As the switchbacks get steeper, I seem to be getting faster. I'm only walking, but I'm not sure I could run up this beast much faster than I'm walking. It feels so comfortable and efficient. I stop at each mile only to slug down another Coke and some water. Trees! For the first time I see trees. It starts to sprinkle a bit of rain and I feel my first cool breeze as we enter the trees. Rich drives ahead to find a parking spot so he can be at the finish when I cross. I start seeing parked cars and think we're there, but we still have another steep switchback to go up. Pushing as hard as I can I start running, but I'm forced by the steepness back into a fast walk. Screaming with anticipation, my rhythm all-akimbo, I break into a run when I finally see the finish. Joyce is right next to me as she has been for the last 50 miles and the smile stays on her face now even when she starts crying. Everything I feel is bottled up inside, too tired to do more than grunt. We cross the finish at 1:15 p.m. with a time of 53:15. I can finally sit down. The crew was the best! The weather was the worst! I loved it all but I will never come back to run another 135 mile road race in Death Valley during the summer.

The Benyos where wonderful. The support and friendship I received from them was more than I could have asked for. They gave me a week of their valuable time while I attempted this completely irrational quest, something they fully understood. They became good friends along the way. I will not forget what they did for me. Some of it was heartfelt and some of it was funny enough to keep us laughing for years. Joyce was her usual exceptional self. She continues to support me as I continue to wander about. She ran the last 50 miles of Badwater with me after running 25 miles of Hardrock with me. Her smile is infectious and her desire to see me succeed only drives me harder. All my minor conquests would mean nothing if I could not share them with her. All our adventures are worth more than gold, and held forever in our minds. For myself, I felt more for those around me than I did for myself. There was no enlightenment as well as no hallucinations. Death Valley has an exceptional beauty if you can see through the heat, and the environment itself is something to experience. I had heard of it since I was a child and was always curious. I was anxious to get there just to see and feel of it. Now I have a personal picture of it, not much different than what I expected, but now it is real. It is mine!

2003 Finishing Time – 53:14:54
Thirty-sixth Place

© Thinkstock/iStockphoto/Fluid Illusion

CHAPTER TWENTY-ONE – MARK COCKBAIN

From Mark's 2003 Badwater Application:

Age: 31
Northampton, England

Why I want a slot on the start line of the 2003 Badwater Ultramarathon:

Badwater is a legendary event in the ultra world. I believe my running portfolio would never be complete without it. It's the icing on the cake. The uncertainty of such a non-stop distance combined with the hottest place on earth is surely the ultimate challenge! As well as the opportunity to again raise much-needed money for cancer research.

ONLY MAN DOGS AND ENGLISHMEN *By Mark Cockbain*

On July 21, 2003 I arrived in Death Valley with my crew of Paul Ravenscroft and James D. Carter. I flew in from the United Kingdom, while my New York-based crew flew into Los Angeles.

We rented a mini-van as our support vehicle and promptly stocked it with essentials, which ranged from iceboxes, food, equipment and – of course, approximately 150 liters of water.

Upon arriving in Furnace Creek, we quickly noted that the temperature was already in excess of 100 degrees... and it was 2:30 a.m. in the morning.

I was assigned the 8:00 a.m. starting time. Not so bad, although the 6:00 a.m. starters benefitted from a couple extra hours in the shade. The 10:00 a.m. starters, however, were in the sun from the very beginning.

We arrived at the first checkpoint at Furnace Creek, after running alongside salty flat beds and the basin of Death Valley for 17 miles. Most of us 8:00 a.m. starters began at a fairly steady pace so we could benefit as much as possible from the shade generously provided by the mountains on either side of the road. The shade didn't last long, however, and soon we were subjected to the awesome strength of the Death Valley sun.

The force of the sun was oppressive, trying its best to stop you in your tracks. Soon we were all reduced to a very slow pace. The heat, you see, is no ordinary heat. It's a dry heat with a searing, penetrating wind which, quite honestly, feels similar to the blast you feel when you open the door of a hot oven. With 15% humidity, it was a little less dry than in previous years of the race, but still tremendously difficult to cope with.

My crew would leapfrog me in the van and pass me ice-cold water at the side of the road and throw ice towels over my back while wetting my desert hat. It was obvious they would have to stop at least every mile (or less) for this section of the race, as my core temperature skyrocketed and my water was becoming warm within a few minutes of being in my hands.

I was already cramping due to excessive sweating and heat as I reach the Furnace Creek checkpoint, so I began drinking electrolytes and icing my neck. My stomach muscles were cramping into a ball near the bottom of my ribs and if I didn't know better I would have sworn my stomach was ripping apart.

Temperatures were in excess of 130 degrees and Jay Birmingham, a veteran of the race told me that getting through the next 40 miles of the race to Stovepipe Wells during the heat of the day was the key to having a successful race.

I was feeling very light-headed and dizzy and I could see many other runners also suffering at such an early point in the race. I guessed the majority of the field was forced to walk at this point, while I somehow managed to keep my legs from cramping and continued on for a few more miles.

My crew continued spraying me with water, keeping my clothes saturated and helping my body stay as cool as humanly possible. However, I was still overwhelmed by the oppressive heat and before I knew it, I lost consciousness and collapsed.

This, obviously, was a new experience for my crew, but they acted like professionals and dragged me into the shade of the van (carrying me like a sack of potatoes!) where they revived me by dousing me with ice and water and putting the air conditioning on full blast. Apparently I had been out for around 10 seconds! With ice around my neck and under my armpits, I soon felt much better; however, this served as a vivid reminder of why the conditions of this race rate it as the toughest in the world.

I continued to drink electrolytes and cool down until I regained my focus. I had a lucky escape, but decided it was time to push on... but very cautiously.

At this point I was forced into a walk/run situation for the next 40 miles. As all my fellow competitors were doing at this point, I was trying every method possible to cool off: ice, wet towels, sprays... anything to keep me moving forward. At best I was doing a slow, hard "slog."

The effects of my heatstroke impacted my ability to hear, and then to add insult to injury I couldn't hold down any solids... or fluids either, for that matter. I was, however vomiting. Quite regularly, I might add.

I wasn't doing well. My crew was concerned I might end up totally depleted of fluids if my internal organs didn't jump into action soon. I had only consumed about two liters of fluids in two hours – and at least one of the liters came back up. I really could have used about two liters for every hour in the desert.

I moved on for a few more hours, bumping into other runners along the way, each with their own technique to help them through the race. Joe Prusaitis of Texas was relying on regular meal stops – of burgers and chips, no less – to get through.

My crew continued to douse me with wet towels and ice packs that I wrapped around my neck and wore as a necklace. I was finally starting to absorb fluids and managed to eat a few energy gels to perk me up a bit.

My crew became concerned that we were going to run out of ice, so James and I took a quick break while Paul drove several miles down the road to try and find some ice at the next village. Unfortunately Paul wasn't able to find any, as previous Badwater crews had cleaned out the stores. Fortunately for us, a medic was notified of our ice dilemma and managed to obtain some ice from another crew whose runner had dropped out of the race.

Near mile 35 I reached sea level and managed to fight my way through a sandstorm as night began to fall. We made it into the second checkpoint at Stovepipe Wells and learned that quite a few competitors had pulled out of the race in the difficult section between Furnace Creek and Stovepipe Wells.

After refueling courtesy of a pot of noodles, I began a 17-mile ascent that took us out of the valley. The elevation would rise 5,000 feet during this stretch. I trudged up the mountain all night long, occasionally passing other runners and crews who were as supportive of us as we were of them. Nearing the 24-hour mark of our journey we were nearing the top of the mountain, at which point I decided to get a power nap of a few minutes after getting some more food. My body was now more stabilized – thanks to the food and the slight drop in the temperature at night. It was a mere 90 minutes until we would see the sun rise, signifying the beginning of our second day in the desert.

I completed my ascent of the mountain with the sun already ominously overhead. I took a moment to look back at the first 60 miles of the road to hell that were now thankfully behind us. However, we still had another 75 miles to go.

My feet were badly blistered and the next winding section back to the floor of the valley was a refreshing change – but also very painful.

Down and through the Panamint Valley, the temperature had peaked yet again and the crew became worried about the time it was taking to get through the race. I tried to pick up my pace, virtually running once again towards the next checkpoint at Panamint Springs. Runners who had dropped out of the race were driving by with their respective crews shouting lots of encouragement. Among them was the other entrant from the United Kingdom, Wayne Simpson, who was suffering from severe dehydration. Wayne had tried to return to the course three times, but eventually succumbed to the heat. Six bags of intravenous fluids were given to Wayne at a local hospital.

I knew I had to stay ahead of the game and get out of the valley and over the next mountain range as quickly as possible so as to avoid burning out again. A long, steep and winding set of switchbacks led me up and over the range in a few hours while the sun continued to beat down on me with enough power to expand the steel barriers along the side of the road, which gave them a distinctive "ping, ping" sound.

Joe and I took turns passing each other along the flat road that would eventually lead us all the way to the pass of Mount Whitney at Lone Pine. With about 40 miles remaining, nightfall was approaching so James moved on ahead to get another pot of noodles ready for me.

I was now totally exhausted. Paul explained to me that the distance I gained during the second night would either make me or break me. At this point my legs were in total agony and my feet were on fire... with deep blisters. I decided I had to regularly cool my feet in a bucket of ice water and change socks if I hoped to get any further in the race.

Darkness came for the second time and I forced myself to run at a decent pace in an attempt to eat up the remaining mileage. Hour after hour Paul gave me an update on the distance covered, as well as my goal for the next hour. I was slowly getting through the miles physically; mentally I was exhausted.

Paul gave me some of his double espresso and I soon began to focus again. Over 40 hours into the race, I was now struggling to concentrate. In fact, I wasn't completely sure what I was doing. I started to hallucinate, seeing a set of giant squirrels sitting along the road. They were chattering and smiling – vividly. I kept myself amused by tracking the numerous small translucent scorpions scurrying in and out of my path on the road courtesy of my headlamp. While the rocks and sand dunes continued to play tricks on me all through the night, I found myself making good time and becoming more determined than ever to finish.

Morning broke yet again, and Paul said we really had a good chance (of finishing) now... just as long as I kept moving forward. I had even overtaken a few other competitors along the way and we predicted we'd reach Lone Pine by 7:00 a.m. that would allow the suggested "one-mile per hour" required to get up the virtually vertical 13 mile climb to the finish up Mount Whitney.

As expected, we made it into Lone Pine (and civilization!) at 7:00 a.m. Fortunately for us, one of the checkpoint volunteers let us use his hotel room to cool off for 30 minutes before my imminent 13-mile climb.

It was going to be hot climbing the mountain. My crew didn't want to take any chances at this point, so they covered me with wet towels from the start. My legs were aching with the constant trudging motion required to move vertically up Mount Whitney. I was, however on autopilot and knew that victory was just a few hours away.

Mount Whitney was absolutely beautiful: waterfalls, greenery, and an overwhelming aroma of pine trees.

Joe came powering up the hill behind me and it was obvious he was full of confidence as the finish line was getting nearer and nearer. Crews passed by in their vans, providing us with lots of encouragement that made me more determined than ever to finish.

After six grueling hours of climbing, the end was in sight!

Paul and James parked the van and returned to me so that we could all cross the finish line together. *We did it!*

Wayne, who was back on his feet again after his IVs, greeted me with a bottle of champagne and a union jack. He even managed to walk a few miles in the later stages of the race with me. His crew, who were clearly glad to see that a Brit was still in the race, helped us out with ice and encouragement. Wayne's crew chief, the inimitable Jack Dennes was out in front cheering me on. Once we made it across the line, congratulations were tossed all around.

I finished 40th in 54 hours. This was by far the biggest test for me at this point in my running career. I experienced a rollercoaster of emotions, ranging from the sheer shock and frustration provided by such hostile conditions, to the sheer elation and relief of crossing the finish line. And, of course, everything in between.

The support was amazing by everyone involved in the race, from the marshals to the crews to the other runners. This was an amazing personal achievement for me – only made possible by having the best crew that any competitor could have asked for.
Thanks, boys. I owe you one!

2003 Finishing Time – 54:01:13
Thirty-ninth Place

© Thinkstock/iStockphoto/Fluid Illusion

CHAPTER TWENTY-TWO – JAN LEVET

From Jan's 2003 Badwater Application:

Age: 52
Pollock Pines, California

Why I want a slot on the start line of the 2003 Badwater Ultramarathon:

The Badwater Ultramarathon will take me down a new path in stretching myself, taking a different risk than most of those I've encountered during my 22-year longevity of ultras. With risk-taking we can grow through the process of being uncertain of the outcome of heading down that open road. Badwater will offer me up a plate of numerous risks, some new to me – the heat, the potential foot problems, the challenges of staying hydrated and well-fueled, the continual mind-numbing pavement – which I'll openly embrace to stretch myself beyond the comfortable envelope in which we find ourselves, to seek out the frontier of my spirit. Helen Keller said "Avoiding danger is no safer in the long run than outright exposure." If I don't push myself to meet a goal, then years down the road I'll find myself regretting that I never tried.

FUN IN THE SUN: BIG HEAT AND SORE FEET *By Jan Levet*

2003

One step after another. "Poco a poco se va lejos." A step at a time and you'll go far. One step, then another. "Poco a poco se va lejos." The inky, black night star display overwhelms my senses, taking my mind from the sledgehammered soles of my feet to a vision of a journey completed. Furnace Creek. Stovepipe Wells. Townes Pass. Panamint Springs. Father Crowley Point. Darwin. Keeler. Lone Pine. Eastern Sierra Escarpment. Blessed Granite. Thunder, lightning, rain splatters. Flowering Columbine. Finish tape. Exultation.

2002

Ultra athlete Barb Elia runs her umpteenth Badwater Ultramarathon. I am flattered as she asks me to join her crew of desert life-sustaining support and pacing. Barb finishes and is clearly elated. The entire sweaty experience lights a fire in me. I am hooked. Soon it will be my turn! And so I begin the lengthy process of preparation of body and spirit... of mind and soul. I never question my sanity in telling family and friends that I'm about to tackle this monster of all ultras. No family members question my sanity – they've grown to accept my ongoing quest to push the endurance envelope, and so they take my decision in stride, no different than they might react if I announced I was about to take out the garbage. A few of my friends – some of them ultrarunners – raise some eyebrows behind my back, and a few point blank tell me I've gone over the edge. So much for me thinking how easy it is going to be to assemble a support crew.

I'd already completed over 130 ultras, ranging from the standard 50K distance up to timed runs of 24 and 48 hours. I was the first woman finisher in 29 of them, of which 17 resulted in new women's course records. How hard could this Badwater thing be? I had already laid the groundwork of time-on-my-feet during 22 years of running ultras. My American River 50 Miler personal best of 7:46 was established in temperatures in excess of 100 degrees. I decided I had the heat factor dialed in. I'd never even had blisters before, not even when I hiked 2,700 miles from Canada to Mexico. Badwater? Shouldn't be a problem.

Early 2003

Never the type to rest on past laurels of achievement and event finishes, I dutifully did my homework with practicing and repeating this "heat thing," not only with running on numerous hot days in May between Badwater and Townes Pass (for which I'm grateful to Ben and Denise Jones for their advice and expertise in logistics preparation), but also with specific training in the Sacramento Valley of California near my home (90+ degrees in the spring and early summer) on asphalt... alone... sometimes covering 50 miles at a stretch running out-and-backs far too numerous to count. My car served as my sole support, as I wasn't able to convince anyone to volunteer to drive me and then sit around and wait for me all day. Fluids and food were available in my car when I needed them. Others training for Badwater may have used saunas to acclimate themselves to the heat. Me? I drove the hour home with the car windows up and the heater set on "high," which always got me nice and wet – the perspiration rolling off of me everywhere and pooling up in salty puddles in my sandals. Badwater, bring it on!

Pre-Race Night 2003 – Furnace Creek

I can't sleep as it's so hot in the motel room... not to mention the air conditioner is too noisy as well. Fitfully I lie in bed, hoping my crew – Rae Clark, Errol Jones, Carola Laumann, and Bill and Diane Dixon-Johnson – have it all together so all I need to think about tomorrow is putting one foot in front of the other. How much trouble could it be for them? They've either run the race before, crewed it, or had a slew of substantive ultra credentials on their resumes. And how about that terrific crew manual I created for them, complete with cartoons and funny ha-ha's to entertain them during the course of our "fun hours" (and hours and hours...) out in the desert?

Race Morning – Badwater

I am assigned the 8:00 a.m. start, probably dictated by my projection of a 47:59 finish time for myself. I've heard that you have to do Badwater once before you're able to have an idea of what the whole experience is about. I guess that means next time I'll be placed in the 6:00 a.m. start so the finish line crew won't need to wait around for me to finish. Relaxed spectators are snapping the requisite pre-start photos of runners nervously pacing; I'm already perspiring and worrying about where the can opener is which will be needed for my electrolyte powders, whether we have enough ice, and if I've spent enough time in the heat leading up to this Day of Days.

It's warm. I'm anxious and run slowly and cautiously. With a final wave and the best smile I can manage (am I perhaps anticipating my impending doom) for the camera, I'm heading down the road.

Furnace Creek

It's time for a turkey, ketchup and mustard burrito break. Carola tries to offer me some apple slices, but it looks too difficult to chew at this point. Besides, whoever heard of runners eating apples during an event anyway?

It's hot as we go through the valley towards Stovepipe Wells. I heard someone say it's already up to 124 degrees. I continue my water, Cytomax and Gu regimen, and every 20 minutes manage to pee (still clear!). I've never pee'd so much in my life! I give up on the occasional cup of tomato juice after one giant, burning acidic intestinal experience I leave on the side of the road. I welcome my old buddy Bag Balm back into my life, and thereafter count on electrolyte capsules to provide me the necessary sodium. One step. Then another. And another.

Stovepipe Wells

A disappointingly long stop here at dusk to tend to my first case *ever* of budding blisters on my heels. I give in: Apparently I'm not immune to the beasties after all. I'm overanalyzing whether it's best to wear two pairs of socks on each foot or change to one pair; meanwhile, I'm fidgeting to get back out on the road. The clock is advancing, and I'm not. It's now dark. Diane joins me on the way to Townes pass after having played laundress with my gunky shorts and now-no-longer-white Solumbra pants (I shortly thereafter canonized her to sainthood).

Crewmembers deliberate on and on, it seems, about who's to do what. Help Jan? Rest? Eat? Get Jan oatmeal? Drive ahead? I thought I'd put together a pretty sound manual for all of them to follow. Perhaps they didn't read it. I sense their dissolution, and consequently end up spending more time preoccupied with their discussions amongst themselves than with my own forward progress. Bill and Diane depart shortly thereafter for a previously arranged medical appointment in Southern California, leaving Rae, Errol and Carola to shoulder all the responsibilities. But a runner can't wallow in her crew's deliberations, whatever they may entail. One step more. "Poco a poco se va lejos." Although I do sense the tension among my crew, I suck it up and move on.

Townes Pass

We pass Townes Pass, and oatmeal waits down the hill so I can recharge before the journey to Panamint Springs. Again, a disappointingly long respite finds me dissecting the back of my heel to extract a seemingly ungodly amount of fluid from an even-larger-than-planet-earth-sized blister.

We are now into our second day. I head up to Father Crowley Point for a break. "Jan, do you want to ice your feet?" "No, I don't want to take the time. But I *will* have some of those French Fries that lady offered." So there goes my healthy eating regimen. But they tasted mighty fine.

Another step. And another. And another.

Errol now joins me up to Darwin through magnificent thunder and lightning and a spitting rain. More oatmeal and ramen soothe the spirit and tummy, but a tortoise's pace is quickly morphing into that more indicative of a snail as the soles of my feet – sledge-hammered by the hours on the hot asphalt – cause me to wonder if the "poco a poco se va lejos" is morphing as well into a "poco a poco se vuelve para atras"*(progress backward, rather than forward)*.

Saint Denise (Jones) helps out around the 100-mile mark with her characteristically queenly expert taping of my feet in an attempt to minimize the effects of the pounding that still remained. She adds: "But, if it doesn't help, then just suck it up and keep going." Nicely, albeit bluntly stated. I take her advice, take a deep breath while the clock is progressing (and I'm not) and head on out for more fun on the road in the dark. Poco a poco...

The star show, the sidewinders, the horny toads and Rae accompany me on a journey through a fantasyland of desert awe.

Whitney Portal Road

We are now into our third day. I view my beloved Sierra east side granite, pass Carola sleeping in one of our crew vehicles along the shoulder of the road, and am joined by Errol as we make our way into an awakening Owens Valley. The masses of bugs I'd been expecting along the high stretch of willows just before Highway 395 never materialize. We cross a highway, Errol takes my shirt somewhere to wet it down, and Rae offers me a hamburger (yeah, there's that healthy eating regimen again... right down the drain) as I progress up the Whitney Portal Road. Carola's face reappears from the driver's seat of her vehicle as it pulls alongside to yell (as in a *real* **YELL** sounding sort of scary) a warning to me of the impending time limit to reach the finish before 60 hours and to, basically, PICK UP THE PACE! Another step. And another. And another.

Errol keeps me upright (well, as best he – or I am able) as I'm overcome with a case of "leaning-to-the-starboard." He encourages me to run (hmmm... at this point "run" is certainly debatable) from one behind the black curtain of clouds above me. Lightning flashes, and oddly enough an aura of calm serenity washes over me. I pause, turn around to the east toward where this adventure began hours (no, days!) earlier, and feel an immense satisfaction and pride in not having given in, not having succumbed, in having kept on, having sucked up the aches in the swollen feet to continue, step after step, to complete this thing called Badwater. Sure, it would be easier to quit if things hurt or if you're exhausted. But why? There's always more left in your body than your brain – or anyone else is telling you. That's what you learn from ultras, right? So just keep on keepin' on. If there ain't no bone showin', then you gotta keep on goin',

Finish Line

I break through the tape triumphantly. How cool! Even the slowest finishers of this event will ultimately feel victorious when they break their very own finisher's tape, so that every last one of them can celebrate their individual triumph over the harsh environment, difficult terrain and personal demons. My eyes are bleary after only having a single 10-minute nap during the previous 55 hours. My feet and legs are swollen from... the heat, I'm assuming? Or perhaps because they were pounding on pavement for what felt like forever. Whatever the case, I finished under 60 hours. I'm elated. I took one step after another, and bit-by-bit I went for it. I went far. "Poco a puco me fui lejos."

Would I do it again? You bet! There aren't many other activities we can engage in amongst this societally-fabricated world in which we live that offers up a plate as rich in self-exploration and fulfillment as this thing known as Badwater.

2003 Finishing Time – 55:11:38
Forty-first Place

© Thinkstock/iStockphoto/Fluid Illusion

CHAPTER TWENTY-THREE – JIM BODOH

From Jim's 2003 Badwater Application:

Age: 50
Tampa, Florida

Why I want a slot on the start line of the 2003 Badwater Ultramarathon:

Badwater is the most demanding and extreme running race anywhere on the planet. I think I am capable of meeting its challenge and I want to prove it to myself. I think my tenacity and the heat training I can get by living in Florida will get me though.

WHAT AM I DOING HERE? *By Jim Bodoh*

I very distinctly remember standing on the beach at my first Ironman Triathlon. The public address system was playing "Lunatic Fringe" and I was asking myself "what have you gotten yourself into? You don't belong here!"

I don't consider myself an athlete. As a child I was diagnosed with asthma so I didn't take "Phys Ed" (that's what it was called in the 1960's), much less any team sports like football or cross-country. In college I took bowling and beginning swimming; just enough to meet the basic requirements. After graduating from college in 1975 I started working at a desk job. Soon I started to gain a little weight. I decided to give running a try. On that first run I ran one block, only to end up walking the remaining three blocks back to my apartment. But I kept at it and within a few years was I was running 5K and 10K races. I was living in Wisconsin at the time and during the summer I started riding my bicycle to work.

In 1980 I moved to Florida and kept running, but never anything longer than 15 kilometers (9.3 miles). In the late 1980's someone suggested I try a triathlon. I knew I could run and ride a bike – and I thought I could swim, so I signed up for a sprint triathlon. I discovered I could in fact swim, but only enough to save my life. I was the second to last person to exit the water. At least I got to pass a lot of people during the bike and run sections. Someone suggested I join a Masters Swim program. I spent several years in the beginner's lane during which I started running and cycling with other people in the program. They were doing half-ironman triathlons, so I tried one as well. I never was very fast; I just never quit, so I never had a DNF ("did not finish'). Then one of my training partners finished a full Ironman and told me I could do it too. And that's how I found myself standing on the beach at Ironman Canada in 1990 wondering what I'd gotten myself into. I finished that race and four more Ironman races over the next few years.

In 1992 after doing a few marathons I found myself at my first ultra, "Passing for Sane,"a 50K trail run. I followed that with a few more 50K's, a few 50 milers and went to Western States in 2000 to pace a friend. He DNF'ed, but I decided to give it a try myself one year later and both of us finished, although I was just barely under the 30 hour cut off.

The following year someone gave one of my training partners a copy of Kirk Johnson's *To The Edge* to read. He read it, gave it to another one of my training partners, and finally they gave it to me and said I should do the race featured in the book: Badwater.

I read the book and thought: Kirk finished the race with less of an ultrarunning background than me; maybe I *can* finish Badwater. I sent in an application for the 2003 race and considering my limited qualifications (only one 100-mile race) I didn't expect to receive an invitation. I thought I'd have to work on my qualifications and apply again in the future. But to my surprise I got invited.

I consider myself a better planner than runner, so I started doing research on the race. I trained in the dry sauna and gathered gear for my support vehicles. Two of my training partners and my wife Michelle (a nurse) volunteered to be my crew. Michelle and I attended Ben Jones 4th of July training camp where I ran the first 42 miles of the course.

At 6 a.m. on Tuesday July 22, 2003 I found myself standing on the road at Badwater. Adam Bookspan was playing the *Star Spangled Banner* on his trumpet and I found myself asking once again: "what have you gotten yourself into? You don't belong here!"

I wanted to start out very conservatively, but it seemed like everyone else had the same plan. In order to avoid taking the early lead I was running at a slower pace that was uncomfortable. It didn't seem like the right thing to do, so I started running at the pace I felt most comfortable. I started to pass other runners. When I got to Furnace Creek at 9:09 a.m. I thought I was leading the race; it soon was confirmed I was right. I knew my sister would be following the race live on the webcast and I remarked that when she read I was leading the race she must have fallen out of her chair.

One of the guys I train with can remember every step of a race – or so it seems when he describes a race to us. I can't. I do remember it getting hot, really hot. I remember when I went by the large sand dunes outside Stovepipe Wells that the wind was blowing so much sand across the road I put on a pair of swim goggles I had brought along for that very purpose. I did a lot of walking and my crew did a great job of spraying me down and keeping me supplied with ice filled bandanas and drinks.

I got into Stovepipe Wells at 4:35 p.m. Michelle insisted I take a dip in the pool to cool off. I had taped some blister prone areas of my feet before the race and the swim caused the tape to peel off, so that had to be redone before I continued. I spent well over an hour there to rest; much longer than I should have.

We started up Townes Pass with much anticipation of the sunset and the subsequent lowering of the temperature. It was not to be: When the sun set, the wind started to come down the pass, straight into our faces. I later returned to Badwater on three more occasions, and have never had an experience like that one: it felt like we were literally running directly into a blazing hot hair dryer.

While going up Townes Pass the devastating heat soon took a back seat to the severe blisters I was developing. This was rather surprising to me because during my training runs I had no such problems. Going down the far side of Townes Pass the blisters worsened and eventually covered the heels and balls of both feet. As I was crossing the Panamint Valley, running on the left edge of the road in the dark I didn't see a spot where the edge of the blacktop was broken off. Stepping on the broken edge, I rolled onto the side of my left foot and was suddenly in a lot of pain. I thought my race was over, but after a few minutes I tried to walk and, although my ankle hurt quite a bit, the blisters hurt more and I was able to continue towards the Panamint Resort. Several weeks after the race I had recovered from my blisters, but my left ankle still hurt, so I made an appointment with a doctor. An X-ray revealed that I'd fractured my ankle. It had already healed to the point that a cast wouldn't be necessary, but I was told had I come in right after the race I would have needed one.

In 2003 a generator powered the Panamint Springs resort, and it failed the day of the race. Their ice stockpile melted (leaving no ice between Stovepipe Wells and Lone Pine) and the swamp coolers in the rooms stopped working. I hobbled into the room we had reserved. Because there was no air conditioning, they kept the door open and (I was later told) earlier in the evening a wild donkey had stuck its head into the room. I slept about an hour, went to the restaurant for a bowl of oatmeal (which took a long time to get because they had no power) and shortly after sunrise, headed for Father Crowley and Panamint Pass.

Although I don't remember much about the climbs, I remember three incidents. The first was getting caught by Chris "The Mayor of Malibu" Frost and being told of the "Carnage in Stovepipe Wells." Chris told us of the large number of runners who never made it out of Stovepipe Wells. Guest rooms at the hotel were being taken over to treat crewmembers who "went down;" some had even been taken to the Pahrump hospital. Knowing I had escaped the "carnage" boosted my moral. Because of my blisters, which by now had been covered with duct tape by my crew, I was walking pretty slowly and I couldn't keep up with Chris.

The second incident: Late in the afternoon of the second day I was caught by one of my heroes, Marshall Ulrich. I feel like I have some sort of connection to Marshall although all we really have in common is being close in age. He is an extraordinary athlete, and I'm not. But we talked for a few minutes and then he too quickly pulled away from me.

The final incident I remember vividly is the hallucination I had that second night in the Owens Valley. Whenever I looked to the right side of the road I saw an old steam locomotive, complete with coal car, going towards Lone Pine with me. I knew it wasn't there, but every time I looked, there it was. The hallucination went on for hours.

From the Owens Valley at night you can see the traffic on Highway 395 going through Lone Pine from a long, long way off. I was hobbling along very slowly and endured one of the longest nights of my life before collapsing into the bed in a hotel room in Lone Pine. My crew was, rightfully so, worried that at the pace I was moving I was not going to finish before the 60-hour time limit. While I slept, my wife Michelle fetched two members of the Badwater medical crew. They came to our room and using nail polish remover, they removed the duct tape from my feet, and then properly re-taped my feet while I slept.

They let me sleep for about three hours. I felt much better, and so did my feet. At 8:44 a.m. I went past the Lone Pine checkpoint and headed up Portal Road in good spirits.

Although the final section of the race from Lone Pine to Whitney Portal isn't that far (comprising only about 10% of the entire race), it's one very long climb. My crew and I were now pretty confident I was going to be an official finisher. They took turns walking with me, giving me encouragement and fluids. At 1:54 p.m. my crew and I crossed the finish line together. I immediately grabbed Michelle and hugged her because I was so happy and also because I was also very close to falling down. I whispered into her ear: "That was a LOT harder than I thought it would be." Then my eyes teared up.

We stood there hugging for quite a long time. Then I hobbled over to "the chair," the Race Director took a few photographs, and I hobbled over to our support vehicle and we headed down to Lone Pine.

Has anyone told you that "some day your life will flash before your eyes and that you should make sure it's worth watching?" When mine does, the 2003 Badwater Ultramarathon will be in it.

2003 Finishing Time – 55:54:15
Forty-second Place

© Thinkstock/iStockphoto/Fluid Illusion

CHAPTER TWENTY-FOUR – CHRIS HENDLEY

From Chris' 2003 Badwater Application:

Age: 40
Las Vegas, Nevada

My Badwater Finishing Prediction:

I anticipate my finishing time to be under 40 hours. Going into the 2001 Badwater race I had less than 500 total training miles for the year due to several reasons that are not issues this year. My current training mileage has been consistently at a minimum of 40-60 miles per week for months. In my under-training condition, I made it to about the 116-mile point of Badwater 2001 in about 36 hours. I did have to leave the course due to dehydration at 116, but will be better prepared this year. So with the increased conditioning and preparation, experience of Badwater 2001 and Western States 2002, I am confident that I will finish under 40 hours.

FROM DOING EVERYTHING WRONG AND FINISHING…
TO DOING EVERYTHING RIGHT AND EVERYTHING GOING WRONG AND NOT FINISHING! *By Chris Hendley*

During my initial attempt at Badwater in 2001, there were several things that could have been done differently. I remember going to the starting line, looking around and seeing I was definitely not like the others. I was surrounded by racers wearing hats, covering their necks and wearing long-sleeved shirts; many were even wearing pants to protect themselves from the sun. I had on shorts and a bandana tied around my head. The only thing on my upper body was sunscreen. I felt the best way to beat the heat was to allow the heat *out*, and what better way to do that than to provide no barriers at all. This was only one of the many things that singled me out from the others. So there I was half-naked and ready to set the course on fire with my top-notch crew.

My crew consisted of the same group of friends for Badwater in both 2001 and 2003. A better group of people would be tough to find. Three of the four crewmembers flew in from the Detroit Metropolitan Area the day before each race. Jeff Ruiz, alias Red Bull seemed to take the crew chief role. He researched the race, analyzed the course, became the supplement guru and took care of all the other aspects that involved homework leading into the event. Gregg Golden, alias Cutman took the role of course medic. Being a physical therapist and track/cross country coach, he was the perfect man for the job. Dave Angileri, a.k.a. "Baby Bear" is a city manager, and he brought a calm head under stress, was the voice of reason and provided the glue holding things together. The fourth member, Jackie Strobel, alias Birdie, rounded out the crew and joined us in the middle of the first night of the 2001 race. Jackie was my fiancé at the time and became the crew's saving grace and my inspiration when things got tough.

Despite my awesome crew's abilities and talents, there were problems. Somewhere between Furnace Creek and Stovepipe, Baby Bear started to experience symptoms of severe heat exhaustion. Only having the one support vehicle, which was one of the fixes needed for any future attempts at the race, there was no way to get Dave to Stovepipe to get him out of the sun and cool him down. We had to keep him in the vehicle with the air conditioning running with hopes we could get to Stovepipe before the truck overheated or ran low on fuel. Dave bounced back in a few miles by keeping ice on his head and neck and staying in the cool comfort of the vehicle. Somewhere between Stovepipe and Panamint Cutman started to experience from exhaustion and nausea due to a severe lack of rest (nearly 20 hours into the race) and extreme heat. Again, only having the one support vehicle made it impossible to get Gregg off the course without coming off the course myself or risk being out on the course without support for the time it would take to drive the struggling crewmember to the next possible rest stop. As Gregg's condition worsened, a decision was going to have to be made about what to do. Just as the moment of truth arrived, Jackie came driving up out of the darkness to join us. She scooped up Gregg and took him to Panamint for his much-needed rest. The second night on the course required a trip to Lone Pine for Jackie and Jeff (again, for rest) that became a nonissue once we had a second vehicle. 2003's Badwater would have a second vehicle from the start – no matter what!

Not only did my crewmembers have problems on the course in 2001, I had more than my share of issues as well. I started out too fast and drank too little, two more issues that needed to be fixed before any future attempts at this demanding race. By the time I hit Stovepipe, I had gone several miles without urinating. I knew this was a serious concern and there was no moving forward until I was sure I was hydrated again. My first attempt to go to the restroom in Stovepipe resulted in a few drops of what looked like a thick, dark syrup. I was bothered by the leg cramps that were popping as I tried to recharge for the upcoming charge on Panamint, but now I was really concerned that I may be causing damage to my kidneys and register my first "did not finish" (DNF) of my nearly 25 years of racing. Downtime in Stovepipe's pool while taking in as much fluids I could stand appeared to do the trick.

After an extended period of time in Stovepipe, it was back to the mission at hand... GET TO WHITNEY! The pace slowed and greater efforts were made to stay hydrated, but eating became more and more difficult until it was nonexistent due to a very irritated GI system and everything that went in came back out. Somewhere around the 70-mile area of the race my running deteriorated to a run/walk, which soon digressed to only a walk and then finally around 116 miles my pace turned into a *stagger*. My crew had to stay on my shoulder to provide a barrier that would keep me from staggering off the road. Not only had the race drained me of my energy to move forward but it also took my ability to talk. I can remember Dave and Gregg sitting me down at the 116-mile mark and asking me how I was doing. I can remember getting frustrated with them because they could not understand me. Later they explained to me that my responses to their questions involved little more than grabbled nonsense like "ahhgeegabaheeahh." It was at this point they decided it was time to drive the stake into the side of the road and take me to Lone Pine to try to recharge for the last 20 miles or so.

In addition to being virtually void of energy at the 116 mile mark, my feet were destroyed and my behind and groin area were raw. It was impossible to distinguish between blistered skin, gel pads and bandages on my feet. Everything was just fused together. Not wanting to get into details of my other issues, just let me say that being in your late 30's is no time to be experiencing severe diaper rash. Anyway, a few hours of rest in Lone Pine, a shower, some foot and bottom care, along with some inspirational words from the crew got me back out on the course and eventually finish in 52 hours and 57 minutes, Although getting to the finish was a very special accomplishment, there was some disappointment missing out on the sub-48-hour buckle and knowing that so many things could have been done differently that would have gotten us to the finish so much quicker.

In 2002 I decided to continue with the ultramarathon scene and completed and buckled at the Western States Endurance Run. As I reflected on the 100 miles of Western States and the 2001 Badwater races, I saw how much I could improve with what I had learned. I decided I needed to rally the troops together and try Badwater again the right way. My buddies and Jackie were "in" and the preparation for the 2003 Badwater was on!

I looked forward to another chance to do well at Badwater, and to do well I knew I needed to change some things. I had never been a high mileage runner, but I realized my yearly mileage (369 miles) going into the 2001 Badwater was not enough. I have usually done pretty well as an age-grouper with training mileage weeks averaging just 30-35 miles. I had completed dozens of marathons, including Boston, with a personal best of 2:45. I had also completed three Ironman triathlons with a marathon split in the 3:30's after the 2.4-mile swim and 112-mile bicycle ride. Other than Badwater and Western States, my only other experience with ultramarathons was at the Dick Collins Fire Trail 50 miler in Castro Valley, California. I completed that in less than eight hours and saw it as added evidence that my hopes of finishing the 2003 Badwater much faster than my previous finish of nearly 53 hours was very possible. So I felt if I did everything right during Badwater a 30 to 36 hour finish should not be out of the question.

Going into Badwater I felt the training could have been stepped up more than it was but it was way ahead of what it was in 2001. I was bringing 860 miles of training miles for the year to the starting line this time instead of the 369 the last time. I knew this was still on the low end for an ultramarathon but it was more than twice as much as my prior attempt at Badwater. The training was in and my crew and I were ready. This time we would be dressed right, we would drink right, eat right, pace myself right; we would just do *everything* right!

The day before the race Jackie and I were going to get settled in early at Death Valley before the prerace meeting. The guys were coming into Las Vegas from Detroit a little later that day so I left my "new" truck at the airport for the guys to jump in and meet us in Death Valley for the prerace meeting. The foreshadowing of how things that were planned to go right could turn into going wrong was in the making.

I just bought a newer model SUV to replace the one I had at Badwater 2001. That SUV had been extremely reliable but it had over 180,000 miles on it and I did not want to take any chances with it. I got the exact same model but it was a couple of years newer and only had 12,500 miles on it. This is the vehicle I left for the guys at the airport. When the guys joined Jackie and me in Death Valley for the prerace meeting, they were joking about how we were trying to acclimate them to the heat and how not funny it was. We both looked at them wondering what they were talking about. Well, it turned out that not only did the air conditioning not work but also the engine temperature was climbing into the red zone and they had to drive out to Death Valley from Las Vegas with the heat running to keep the SUV from overheating. They thought I had rigged things that way as a "welcome to Death Valley" joke.

As a group we decided we were still better off taking both vehicles on the course as long as one had AC in case someone got overheated. This little glitch in the perfect race would not be an obstacle to our attempts to get to Whitney before the second nightfall. We still were better trained, better dressed, and had a better race strategy with pace, food, fluids, and electrolytes.

Race morning came and we were ready. I had on my hat provided by the race that also protected the back of your neck. I purchased a special shirt/jacket designed for sun protection and wicking to keep the body cool and light weight wicking shorts. I also had toed socks to try to keep the blistering between my toes to a minimum. There were multiple running shoes in the truck with some in larger sizes in case of swollen feet. The crew and I looked like a completely different team than we did in 2001... *WE WERE READY!*

The race started and I was off. The support vehicles were going to leap frog by the mile. I was to start without pacers; it was my job to keep the pace comfortable and easy. The crew kept detailed notes on pace, calories in, fluids in, types of fluids in, urine out along with color, and periodic weigh ins at the side of the road. I carried a walkie-talkie in case I needed something before I got to the leap-frogging support vehicles. Everything was going as planned and things looked good early in the race.

At some point between Furnace Creek and Stovepipe, the late morning and then afternoon sun seemed to be way more intense than I had ever experienced in the past. At this time I had been living in Las Vegas for about four years and had visited Death Valley multiple times (including the 2001 Badwater) and never felt this overwhelmed by the heat. As crazy as it sounds, it seemed humid hot... it was suffocating!

I started loading my hat with ice at every mile stop but that never lasted for more than a quarter mile or so. The shirt and hat I was wearing to protect me from the sun seemed like they were holding in the heat. I started to deeply second-guess my decision to dress differently than I had in 2001. No shirt and hat sounded pretty good to me, but as I felt my blood boil I knew it was the right thing to do and kept them on. As I heated up, my ability to eat decreased but I did continue to drink. My urination became an issue but was still much better than 2001. I felt that if I could just get to Stovepipe, regroup, cool off in the pool and start out after the sun set, we could get things back on track. But right now I was cooking from the inside out! As I struggled through the last few miles to Stovepipe, Jackie, Dave, Gregg, and Jeff would pace me in an attempt to keep me going and make sure I didn't crash between the leap-frogged stops. I could not believe I was coming unglued...especially so early in the race that was in so many ways supposed to go better than the last Badwater. I had never DNF'd before but there was no way I could go on this way for another 90 or so miles. I JUST NEEDED TO GET TO STOVEPIPE!

We finally got to Stovepipe. We lost some time but we got there and now it was time to shake off the near meltdown we had just survived and get things back on track. Once I stopped moving I would get incredible cramps in my legs. Hamstrings, quads, calves, lower back, lats; it did not matter. If I stood still and flexed to keep my balance, something would cramp. If I adjusted to that, something else would cramp. If I got into the pool and stepped or stood a certain way, I would cramp. Hydration was my biggest concern going into this race, but now it was these incredible cramps that just stopped me dead and they were killers that absolutely took my breath away. It appeared my electrolytes were out of whack despite our efforts to keep the fluids and supplements going as directed by the labels. I guess the labels did not take into consideration the dreaded and unknown "Death Valley in July" variable. As time passed, efforts to get back on track did not work. The cramping just got worse along with my GI problems. After a few hours of trying to turn things around with fluids, electrolytes, pool, stretching, etc., it was time to check in with the medical team at Stovepipe.

It was not long before the medical team had me lying down in one of the beds. There I had my femoral area packed in ice and two bags of IV solution running. Instead of pacing me to Whitney, my crew was taking turns acting as IV stands holding the bags of IV solution in the air as they drained into my arm. And just that quick, our efforts to get to Whitney were over. My first DNF! It was surreal. I could not believe it. We were doing everything right... last time we did so much wrong and we got to Whitney. This time we did not even make it out of Stovepipe. It is hard to describe the disappointment. I never had to stop anything before. I also felt like I let my friends down. The time... the expense... they flew in from Detroit to be a part of something special and it ended unfinished!

My 2003 Badwater attempt fell short for sure. I had high expectations. Some say the conditions were more extreme in 2003 than any other year. Maybe that is what happened. All I know is that I was cooking from the inside out while I was making my way to Stovepipe. I still joke with Jackie about the shirt/jacket I wore at the start of that race in my attempt to do everything right. I have never worn that shirt since but she has. I refer to it as the "Widow Maker!" Badwater 2003 almost killed me...was it the conditions? Over or under prepared? Over dressed/Widow Maker? You decide.

Badwater 2003 taught me a couple of things. One, I have some of the greatest friends in the world! Jackie, Dave, Gregg, and Jeff: Thank you so much for all of your support through the years. Two, I don't think that you can prepare for everything because so many things are out of your control. All you can do is your best and see where it takes you and be happy with the journey. Three, we all have limits and part of life should involve the enjoyment of exploring those limits. Cheers!!

2003 Result – Did Not Finish

CHAPTER TWENTY-FIVE – BEN JONES

From Bens' 2003 Badwater Application:

Age: 70
Lone Pine, California

Why I want a slot on the start line of the 2003 Badwater Ultramarathon:

I want to be the first person over age 70 (birth date: December 26, 1932) to complete the course. No one else has tried it at this age.

IT WAS 135 AT THE BADWATER 135 *By Ben Jones*

The alarm was set for 4:00 a.m. on Tuesday, July 22. My feet were pre-taped two days earlier by my wife Denise, so that saved a lot of time. All I had to do was get on my solar protection gear along with the bright yellow and green John Deere tractor suspenders and insert my Louis Skolnik pocket protector with the rectal thermometer. As I turned over my wallet, money, credit cards, cell phone, and pager to Denise I thought to myself that for once I didn't need these material things and they wouldn't do any good here anyway. It was a great feeling. I was turning myself over to my wife and crew... and to the environment.

I had a bagel and some juice and then started drinking water and Gatorade as we headed for Badwater around 5:00 a.m. I was assigned to the 6:00 start. It was great as we visited and gathered for the voluntary/obligatory photo shoots. Several official-looking people singled me out for pictures and interviews, which pleased me. I had stuck my neck out to be the first 70-year old to compete in the Badwater Ultramarathon. I headed for my "office" to make a last-minute deposit and to make sure no misspelled graffiti had been added to the walls. Recent paving obliterated the starting line, and I was hopeful that the official distance wouldn't be challenged. There had not been enough time to wheel the course in reverse to establish the accurate 135-mile distance. "This might be one of those asterisk (*) years," I thought to myself. Adam Bookspan played the Star Spangled Banner on his trumpet and it was inspirational. Race Director Chris Kostman did a countdown using his radio-controlled clock for an accurate 6:00 start.

Several runners streaked out as Ken Eielson shuffled off. A little while later I found I had worked my way into last place. My crew leap-frogged ahead —one mile at a time to make sure I was properly fueled. I managed to pee every 15 minutes for many hours thereafter. (In 1994 I was under-hydrated and faced the danger of renal shutdown and rhabdomyolysis and had to drop out of the race after 41 miles). The CBS crew headed by Linda Alvarez visited me for a few minutes several times in the first 10 miles. I really liked them. I didn't tell them I was practicing to be on the David Letterman Show. Near Mushroom Rock at 12 miles I looked out over the salt flats where two separate motor vehicle accidents had taken place last summer, each one involving a death and requiring my services. I also looked west to the foot of Telescope Peak where a Swiss professor had tried to climb up and down from the Valley floor. He almost made it back to his vehicle and was found dead after having been reported missing. This was during the race in 2002. It was necessary for me, the only medical doctor in the area, to perform the autopsy.

The 8:00 a.m. starters began to pass me by and we all exchanged friendly and encouraging waves. This was repeated two hours later with the 10:00 a.m. starters. It wasn't long before the first 8:00 starter, Blade Norman, streaked by as if he were on his way to a surfing contest. I cautioned him about his speed and lack of clothing as I was buffeted in his vortices. A few others passed me from the 8:00 start before I got to Furnace Creek. The time station registered my time there in 5:38 so I had done a 20-minute-per-mile pace up to that point. The shade of a palm tree was inviting for a brief cool down. I decided not to rest in the irrigation ditch at the palm orchard this year. At the Harmony Borax works I looked west to see if the Central Asians were practicing with their crop dusters over the borate flats. It was hard to tell anything through the mirage. At around 20 miles the 10:00 start runners started to pass me. I recognized

Rudy Afanador and shouted him words of encouragement. Later Pam Reed approached and I am proud to have been side-by-side with her for a few nanoseconds. I have a picture proving it.

Between the marathon mark and the 50K mark I noticed I needed five-to-ten minute rests and was only averaging 30-minute miles. Gary Morris strolled with me for a mile and it was inspirational to have him at my side. He has the concept that this race is strictly between man and his environment. Mentally I was dreading the "hill" between the sea level signs before rounding the turn to Stovepipe Wells (SPW) from mile 31 to mile 35. It was as hot as it has ever been in my 40 years of going to Death Valley. Kari Marchant informed me that her van sensor reached 135 degrees. Besides that, the humidity was relatively high, somewhere near 25%. So now the heat index figured into the situation. (After the race, Jay Anderson reported a temperature of 139!)

Employees at Stovepipe Wells were sweltering and one had to be evacuated to the hospital for IVs. Crewmembers were being shuttled to rooms at Stovepipe for paramedic evaluations and IVs. Forty percent of the paramedic responses were for crewmembers. As I was being "put down" in the van, I felt as if I were about to undergo anesthesia either for electroshock therapy or for some sort of procedure. I began imagining angels were coming to my rescue and that I was in the Garden of Gethsemane. Mary Magdalena was there. I thought I was still rational and also felt my body temperature was up.

Usually I don't tolerate a slight fever and am often at 96 degrees. The sun was behind the clouds but that didn't seem to help. I put in a request to be taken from the 35-mile mark to Stovepipe to have my temperature taken. The rectal thermometer had exploded in my pocket protector earlier. The reading was 101 plus. Next it seemed as if I were being prepared for embalming. I was wrapped in cold towels and packed with ice bags. A photograph was taken, and upon reviewing it later it seemed as if I was wrapped in the Shroud of Turin. When I came to, I looked for my imprint but had trouble seeing it through the cataracts. The shroud is being saved for carbon dating in case the Messiah thing comes up. After my temperature dropped to 98.1, I asked to be dumped back on the course at the Scotty's Castle turnoff. I lasted two miles. Several weeks earlier I did a coroner's autopsy on a 79-year old tourist who had dropped dead between the Devil's Cornfield and the Stovepipe dunes when it was 115 degrees. I am the only autopsy surgeon in Inyo and Mono Counties and decided I didn't want to do an autopsy on myself. I did notice I had cadaver legs at that point. I pulled myself at 37 miles and 17 hours. I could tell other runners were going down for the count. I had no idea what was going on ahead or behind me.

Here is a summary of my reasons for not continuing:
- Hyperthermia

- World record temperatures. Jay Anderson reported a van-reading temperature of 139. Others reported their sensor was pegged out at 130. (The only official recording devices are at the Death Valley National Park Visitors Center)

- Reports of struggling runners and crewmembers

- IV fluid administration to employees (Xanterra), runners, and crewmembers.

- Blast furnace winds

- Humidity of 25% (versus a normal humidity of 5-10%)

- Sense of fever confirmed at 101+ and inability to maintain a normal temperature

- Visions of angel, Mary Magdalene and the Garden of Gethsemane

- Being wrapped in the Shroud of Turin

- Seeing my imprint on the shroud – saved for carbon dating

- The Messiah

- Autopsy performed on heat stroke victim

- Unable to perform autopsy on self

- Cadaver legs

Now the Fun Starts

I would like to again thank my wife for helping me get trough the races from Badwater to the top of Whitney in 1991, 1992 and 1993. Without her I would not have had those successes in the earlier years. I now have a 50% success rate with failures in 1994, 1996 and now this year. I am not unhappy this year as I felt I gave it my best while under intense scrutiny but I know I let a lot of people down by not finishing. I thank my crew:

- Denise Jones, Badwater veteran, First Lady of Badwater, and Blister Queen

- Dave Thorpe, Badwater veteran, who has been with me every year

- Katie Rose Thorpe, Dave's daughter, age 19, who helped me also in the earlier years

- John Rosmus, Badwater veteran

- Rick Nawrocki, Badwater veteran and cancer survivor

- Brian Troupin, son of my neuropsychiatrist, insomniac and night driver.

My team heard an echo emanating from the sarcophagus. Someone took the lid off and I climbed out on Wednesday morning, July 23. We stumbled over each other in our room at Stovepipe for a while.

I staggered outside into a frenzy of swarming locust. It was like a pestilence. (The bugs were actually dragonflies) Besides that the sky seemed ominous with black clouds and threatening rain and thundershowers. It seemed as if Armageddon were about to happen... or perhaps already had happened. We decided to pull out and cruise the course in our three different vehicles. As I went up to Towne Pass the first runner I saw was Jay Birmingham. I was really pleased to meet him after all of these years and happy to see him still in the Race. There were at least 20 runners between there and Panamint Springs Resort (PSR). I would have loved to be in their midst. At Panamint we congratulated all of those who had made it that far and were about to proceed. I had a chance to more formally meet some of the crewmembers.

Denise went to various rooms to examine and patch up some feet and get them going again. We proceeded westward seeing those brave souls trudging and some even running up the west Panamint grade. At Father Crowley I bumped into Chris Frost and his three vehicles. I visited with him briefly the day before at around 30 miles where he informed me he was feeling great and was two hours ahead of last year. This was rather demoralizing to me at the time but I was really happy for him regardless. He was on the cell phone with his office in Malibu probably clinching some real estate deals.

The Darwin time station race data was interesting as it was being timed on Darwin-time, which is twelve hours different from the rest of the west coast. I tried to do some interpolating and extrapolating to figure things out so I could present realistic data to the webcast room at the Dow Villa in Lone Pine. Many other runners were between Darwin and Lone Pine as I went by. It was great seeing how well the lead runners were doing after 24+ hours. Monica Scholz and Chris Bergland looked good at Keeler and Dolomite, respectively. Pam Reed and Dean Karnazes were on the Portal Road and looked awesome. I was proud to be at the finish line when they arrived.

Later in the day (Wednesday - day #2) I doubled back out on the course and checked on the middle-of-the-pack runners. By then the sky exhibited one of the prettiest sunsets I have witnessed in Owens Valley and the Sierra. I thanked the Lone Pine Chamber of Commerce for this wonderful display, only to discover that rain showers and colorful clouds had been added to the spectacle. In the meantime Denise was still checking on feet and Dave and Katie were delivering Popsicles and distributing our leftover ice. We all praised their efforts and encouraged them on.

Early the next morning (Thursday - Day #3) I headed back out on the course to the back-of-the-pack runners. It seemed as if some would not get to the Portals within the 60-hour cutoff. Fortunately I was wrong and was very impressed with their fortitude. We all did the same things as before. Rick Nawrocki paced Ken Eielson who had paced him the year before. John Rosmus got our rented van spic and span and ready for return to the rental place in Bishop and then he had to depart for home. Later in the day we all went back to the Portals to witness many more finishes, which were all dramatic. Going back down the Portal Road I informed the final runners how much further they had to go and how many minutes-per-mile had to be done according to my pace chart in order to break 60 hours. I think most of them appreciated these facts. The multipurpose room at the Lo-Inyo School in Lone Pine was packed for the dinner and awards ceremony. Denise and I were proud to be on the same stage with Pam Reed, Dean Karnazes, Jay Birmingham, and Gary Morris. Each was presented with a petroglyph representing life in the area before the white man.

The next morning we had a nice breakfast at Seasons Restaurant provided by Jeff and Trina Tropple, who are great supporters of the Badwater Ultramarathon. Things really got quiet the next few days as the stragglers dropped by to bid farewell until next year. We always enjoy Marshall Ulrich and his performances on the course. I met his new wife Heather for the first time and found her to be quite charming. Art Webb told us about his segmental approach to the course this year. Adam Bookspan, along with his crew of David and Curt, has some secret plans for assaulting the desert again. I received many E-mails about the race. I spent quite a bit of time reviewing all of the pictures on the website. I look forward to the CBS coverage of the race on the David Letterman Show... even if I wasn't invited. My rectal thermometer exploded near the Beatty turnoff.

And... I still have some unused garlic suppositories if anyone is interested.

2003 Result – Did Not Finish

© Thinkstock/Stockphotos and illusion

CHAPTER TWENTY-SIX
– A VIEW FROM THE CREW

The following is a narrative of Badwater from the

perspective of the crew: specifically the crew chief for

Ruben Cantu.

GO AHEAD, CALL ME CRAZY TO VOLUNTEER TO HELP SOMEONE RUN ACROSS DEATH VALLEY IN JULY, BUT YOU JUST DON'T KNOW WHAT YOU'RE MISSING...

The Badwater Ultramarathon is known to be the world's toughest footrace, due to its incredibly harsh Death Valley environment in late July, the elevation gain, the length of the race and temperatures as extreme as the 130's. Do you have to be crazy to run this race? I've thought about this and been to the Badwater Ultramarathon as a crewmember twice and my firm answer is no. I can't answer firsthand why the runners do it, but I know why I return, and why I would go again as a crewmember if given the chance.

The race starts within Death Valley National Park at Badwater, California, 282 feet below sea level and hemmed in by nearby mountains over 11,000 feet high. It leads you on a paved road 135 miles through Death Valley, over two mountain passes each gaining nearly 5,000 feet in elevation, through the town of Lone Pine, California and up the steeply switch backed Portals Road. The Portals Road starts at 3,700 feet and ascends 13 winding miles to 8,360 feet ending at the trailhead to Mount Whitney, the highest peak in the contiguous United States at 14,496 feet.

From the dramatic dry basin of Badwater through the sand dunes, up and over steep and long sandstone mountain passes, through Joshua tree forests, across the dry bed of Owens Lake, through the famous Alabama Hills and climbing into the majestic Ponderosa Pine forests of the Sierra Nevada's, the Badwater Ultramarathon is both beautiful and extremely demanding.

The spiritual growth that I experienced at Badwater is quite indescribable. The sheer beauty of the environment during a season which showcases the best and worst Death Valley has to offer would be enough for me. Yet the true reason I go is to experience the raw emotion that accompanies crewing and caring for a runner, and being a critical part of his or her success. Everything from real life is stripped – there are no jobs or careers, no titles, no status symbols, no suits or ties, no bosses, no E-mail, nothing high tech. You don't sleep in a bed, eat in a kitchen or restaurant or follow a normal routine by the clock or the sun. Your watch means only one thing – a way to measure your runner's progress. Hours slip by and the sun rises and sets, and rises again. Entire time periods become a blur but one responsibility remains – caring for your runner.

Runners, crew, race staff and supporters are known only for their character and actions alone, and kindness seems to run amok at Badwater. For me, Badwater is an adventure, an escape and a time to renew my spirit and fill my emotional reservoir. Badwater 2003 truly was an incredible, unforgettable, and breathtakingly beautiful experience. 2003 was so different, so much more emotional and challenging for me than the previous races I had crewed for ultrarunner Ruben Cantu. There are reasons why it was different this time that I hope to explain. I could not imagine having a more incredible, more spiritual time.

A vacation on a quiet beach, a sightseeing tour of a big city, watching movies, reading books or simply going for a run – people escape life in countless ways. A typical escape for me is a backpacking trip in the Colorado Rockies to a place where I won't see anyone except the folks I brought with me. The silence and beauty of the natural surroundings and wildlife relaxes and energizes me.

But the older I get the more I realize I have to make my every day life feel this good by eliminating or minimizing stress and unnecessary actions and pointing my efforts towards letting every moment give me pleasure, not just the brief periods of escape. To this point, I try to bring as much Badwater home with me as I can.

What happens on the Badwater Ultramarathon road is known only to the road and the people who travel it. I've often heard in the context of ultrarunning *"What's said on the trail stays on the trail."* Decisions are made by the runner and the crew under the vast desert sky. There's no one to consult and very few rules to consider. What's important are your physical and mental health, hydration, nutrition, and protection from the elements. Nothing else matters and for me, it's all part of the allure.

Ruben is an amazing athlete and inspirational human being. In the last four years I have come to know him it didn't take me long to understand he is serious about his training and ultra events while still keeping in focus that life is for living and enjoying. His mental fortitude has no bounds and quitting is not part of his makeup. He's taught me so much that I can't ever hope to repay him. I crewed for him at the Leadville Trail 100 in 1999 and at Badwater in 2000 so when he called in June 2003 and asked me to come to Badwater in July, I jumped at the chance.

Although I dedicate hard–earned vacation time and money to be able to support him at Badwater, I get back so much more than I put in and I think sometimes he just doesn't understand that the trade–off is a good one for me.

Badwater – Prerace Preparations

Ruben is a demanding and successful runner and requires a very hardworking crew. I go to Badwater with the full knowledge I will give 110% to Ruben and his effort, physically and mentally, while at the same time taking the utmost care of myself and my fellow crewmembers.

Throughout the entire race one person will pace him on foot or bicycle and the other crewmembers will drive the vehicles one mile, then give him aid when he gets there without breaking a step of his stride. And I've learned from experience that he doesn't take many breaks!

Each mile the pacer with Ruben calls the car on the walkie-talkie a few minutes before their arrival at the car and tells them what Ruben needs. It is almost always a specific combination of ice and water, but could also be diluted Gatorade, Kern's juice, Coke, any of the three flavors of Mountain Dew, Capri Sun, pita chips, cookies, pretzels, gum drops, Reese's chocolate balls, watermelon, oranges, or a peanut butter sandwich. Non–food requests include a change of clothing, sunscreen, a different hat, ice in a neck wrap, ice for his hat, a fresh washcloth for his face or a fresh handkerchief, electrolyte tablets, or Advil. You've got to locate what he wants quickly, get it ready, look for traffic, cross the road and deliver it to him without making him slow down or stop. You've also got to anticipate what he hasn't asked for and have it ready without bombarding him with unnecessary questions.

We spent hours going over his gear the day before the race and understanding which bin it was stored in, and yet still once the race began we had trouble finding everything due to the cramped and packed quarters of the Subaru wagon. In addition to food and clothing there is an entire first aid bin full of band aids, gauze wrap, tape, special blister treatment, powder, Vaseline, Bag Balm (anti–chafing jelly), sunscreen, triple antibiotic, IV saline solution kit, and nighttime specific equipment such as red clip–on flashers, headlamps, flashlights, reflective vests, ankle straps and bug spray. There are also three extra pairs of running shoes and a folding chair for Ruben's rest breaks.

It's a lot of gear but it probably doesn't sound like all that much to do if you've never done it before. But when you break it down you have 10 to 15 minutes to pack up your car after the last stop, drive exactly one mile (no more and no less!) on the odometer and find a decent part of the shoulder to park on, open the car back up, fill the bottles with ice, answer the walkie-talkie call and find and prepare anything he asks for. In addition you've got to remember all the other things like giving him an electrolyte tab every third mile and keeping tabs on his fluid input and output. It's also very helpful to know what mile he is on, how many miles to the next time station, what time it is and what his pace is. Approaching time stations you should compare how he's doing to his times from the last three years. Most importantly you've got to take impeccable care of your own body with sunscreen, water, electrolytes and food. With this much to do each mile goes by very quickly.

I'm not a worrying person by nature, but when I assume the lead crew position I carry the weight of my runner and their health and well being on my shoulders. Of course if serious problems arose, I likely wouldn't be the final decision–maker, but nonetheless I feel as if I am fully responsible. I believe that the crew should take care of everything so the runner has one focus only: the run.

I believe this is how a crew leader needs to act in order to acknowledge the seriousness and risk of Badwater. During her flight attendant days, my mother used to tell me how she felt 100% responsible for the safety of every flight and every person on the plane. I thought her attitude and dedication was great but that she shouldn't carry such a huge burden herself. Now I have a different view because at Badwater I do the same: work as a team, but act as if you carry the responsibility yourself. I think it's an honorable thing to take your job this seriously, as long as you don't forget to be a team player.

Crewing is much less stressful if you have enough people and enough space in your vehicles and the crew is organized and upbeat and knows what to do. It's still a lot of work but once you get your system mastered, it's not a problem.

Badwater – The Start
Tuesday 6 a.m.

We were part of the 6 a.m. start group supporting our 60–year–old ultrarunner, Ruben Cantu. Shortly before the official start time it was 106° F already but it felt pretty nice after noting 128° F in the shade at the Death Valley National Park Visitor's Center at 5 p.m. the previous day.

We had risen at 4:30 a.m. on race day and packed the coolers and the rest of the gear in the car. Ruben was fired up and ready to go. The pre–dawn night was dark but already starting to lighten. I am not sure exactly what Ruben was feeling, but as a team we were charged with a combination of excitement and anxiety and I could feel both in the air.

The little Subaru wagon was packed so full of gear that I had to sit crammed on the center console between Bram and Ruben, both good–sized guys. Normally there are two crew vehicles so one can stay near the runner and one can drive to get ice and check in and out of hotel rooms, run other errands and provide additional support. We had planned to cover the start with Bram and I in one vehicle, and then a second veteran crewmember, H.E. West, was to arrive in Death Valley with a pickup filled with additional ice sometime later that morning. I was expecting him by early afternoon and hoping he would make it by noon.

We had the Subaru packed tight with three bicycles on the roof and all the extra gear we could put up there that wouldn't be damaged by the searing heat. We couldn't even put tennis shoes up there since the soles would melt. So we put clothes and camping gear and a few other things to make room for four huge coolers and many food and gear bins inside the car. I knew we would be fine until H.E. arrived, and then things would be a lot easier. We were mostly quiet on the 20 minute drive from our resort hotel oasis at Furnace Creek to the start at Badwater, driving through the eerie landscape of the hottest temperature recorded in the Western Hemisphere: 134° F in 1913 (only exceeded by a reading of 136° F in Libya in 1922).

At 5 a.m. the sky was bright, and coming from a person who is normally asleep at sunrise, for what it's worth, a Badwater sunrise is one of the most beautiful I've ever seen. Badwater is 282 feet below sea level in a flat and barren desert valley surrounded closely on all sides by tall mountains, including Telescope Peak at 11,049 feet, a dramatic elevation gain from the basin. If you strain your eyes in the light you can trace the race path through the tiny villages of Furnace Creek and Stovepipe Wells and imagine the cut in the mountains where we will climb Townes Pass in 40 miles.

The start at Badwater is very relaxed as far as races go and has a happy vibe. Although the runners must feel a lot of fear and anxiety it seems that once it officially starts they are relieved. Runner Adam Bookspan played the Star Spangled Banner beautifully on his trumpet into the wide-open spaces and to a solemn crowd, and afterwards the race began. Ruben ran the first four miles by himself and then we began pacing him.

Runners can only be paced after mile 17 at Furnace Creek, unless they are 60 years old or older and in that case they are allowed to be paced the entire race. I had the first shift pacing Ruben but during these early miles he is running at a quick pace and neither Bram nor I can keep up with him for very long. Bram got my bike off the roof rack and I began to ride with Ruben. But something was wrong with my bike; there was a bad rubbing sound on the tire. While riding I released the front brake cable, thinking the heat had caused it to become misaligned. In this harsh environment with heat and sand you quickly learn that your equipment behaves differently out here. The noise persisted so I stopped and took off the front wheel and put it back on. After two miles the bike would no longer roll because the rubbing was so fierce. I dropped the bike off at the car explained the problem to Bram and ran to catch up and continue on foot with Ruben.

At the next mile Bram had figured out that mysteriously the back wheel had come slightly loose from the frame, so he tightened it and I was thankfully back in business. But a few miles later I got my first flat tire. Bram quickly surrendered the front tire from his bike and I continued riding. We thought we might be experiencing a loss of air pressure in our bike tires due to the heat or low elevation. So besides preparing for Ruben each mile we had to deal with pumping up and switching bike tires. After another frustrating flat I switched to Bram's mountain bike.

In the meantime we were working in the very tightly packed space of the Subaru wagon and had a difficult time finding things. Many times when Ruben called for something to eat we would have to unload four or five Rubbermaid bins to get to what we were looking for and all of this in record time trying to maintain his pace. And if he asked for watermelon, we had to locate the right cooler, find a knife, cut it into a bite sized piece and put it in a baggie for him, all under the blistering desert sun and sandy wind. Most crews have larger vehicles and sometimes even cargo vans or RV's. It's easier to be highly organized when you've got some space.

The start of the race definitely holds an adjustment period for the crew. I kept telling Bram that after a few miles or an hour we'd have our system mastered and it would be easy from there on out. But the bike problems threw us a curve and just the simple fact that Bram was new at crewing made us slower to adjust. The extreme heat that was building as the day progressed melted our ice quicker than we had guessed, in part because the Subaru's air conditioner was not able to keep up with the doors and hatch being open much of the time. The first 17 miles are relatively flat with a dramatic view across Badwater Basin to the majestic and towering mountain ranges. The oasis at Furnace Creek becomes visible with lush trees looking foreign in this landscape. With the barrier of the 5,700-foot Dante's Peak in the Black Mountains directly on our east flank, the sun pokes out and hits us full force at around 9 a.m. That is the point at which for me the race officially starts, as we are no longer sheltered from the brutal sun and won't be again until the first night falls.

Near the end of Badwater Road, about three miles from the first time station at Furnace Creek, we already needed ice so Bram took off with the car and I loaded up with extra water bottles and rode with Ruben while Bram hurried to get ice and check out of last night's hotel room. We had kept the room keys in case Ruben wanted to use a real bathroom. After a few miles Ruben sent me ahead on the bike to help Bram. I pedaled away hard and kept my mouth closed and my hat pulled down low as I bombed on the mountain bike as fast as I could against the brutal superheated wind into Furnace Creek. I notified the time station that Ruben was coming and gave the bike to Bram and then drove a short block to the icehouse to buy bags of ice. I didn't feel like I was running on adrenaline but we were definitely going at warp speed to keep up with our duties and Ruben's pace.

Furnace Creek
Tuesday Morning

Ruben arrived at the Furnace Creek time station at 9:38 a.m., 17 miles and 3 ½ hours into the race. The day was definitely heating up. Bram had checked out of the hotel and ran into the store to buy a wide–brimmed hat since he couldn't find his, and then pedaled down to the icehouse to help me fill the coolers with four huge bags of ice. We were fast and busy and caught up with Ruben again just outside of Furnace Creek. With only one vehicle and two crewmembers it is difficult to get everything done without leaving the runner alone on the road. We did what we could to make sure he would only be out there unsupported for a few minutes.

It started to get windy and unbearably hot around noon. Heat is relative, we learned. I smiled and told the sun it couldn't touch me. We had learned that 115° F wasn't so bad when we mountain biked in the mountains west of Las Vegas three days ago to continue our heat acclimation. I'd been running in Colorado during the heat of the day to train for Badwater, sometimes in 100° F weather. I also drove in my car with the windows up and the heat on high that, without exception, people found strange when I exited the car dripping with perspiration. But as crazy as it seemed it was all necessary to successfully acclimate to this extreme heat as I learned on my trip to Death Valley in 2000 when the temperature was 129° F.

As the sun delivered its worst to us we heard rumors that it was 133° F. It was frightening to hear but also empowering to realize it hadn't gotten the best of us and we were surviving. The wind was brutal and relentless as we crossed the sand dunes. The road was a brand new, shiny blacktop and the heat coming off of it seemed to approach 200° F. In Death Valley the ground temperature is typically 40% higher than the air, which equates to 186° F but I imagine it was even higher due to the blackness of the road. It felt like standing in front of the ovens at Dominos Pizza when I worked there as a teenager, except here there was no relief and no walk–in freezer to escape the heat.

We had been monitoring the humidity before the race with a handheld gauge, knowing it was hovering around 15%, much higher than the normal 3% in Death Valley. We noticed our bodies perspiring when normally the perspiration would evaporate before it was ever felt. By now on the hot road we could feel the added effect the humidity was giving us. The heat index or "feels like" factor with the wind and humidity must have been in excess of 140° F. It was unbelievable. Getting into the car was only marginally better because it provided relief from the wind. The sun was beating straight into the driver's side window and even a rollup shade didn't help much. The temperature in the car hovered around

120° F and wasn't unbearable, but it was literally hell on the ice in the coolers. The car was faithfully struggling with its air conditioner, even with the fan on low. We had a very large and heavy load for the little four-cylinder car; it was a low-rider piled high with bikes and gear on top. The temperature inside the car with the air conditioner on was as high as 126° F that day. Most of the time it was around 115° F and that at times felt good compared to the outside.

But at times the car's temperature gauge would creep above normal and we would turn off the air for a while until it returned. Knowing we were taxing the car probably close to its limit with the heavy load, the intense heat, the strain on the air conditioner, opening the doors frequently and the constant starting and stopping of the car, I prayed we wouldn't have any problems. Without H.E.'s arrival, a broken car might mean Ruben would have to drop out of the race and I dreaded the thought.

The stretch between Furnace Creek and Stovepipe Wells is the leg that Ruben most despises. We pass by areas aptly named: Devil's Golf Course and Devil's Cornfield, both endlessly beautiful sand dunes. We had finally climbed high enough to be at sea level. It truly is a stretch that tries to kill you in the peak heat of the day. Ruben had switched to his full desert outfit: white UV protected long pants and pullover top, and a white hat with side curtains. We added to it a neck towel filled with ice every few miles and a washcloth inside his hat to contain more ice. I switched to ¾ length pants and a ¾ sleeve cotton white shirt and a floppy hat. After an hour of riding the bike with Ruben, the exposed skin on my ankles started to feel like it was literally cooking and was red so I quickly donned full length pants and a UV pullover, soaked myself with water and cooled down quickly and thankfully. Most of the time I had ice riding in the top of my hat and kept my clothing wet to stay cool. That was my worst physical point of the entire race. I could feel the stress and the heat catching me, but once I changed clothes and soaked myself and took a break driving the car I felt a lot better.

At 130° F ice melts quickly! We did not have space in the coolers to store the jugs of Ruben's drinking water so they had to sit in the hot car. We would fill his bottles with ice and when he approached we'd top them off with water. But the water was so hot it would melt half the ice so we had to fill them back up with ice, pour a little more water and repeat. This tripled the work we ordinarily had to do. Ruben would be sure to tell us if we didn't have enough ice in there. You've got to respect his methods – he's crossed the Badwater finish line four times and he knows what he's doing. But in this temperature it was a struggle just to keep the bottles filled with ice.

The bike problems continued and this daytime section was a bit of a blur to me. Bram had outfitted the bar ends of the bicycle handlebars with white socks since they were burning our hands. Eight hours into the race we had decommissioned two of our bikes with four flat tires. Early on the race officials told us we had to ride in the gravel on the side of the road and we learned the hard way there were tough thorns out there that had no problem piercing the hot rubber of our tires and tubes. We now had just Bram's road bike left and we decided we would walk with Ruben now and save the road bike for tonight in case H.E. didn't show up. In addition, H.E. was a driving crewmember, and not a riding or walking one. Without a bicycle and with only two pacers we would have a tough time crewing Ruben on foot every mile of the way. So for what we all considered the most brutal and hated section of the course, we joined Ruben on foot. At one point Ruben looked at me and said "I've trained for this and I'm miserable; you get into the car and take a break." I took his advice and knowing we were nearing the next rest spot, we left him without a pacer for a few miles.

As the afternoon wore on I wondered about H.E. from time to time. I was starting to lose faith he would arrive and began to plan ahead in case he didn't show. We didn't have a way to contact him; we just had to wait. I set my sights instead on Mike and Jeanne's arrival this evening, and I knew we could make it until then as long as we had a working bicycle. Although it isn't critically necessary for Ruben to have a pacer every mile of the way, I know that he thrives with the company, whether talking or not, and prefers it to being alone. It was our goal to pace him as much as we possibly could.

Stovepipe Wells
Tuesday afternoon

We arrived to the chaos of the tiny village at Stovepipe Wells (mile 41) at 4:44 p.m. and Bram and I ran around at warp speed checking into the hotel, staking the spot Ruben left the course, driving him 100 yards to the room, then getting him food and drinks. While Ruben rested in the air conditioned room, we were busy getting 15 more bags of ice, fueling the car, calling Ruben's wife and Mike on a pay phone, rearranging and cleaning the car, throwing away trash, and draining and repacking the coolers. The lone motel in Stovepipe Wells has a pool and a gas station, all swarming with crews and their vehicles trying to get gas and frantically grabbing the last bags of ice. I heard later they ran out of ice shortly after we left. That means half of the runners" crews would have had to go 25 miles back to Furnace Creek, or 31 miles ahead to Panamint Springs to look for ice. These are long miles to drive when the temperature is in the 130's, your runner and crew are desperate for ice and these desert outposts can't always be depended on to have ice.

The goal of the hotel break is to get Ruben horizontal on a bed, cool him off and give him a much-deserved rest. We were there just less than two hours and he did sleep a bit. He's trained his body to shut down for short periods of time, then quickly recover and get back to the race. He seemed to catch small catnaps in between me checking on him or trying to get him to eat. At times we just sat and lightly chatted, a few words at a time. He acknowledged the run had taken its toll on him and he was slower than previous years. I reminded him the extreme heat and unusual humidity was slowing everyone down and that he was actually doing quite well. Bram bought the first round of ice while I tended to Ruben and tried to make some overdue phone calls. Getting ice was an ordeal that involved waiting in line at the gas station, paying for the ice then driving across the street to the hotel and waiting in line again for "Dot" to bring your ice out from the kitchen in the back. Dot was an older lady who seemed to have been working a double shift and was so helpful and nice that she would not only retrieve your ice from the kitchen, but she'd also wheel the bags out to the end of the pavement on a cart and help you carry it to your car. Most of the hotel and services staff along the Badwater route are nothing short of amazing.

I did quite a bit of walking back and forth across the hotel grounds – to the gas station to talk to Bram, to the hotel room and to the pay phone. The wind whipped through the dirt parking lots of the hotel and

I have never felt such an inferno. It is difficult to merely take a breath in such conditions. Waiting in line for ice with other crewmembers the talk was limited to the heat, wind, humidity and the performance of our runners. I hoped that as we advanced into the evening and Ruben rested for a while we would get at least a five-degree break before he started back on the road. While I walked with my head bent down against the wind I focused on the beautiful backdrop of mountains instead of the heat, and thought about how we would soon be leaving Stovepipe Wells. By then I agreed with Ruben: This was indeed the worst part of the race!

I waited at least 20 minutes outside in the heat for the pay phone while someone else's crewmember chatted in tones I couldn't quite capture, even though I strained to eavesdrop to pass the time. I finally got a hold of Ruben's wife and gave her the update, but did not tell her exactly how hot it was. I really didn't know the exact temperature and so I neglected to tell her the rumors of temperatures greater than 130° F because Ruben simply did not want her to worry more than she already did. At this point Ruben was performing very well, although a little slower than he had hoped, but with the added factor of the extreme heat and unusual humidity I believed he was right on track.

After talking to Carol and ensuring her that Ruben was fine and that we would take the best care of him and promising to make him eat, I finally got hold of Mike, who was still at home in San Diego and had at least two more hours of work to take care of before packing and hitting the road with Jeanne. Ruben told me to tell Mike of the extreme heat and how it slowed Ruben down and how H.E. hadn't shown up.

This week had found Mike buried in work he couldn't ignore. He projected leaving for the five-hour drive in a few hours, which would put him in our area around midnight. This is the time I then looked forward to, a time for us to regroup and take a breather and crew Ruben without the adrenaline rush we had been operating on so far. We were so far into the evening that we had written off the arrival of H.E. and were now operating as though he wasn't going to show up at all. I was disappointed with Mike's news that he wouldn't be there any earlier, but there was nothing I could do except be grateful that he was coming, and look forward to seeing someone I had bonded with and enjoyed at Badwater 2000.

At one point I was sitting on the other bed keeping an eye on Ruben, thinking about him and this crazy race. Strange things happen to a runner and their emotions during a race such as this. Without having experienced this myself, and only as a crewmember, I relate a quote I heard from a mountain climber to explain to myself what it means:

"Strong emotion is what a climber lives for. Fear and joy are the two strongest of all. If he can't feel fear, he can't feel the sublime joy of victory. The climber experiences life to its extreme limits. He is not trying to get himself killed. He knows what life is worth. He is in love with living."

- Italian Alpinist Walter Bonatti

Emotions get stripped down to their rawest forms. Runners have a lot of time to reflect on life and even something like a fellow runner having to drop out of the race can make them cry. It is common during a race for a crewmember to experience intimacies one would normally not have in everyday life – massaging shoulders, neck, arms and legs of the runner, standing nearby with back turned while they urinate on the side of the road and asking them what color it is, or helping them dress or undress. It's all part of the event and we all go with the understanding it is a different world out there and there are different rules.

Townes Pass
Tuesday evening/Wednesday morning

We left Stovepipe Wells at 6 p.m. after checking Ruben back onto the racecourse. We were 12 hours and 45 miles into the race. The temperature had dropped slightly, and we had fresh ice and a refreshed runner who just ate an entire oversized can of soup that had cooked sitting on the dash of the car for a half hour. I had brought the can to him in the room and lifted on the pull tab a little too hard and broke it off, bending only a small hole in the lid. Ruben laughed at me and said "Way to go!" I pulled out a penknife and pushed the lid down splashing chicken noodle soup all over my arm and the nightstand. He laughed at my antics and although he had planned on eating only half of it, after tasting Bram's fine cooking he was prompted to finish the entire can. He smiled and his spirits lifted and I was overjoyed to see him eat that much. We were now ready to roll.

Our next goal was the top of Townes Pass, 4,960 feet in elevation above sea level, where we now stood. It would take us 17 miles to climb that high. The beauty of the climb is that for each 1,000 feet gained in elevation we were certain to enjoy a five-degree temperature drop. That combined with the slowly approaching sunset lifted my spirits. The days are long in Death Valley and the sun beats you down for endless hours. Shade is unheard of as the only trees are few and far between and are often Joshua trees that provide no shade. My immediate goal was for the sun to hide behind the Townes Pass Mountains to provide us with a hint of relief.

I worried about Bram throughout the day; worried that he was working so hard he was forgetting to see the beauty of Death Valley. Bram gets very focused when he works and he's very serious and I see it as my job to remind him of these things. He sometimes forgets to smile and so every once in a while I would make a passing comment on the beauty of the day or the amazing fact we were functioning quite well in 130+° F degree heat. I don't think the beauty was lost on him; I think he's just the kind of person that sees it in retrospect, rather than appreciate it at the exact moment. At the time he was just head-down and intent on giving his best effort.

Ruben plodded on and up the pass as dusk approached. We rode and walked with him, sometimes talking, sometimes not. The relief of the setting sun made crewing easier. Ruben had peeled off his full-length layers and was back to shorts, sleeveless T-shirt and a small white cap. No longer did we have to scramble to fill the neck roll and hat with ice and it gave us a few extra moments to breathe.

Bram rode many of the miles up the pass on his bike. I had trouble riding his bike because it was too big for me and the reach to the handlebars kept me in a very uncomfortable, outstretched position. Darkness fell, the temperature got more and more tolerable and we could hear the scrambling and chirping of the creatures and bugs of the Death Valley night. We got out the flashers and the flashlights and donned reflective gear. Several miles from the top Bram took over driving and I walked the rest of the steep pass with Ruben in the dark. I wore a headlamp that gave us minimal light and the stars were incredible. At times we turned off the light and let our eyes adjust. We didn't see too many runners, and a few crew cars would leapfrog us every mile. We were following runner Ken Eielsen and could see his flashy State of Texas flag shorts waving in the dark ahead of us. He had a bright lamp he would flash erratically over the nearby mountains and cliffs giving us a glimpse of the hidden hills we were passing through. The moon was hiding behind the unusually thick clouds so the night remained very dark. We arrived at the top of the pass at 12:15 a.m. and had a scheduled naptime for Ruben. He had briefly mentioned at midnight that Mike should be there any minute, and I softly warned him not to look for him until around 1 a.m. I wanted to give Mike a buffer and not stifle Ruben's hopes if Mike was running behind. Ruben had quit drinking watered-down Gatorade around 10 p.m., mentioning heartburn.

We pulled the car off the road on a dirt pullout and laid out a Thermarest inflatable camping pad and Ruben's pillow on the hard ground next to the car. We checked the area for scorpions and snakes and prayed he'd be okay. He brought his pillow from home on Mike's advice to bring something from home that smelled like him. Mike, an ultra runner/swimmer/cyclist is Ruben's faithful friend and training partner. Mike spends countless hours on weekends riding his bike and crewing Ruben during his long runs in the desert east of San Diego. On the road they bicker in a humorous way like children and you can feel the strong bond of friendship between them.

Ruben might not admit it, but I believe he will do nearly anything Mike tells him to do during the race. He has a lot of respect for Mike and knows that Mike will do what is best for him.

As he lay down I said to Ruben with a smile, "If Mike was here he'd tell you to smell your pillow before you go to sleep." I imagined in the darkness he smiled and he nodded off to some faraway place for about 90 minutes. Bram and I tended to our blistered feet during our first real sit-down break in 20 long hours and spoke quietly sitting on the other side of the car. All was eerily quiet at almost a mile high into the Death Valley sky. I love this place.

At 2 a.m. sharp I woke Ruben and we got him rolling again. It is still surprising to me that once he gets on his feet it doesn't take much for him to start walking his fast pace again. There's no warm up for him – from sleep right back into race mode. We had a long descent into Panamint Springs to look forward to: 14 miles as steep as 6% at times. Bram was pacing on his road bike and said he felt good enough to continue. I manned the car and due to the lower nighttime temperatures my duties were easier with Ruben drinking less and not requiring ice packs for his neck every mile. For the first time I had moments to myself to sit on the tailgate and star gaze. I imagined it was about 90° F in the pure mountain air and it felt refreshingly cool. It was a brutal day but night allowed me to crack a smile and enjoy what life was offering at that very moment.

In the silence of the long night I once heard rocks crumbling off the mountainside, maybe kicked off by a small animal or maybe it was just their time to fly. I battled hundreds of unidentified bugs and a few mosquitoes trying to swarm around my interior car light and land in the ice chests. I took moments at a time to reflect with wonder at the density of the Milky Way and once in a while in between the towering mountains I could locate the Big Dipper. I periodically took self-portraits with my digital camera to see how tired I looked and to laugh at myself – I looked awful!

It was a long night: Bram spent 4½ hours on his bicycle descending with Ruben into Panamint Springs. The dawn was welcome, giving us a new outlook on the day, but also came with dread knowing that with a new day came more heat. Ruben would briefly mention to Bram his heartburn or upset stomach, but mostly he was quiet about his condition.

Once we descended the pass we landed on a completely flat stretch resembling a ribbon laid across the desert floor. Here we passed through low dunes, dry cracked mud and flash flood areas. The creeping light of the pending sunrise seemed to start prior to 5 a.m. and the magic and slowness of its pace kept me entertained for hours. As the sky lightened I could see the silhouette of the soaring Townes Pass we had just conquered. We were sheltered by mountains all around, so it would be many hours before the sun crested the top and actually hit us.

I could also see the almost oasis of the Panamint Springs Resort up ahead, our next goal and checkpoint. The weather to the west showed unusual clouds and occasional lightning. A passing runner, Anita Fromm, whom I cheered words of encouragement to each time she passed, warned of flash flooding and told us to get our runner to high ground quickly in case of rain. I was glad for her words, as my weary brain had not realized the potential danger.

In the dawn's light we soon noticed the heavy but high cloud cover and were amazed at the strange weather that Death Valley had cooked up for us. The humidity was even more stifling, but luckily the heat hadn't returned yet. I think we all silently worried something had happened to Mike. Ruben said it wasn't like him to not call and let us know what happened. I prayed it wasn't a car accident or something horrible. I tried to put it out of my mind and not think about what might happen should Mike fail to arrive.

During the last four hours coming off of Townes Pass Ruben was plagued with heartburn and upset stomach and we gave him Prevacid but it didn't seem to help. He quit drinking Gatorade feeling the excess sugar may have been adding to his problems and we supplemented him with electrolyte and sodium tablets. His spirits were visibly down and at one point on the flats within eyesight of Panamint Springs, Ruben let us know that he was going to take a significant break there and it was possible he would be dropping out of the race, and that he was sorry. I could see the disappointment and strain in his eyes and knew he felt he was letting us down.

When H.E. failed to show on Tuesday it was a blow to all of us but once I wrote him off and began looking forward to Mike and Jeanne's arrival Tuesday night, things had looked up. I knew we could make it without H.E. But the fact remained we now needed Mike and Jeanne to continue to pace Ruben each and every mile, and we needed the extra vehicle in case of any problems with the stressed Subaru.

All night we had looked for Mike's van, but to no avail. Not many vehicles pass against the flow of the race and at night on the backside of Townes Pass I could see a car approach from as far as ten miles away. But again and again it wasn't Mike and our disappointment collectively grew and we quit mentioning it. On the flats I was finally able to get cell service and called my cousin Julie, telling her I needed prayers for Ruben that he could continue. I told her what we were up against and she gave me great words of encouragement, telling me to not think ahead, but to just take it one mile at a time. I really needed to talk to a loving voice, to someone who would sympathize and give me a voice of reason, someone who had had a good night's sleep! After 24 hours of non-stop activity my brain was in a strange and vulnerable place.

After hanging up I immediately dialed Ruben's wife, but the cell connection was lost, no matter how creatively I held the phone or tilted my head. That seems to be the norm for Death Valley. I learned if you are lucky enough to get a connection, make it quick and don't assume you will be able to make a second call. Ruben was very quiet during this time and I had never seen him this low, but I still didn't have any doubts he would still make a successful finish. We just needed for him to get through this rough spot.

Panamint Springs
Wednesday early morning

Rolling into Panamint Springs at 6:35 a.m. Wednesday morning, we all hoped and thought that Mike would be arriving. We had our doubts and fears something bad had happened. We could not reach him in person and had no voice mails on our phones.

Ruben was really hurting and we set up a chair for him to rest on in the parking lot. Chris Frost's girlfriend Tracy was parked next to us and found some ginger ale for him to try. Chris maintains that ginger is the best thing for a troubled stomach, reminding us that when we were sick as children our mothers always gave us ginger ale. Another crewmember offered their last ounces of Pedialyte. Another helpful person was Leon, the time station official and Badwater veteran. He told Ruben to eat several e–Caps (electrolytes in caplet form) because he was probably low on electrolytes. Ruben listened to him and I quickly got him the e–Caps and a glass of water. Ruben, I think, was taking his condition minute by minute, anticipating Mike's arrival.

He told us that he might not continue if his stomach didn't get better. I told him not to make any decisions right now and we quietly left it at that.

We finally got Mike on the phone and learned that he was still two hours away. It seemed to give Ruben a little peace of mind knowing he was on his way. He also talked to his wife and told her he did not know if he could finish and that he was not going to attempt the double crossing. I went inside the hotel and ordered an egg and cheese sandwich and a bottle of orange juice from the bar. The staff had kept the restaurant open all night and they were frazzled. The cook was fighting with the waitresses and they were full of threats behind his back. I took the juice to Ruben and returned in 15 minutes to pick up the sandwich, which had since been forgotten. I reordered and got the sandwich in five more minutes, hearing the cook cursing in the kitchen the entire time.

Ruben ate the sandwich and then wanted to sleep so we put him in the front seat of the car. He lay sideways with his pillow against the center console and stick shift with his legs hanging out the car door and slept intermittently. A Subaru is really not fit for a resting 6'2' man but somehow he made it work. After a while he asked me to turn on the air and I checked on him every few minutes. At one point he was lying twisted on his back with a terrible expression of pain. I knelt down and touched his knee and gently asked if the stomach cramps were causing it.

He nodded and said he just wanted to sleep. He turned away and curled up into a ball and I took the chance to lie out the windshield sunshade and lie on the pavement next to the car for a nap.

The sun had risen over the mile-high mountains we had just passed and it was about 8 a.m. The temperature was bearable, maybe just under 100° F. The humidity was oppressive after reminding myself I was in the desert. I drifted in and out of sleep for 20 or 30 minutes until I felt what I thought was someone mischievously dripping water on my arms and face. I was too tired to open my eyes to see who was bothering me. Then it began hitting my legs and back and I could no longer ignore it. I opened my eyes and could not believe that it was actually raining! What challenging weather we had so far.

Bram had nearly emptied the entire car's disarrayed contents into the parking lot. Fellow crewmembers walked by shaking their heads in amazement as to how we could make this work with such a tiny car. Bike parts were strewn everywhere with four flat tires in the process of being fixed. Stealing a tube from his road bike Bram was able to get my bike working. With a knife and by hand he pulled around 100 stubborn thorns out of my front tire alone. We hoped we got them all but knew we couldn't assume the new tube would last. Knowing that Mike should arrive around 10 a.m. we hoped we wouldn't need it much longer than that.

Ruben started to stir about 9:30 a.m. and it seemed his stomach had improved slightly. I led him to the bathroom outside the restaurant and when he returned he was a new man. We were not prepared for his energy or eagerness and he let us know that he was ready to go. I remember thinking at the time how tall he was, which is a strange thought. But I think compared to the curled up hurting man we had observed the last couple of hours, this fired up person standing in front of me loomed larger than life.

I quickly test rode the bike and loaded up with water. Ruben said we should wait for Mike since he was due to arrive any minute. I said "To hell with Mike, let's go!" and with that said, Mike's long–awaited green van arrived. We had hugs, quick introductions for Jeanne and Bram and an assessment of the gear in our car. Mike said something like, "Oh, now I see. WOW, this must have been really tough crewing like this!"

Bram and I just smiled. I left Mike and Bram to decide what gear to transfer to the van and Ruben and I began the 18-mile climb up the pass to Father Crowley Point at an elevation of around 5,000 feet. Panamint Springs lies in a valley at 1,970 feet so we had some steep climbing to do. I rode alternately alongside and in front of Ruben, depending on oncoming traffic. The mountain road is narrow and winding with no shoulder. The headwind was strong so I tried to break some of it with my bike. He told me that Bram did such a good job of pacing him all night on the bike because he would ride ahead of

Ruben at just the right length. Ruben and I talked a lot, his mood was good and ornery and I felt his second wind. I knew that Mike's arrival lifted his spirits and would only continue to improve them.

After a few miles Mike drove slowly alongside us exchanging witty comments and I remembered again what fun he is. I commented on the great view I had, and Mike acknowledged not the scenery but Ruben's backside and Ruben responded with a smile and a quick moon for all of us. It was remembered camaraderie from Badwater 2000 and Ruben came alive again with his quick slashing wit and smiles that made all of us feel better. Mike hollered to me to get myself in the car and take Bram to the hotel in Lone Pine and get some rest. I said "Hotel? Hell, we're going to the *bar!*"

Shortly thereafter Mike relieved me of my duties on the bike and I stayed behind with Jeanne at the van to talk about where things were located in the bins, to give them their Death Valley National Park passes, and help affix Ruben's name and number and the "Caution Runner" signs to the car. Bram arrived a few minutes later in the Subaru after repacking and reloading the bikes and we helped Jeanne crew for a few miles. Parked in a turnout on the pass, looking over Panamint Springs and the road crossing the flats and ascending the wicked Townes Pass we had come over last night, the view was incredible. The millions of years of geology exposed in rock and sand and sandstone before our eyes was hard to fathom. The knowledge of Tuesday's brutal heat and wind were now behind us, and we were beginning a new day with the welcome arrival of Mike and Jeanne. And with Ruben on the road and smiling again, we all had confidence for a finish that Ruben would be proud of.

Suddenly we heard the roaring engines of jet fighters and we strained our necks to locate them through the cloud cover and the 360-degree view of mountains. Finally we glimpsed one flying low and shooting through the mountains at a frighteningly low elevation. Shooting the gap is what I call it and it took our breath away – the speed and the closeness to the ground and the sheer thrill and daring of the pilot. We watched as he arched out of the canyon and back up into the sky above the mountain horizon, then circled around and did it again! I fired off as many photos as I could with my zoom lens knowing no photograph would do justice to actually hearing and seeing it so close in person.

We were at the 30-hour mark of the race and with the arrival of Mike and Jeanne came a time for Bram and me to take a much-earned break. We drove 50 miles ahead to the little town of Lone Pine, California, the gateway to Mount Whitney and the Sierra Nevada Mountains. Once over the top of the pass at Father Crowley Point we descended down to Owens Flats and enjoyed our first view of Mount Whitney and the surrounding mountains. The sun was streaming through the clouds and it was gorgeous. I remember this view from 2000 and I swore I'd return to climb that mountain.

We got a tiny room at the historic Dow Villa Hotel, and historic is a good description of the room. While I was checking in another crewmember at the counter looked at me and said with a smile "Hey, I met you at Lost Boys!" I was wearing the Lost Boys shirt from the 50-mile trail run Ruben directs and I let the young man know I had never been to Lost Boys. He looked a little "lost" he when I said this. He stumbled over his words then said he thought I was Ruben's son–in–law's wife, which I translated in my head to mean the wife of Ruben's son Ric. I met them in San Diego almost four years ago in October, after Leadville 1999. I didn't remember her as blonde but rather a tiny dark–haired girl. I didn't think I looked a thing like her and so I chuckled to myself. Maybe sleep deprivation was getting to him too!

When we checked in I hadn't even looked at my watch, but it was only 11 a.m. Since our room wasn't ready yet Bram and I ate lunch at a local old-fashioned ice cream and hamburger stand and after waiting 35 minutes for "fast" food, it tasted great. A big burger and fries was not the healthiest food we could have chosen, but for our first real meal in 40 hours it tasted great. We returned to the hotel and slept for two hours. Death Valley hotel rooms are few and far between and don't offer cold tap water. Surprisingly, it was tough to get hot water too, so we were left with a lukewarm shower, but we were just happy for a shower, period. Afterwards we cleaned out the car, got more bags of ice, checked in at the race headquarters in a suite at Dow Villa and marveled at the magnificent view of Mount Whitney and the surrounding mountains. From 3,700 feet in elevation at Lone Pine the view soars to the 14,000+ foot peaks surrounding Mount Whitney. The mountains tower over the town and look both close and unattainable at the same time.

Father Crowley Point, Darwin, Owens Flats
Wednesday afternoon/evening

We learned at race headquarters that Ruben had passed the time station at Darwin at 2:46 p.m., meaning he had traveled up and over the pass at Father Crowley Point and began the long descent into Lone Pine. We checked in with the wife of runner Art Webb who was having trouble. He had "staked" out at mile 51, rested at the hotel, and then returned to the course. The sign at headquarters said they needed volunteer crewmembers and his wife needed a ride back out to Art. She told me she already got a ride and thanked me for our offer. We had heard rumors of 14 crewmembers suffering heat exhaustion in Stovepipe Wells and one crewmember being airlifted out and given seven liters of IV fluid. No part of the Badwater Ultramarathon can be taken lightly, and this was the immediate, life-threatening proof.

We found Ruben and crew on the Owens Flats, making good time and bad jokes with Mike in the lead. I joined them on foot for just a while, not wanting to get a penalty for having more than one pacer on the road at a time. In the few minutes I enjoyed with Ruben and Mike, Mike's jokes fell from 4th grade to 1st grade level. "Where do the melons go for summer camp? John Cougar Mellencamp. What has 40 legs and eats ants for lunch?? 20 uncles." We laughed in spite of Mike.

The afternoon and early evening were pleasant in temperature with a heavy cloud cover. We enjoyed breathtaking views of the Sierra Nevada's, Mount Whitney and even a rainbow. It spit rain off and on and in the distance in the dry lakebed of Owens Lake we watched ferocious dirt devils spinning around and cells of rain cross the floor. We had time to relax with three crewmembers manning the cars. We laughed at the comical and formal sounding walkie-talkie dialogue between Mike and Jeanne. Invariably it went like this:

Mike: *Jeanne, this is Mike, do you copy? Over.*
Jeanne: *Yes, Mike, I'm here. Over.*
Mike: *Jeanne, hi, Ruben would like water with ice and a handful of Reese's chocolate balls, if you could get that for him? Over.*

191

Jeanne: No problem, Mike, I'll have it ready. Over.
Mike: Thank you very much, Jeanne. Mike, over and out.

We laughed at Mike asking every mile if Jeanne was there or if she copied, and telling her who he was every time. We felt like yelling, of course we are here and we recognize your voice! The two of them are quite a pair, their dry humor and kindness evident in every word.

Bram and I enjoyed the conversation with Jeanne and the much more relaxed atmosphere of crewing, without the need for so much ice: ice in the neck, ice in the hat, sunscreen, a change of clothes, etc. We took time to take in the surroundings and getting to know Jeanne. As we paused near the tiny village of Keeler, a mangy barrel-chested mutt came out of his yard barking at us.

As he crossed onto the highway I said in my mean doggie voice "You go home! Now, go home, you don't need to come over here to say hi to us, GO HOME!" I didn't want to deal with a strange dog and found it funny he took me seriously and turned tail and went back to his yard. Jeanne giggled and I explained that my "mean" dog voice tells them I mean business and they usually listen.

A few miles later I got cell phone service on the flats and called my parents. My stepdad answered with a very croaky "Hello?" and I quickly looked at the clock and realized it was 11 p.m. in Texas and I had woken him up. I apologized profusely and told him I had no sense of time, or common sense for that matter! He was glad to hear we were all okay and that Ruben was doing well. My parents have met Ruben and my mom watches the live webcast and prays for the safety of all of us during the race. She's always grateful for my calls and understands that being able to use the cell phone or finding a pay phone in Death Valley is extremely limited.

As we approached the turn to Lone Pine we had been crewing again for about five hours and although the crewing was easy and relaxed by now, we could feel our fatigue from the previous days and hours. I see now my performance is better when I am going at warp speed with no time to rest. When the pressure was off and I had time to relax I could feel the fatigue coming on and my brain didn't have to be so sharp anymore. On my suggestion, Bram and I returned to our room to Lone Pine to catch another 90 minutes of rest. After checking in at headquarters and learning Ruben had passed the Dow Villa time station at 11:44 p.m., we caught up with the team on the Portals Road at about midnight. We were amazed at the progress Ruben had made since we left him. He was making better than 14-minute miles and on his way to a stellar finish.

Portals Road
Wednesday night/Thursday morning

The Portals Road takes you 13 miles up a steep, winding and switch-backed road to the trailhead of Mount Whitney, gaining almost a mile in elevation. At night you only get an idea of the landscape and the strange rock formations are easily imagined as goblins or creatures of the night. In daytime you can see the Alabama Hill rock formations that are well known as being the backdrop for nearly every old time western movie ever made. Many formations are named for creatures or animals but at night we can only imagine them. The temperature cooled nicely as we climbed and we were soon in a sweet smelling pine forest and could hear but not see a rushing river. Jeanne walked with Ruben most of the Portals and we timed a few of his miles at an incredible 15 to 18 minutes. The road grade here is steep, sometimes 6%. It's not an easy walk, even if you haven't already run continuously for 122 miles.

Ruben went into what I call his "zombie walk" mode. With a sort of tramping gait he plods forward and rarely stops to take a break. Mike, Bram and I spent our time talking, at times under the rain cover of the hatchback of Mike's van while the mountains spit rain at us. We were feeling the finish close in on us in the wee hours of Thursday morning and I was getting more and more excited. Ruben asked to sit in the car for five minutes and he later told me that Jeanne could not believe a person could be that revived after just a few short minutes of rest. He explained to me he has trained his body to rest quickly and then get back on his feet and return to his pace, but it still amazes me.

Within three miles of the finish Ruben asked us to drive ahead, mark the mileage, and tell us how far he had left and where the one-mile mark was. After 45 hours of intense focus and physical and mental effort, these last miles have the utmost importance. We traced the mileage, coming near the finish line in the car and backtracked to Ruben. I wished like hell the mileage were less than three, even two-point-nine, just to sound more optimistic, but it was steady at three-point-zero miles and I told him so. He was disappointed and said "Three full miles?" And we continued.

At the next mile stop we saw the front end of the Subaru spew steam. With dread we opened the hood and noticed coolant spilled over the radiator. It didn't look like much had spilled but the temperature gauge had spiked and we hoped it was a fluke. The car ran fine so we continued.

We rationalized that some coolant had boiled out when we were driving the steep roads up to the finish and since the temperature gauge returned to normal, we worried no more. Mike and I drove our cars and parked at the finish, and then I ran down and joined Ruben and Jeanne. It was a little creepy running in total darkness on such a steep downhill. I think I passed two runners and a group of crew waiting on the side of the road. Mike and Bram joined soon afterwards and the full team of five of us walked the last mile together, according to Badwater tradition. Ruben asked us to gather close and soon the mile could now be measured in feet.

Finish
Thursday 4 a.m.

The finish line is hidden around one last corner and in the darkness of the mountains and thick pines and lack of lights, it is very difficult to identify. Ruben kept asking if that was the finish and I told him not quite yet. But once we saw our cars parked on the side of the road we knew we were within 30 feet and a second later we could see the finish line and the shouts of the race officials trying to identify us as a team. "Ruben Cantu, #6!" we shouted with cameras flashing in our night eyes. It was just a few minutes before 4 a.m., Thursday morning. Ruben asked us, though it wasn't a question, "Are you ready to run?" and without a word we all ran a half step behind Ruben as he crossed the finish line and through the ribbon with his arms up and a big smile on his face! 45:55 was his final 135-mile time – spectacular!

The finish is emotional and also anticlimactic. Ruben sat down on a chair beneath the race banner and was interviewed briefly by a crew with a camera. Chris Kostman, the Race Director, shook Ruben's hand and awarded him with a finisher's medal around his neck. Ruben shouted to him "Can I have my application for next year's race?" A few pictures were taken with the crew and after hugs all-around we got Ruben to the car before the chill of the cool mountain air got to him.

I learned a lot about myself. I learned I could perform under stress and fatigue and sleep deprivation that was pushed beyond all previous levels. I learned how difficult it could be to clearly communicate with my fellow crewmembers and my runner. I learned through watching Ruben struggle with severe stomach problems and cramps from miles 55 through 71, and then getting back on his feet that the human spirit – *his* spirit –is incredible and untouchable.

I enjoyed every minute, every word, every mood, every degree of temperature and every star in the Death Valley sky. I didn't care that it was 133° F with 15% humidity and a headwind on the shiniest and hottest blacktop known to man and that I hadn't slept in two days – I had fun and I would return tomorrow if I could. As a crewmember many of our experiences are outside the realm of the runner and his goal.

They are about the relationships that are formed and bonded waiting for the runner to approach. They are about working together, communicating and keeping a sense of humor through the anxiety and stress of the event. They are about the beauty of the environment, the stark landscape, the brutal and unforgiving weather and noticing every thing I can possibly notice, knowing I have only taken in a tiny fraction of it. I love all of it.

I am again experiencing the letdown of returning to real life and the insignificance of many things; mainly my job. I knew it was coming but know it's not something I can prepare for. I already knew my job was unimportant in the grand scheme of life; now I feel it. Who knows what changes will come out of my life from this? I do know they will be good, thanks to Ruben and the life lessons he has taught me by being who he is and running these races.

Ruben's company does so much to lift my spirit and remind me why I am here on earth. Simply put, who he is does a lot for me and I hope to always have him in my life. These are my heartfelt feelings as a crewmember and friend. I had a righteous time – and my thanks go to Ruben.

Now, after the finish and just steps away from Mike and Jeanne directing Ruben to the van, I simply look forward to my hotel bed and more importantly for Ruben's well earned rest and sense of accomplishment and fulfillment for his 4th successful Badwater Ultramarathon finish.

I walk away with Bram to our car with a smile on my face in the blackness of the Mount Whitney night. I try to acknowledge all that it took for Ruben to cross the finish line... and I cannot.

APPENDIX: 2003 BADWATER ULTRAMARATHON RESULTS

Position	Name	Age	State	Time
1.	Pam Reed	42	Arizona	28:26:52
2.	Dean Karnazes	40	California	28:51:26
3.	Monica Scholz	36	Ontario, Canada	33:41:29
4.	Chris Bergland	37	New York	33:58:37
5.	Tracy Bahr	31	Oregon	35:16:17
6.	Scott Ludwig	48	Georgia	36:32:46
7.	Luis Escobar	40	California	37:19:18
8.	Charlie Engle	40	North Carolina	38:39:38
9.	Louise Cooper	49	California	39:22:14
10.	Bill Lockton	55	California	39:39:32
11.	Sergio Cordeiro	49	Brazil	40:03:44
12.	Christ Rampacek	51	Texas	41:58:31
13.	Joseph DeSena	34	New York	42:03:13
14.	Jay Anderson	47	California	42:18:07
15.	Chris Frost	52	California	42:51:37
16.	John Radich	49	California	43:14:12
17.	Daniel Conrad	54	California	43:30:39
18.	Roger Klein	57	Luxembourg	43:37:09
19.	Patrick Cande	46	Tahiti	43:41:59
20.	Mary Kashurba	47	Pennsylvania	44:08:04
21.	Don Lundell	41	California	45:10:46
22.	Jane Ballantyne	48	BC, Canada	45:23:46

23.	Mark Morris	45	Texas	45:23:58
24.	Marshall Ulrich	52	Colorado	45:30:04
25.	Ruben Cantu	60	California	45:54:01
26.	Lisa Henson	42	California	45:57:20
27.	Adam Bookspan	37	Florida	46:01:42
28.	Bonnie Busch	45	Iowa	46:04:26
29.	Anita Marie Fromm	32	California	46:48:49
30.	Mike Karch	34	New Mexico	47:19:09
31.	Patricia Cook	51	Missouri	48:31:13
32.	Andy Velazco	55	Georgia	48:54:12
33.	Lisa Smith-Batchen	42	Idaho	52:11:39
34.	Nancy Shura	53	California	52:35:36
35.	William LaDieu	53	Pennsylvania	52:49:18
36.	Joe Prusaitis	48	Texas	53:14:54
37.	Ken Eielson	54	Colorado	53:23:36
38.	Dan Marinsik	44	California	53:36:12
39.	Mark Cockbain	31	United Kingdom	55:01:08
40.	Barbara Elia	58	California	55:01:08
41.	Janice Levet	52	California	55:11:38
42.	Jim Bodoh	52	Florida	55:54:15
43.	Ian Parker	52	California	56:48:46
44.	Michael Doppelmayr	42	Austria	57:39:48
45.	Gillian Robinson	36	California	58:38:57
46.	Scott Weber	50	Colorado	58:43:29

26 of the starters did not finish the race.
Art Webb had an honorary finish in 95 hours.

© Thinkstock/iStockphoto/Fluid Illusion

EPILOGUE

THE "LONG, COMFORTABLE ROAD" NEVER ENDS

The Badwater Ultramarathon took center stage after the summer of 2003. Pam Reed appeared on *"Late Night with David Letterman"*(sorry about that, Ben Jones) as well as on the cover of the October 2003 issue of *Ultrarunning Magazine* (I contributed an account of the race for the issue – and was pictured over Pam's left shoulder on the cover: I'm wearing bib # 20). "Dean Karnazes" became a household word. Autobiographies by both Pam (*The Extra Mile: One Woman's Personal Journey to Ultra-Running Greatness*) and Dean (*Ultramarathon Man: Confessions of an All-Night Runner*) became national bestsellers. The legend of Marshall Ulrich became, well, legendary.

Twelve of the 46 Badwater finishers from 2003 would return to Death Valley over the next nine years to compete in the toughest footrace on the planet, accumulating a composite 46 more finishes. Marshall Ulrich led the way with six finishes, Monica Scholz had five and Pam and Dean both had four. Monica and Dean shared a day in the sun in 2004 as they were crowned the women's and men's Badwater Champions, respectively.

But there's more than just Badwater in these runner's lives.

Monica Scholz, who had established the record for the most 100-mile runs (23) in a calendar year in 2001 prior to the 2003 Badwater Ultramarathon, extended her record to by two by completing 25 100-mile runs in 2010.

Dean Karnazes completed the 50/50/50 in 2006: 50 marathons in each of the 50 states in 50 consecutive days to raise awareness of youth obesity and getting America active. Dean wrote a second book documenting his adventure (*50/50: Secrets I Learned Running 50 Marathons in 50 Days*) and followed it up with a third book (*26.2 Stories of Blisters and Bliss*).

Ben and Denise Jones were both inducted into the Badwater Hall of Fame in 2007 for their (at that time) 17 years of service to the race in various capacities.

Lisa Smith-Batchen, supported by good friend Sister Mary Beth Lloyd completed an incredible 62-day odyssey in the summer of 2010 as she ran 50 miles in each of the 50 states in support of AIDS Orphans Rising, an organization providing food, housing and education for children orphaned by AIDS and the Caring House Project, which builds communities in Haiti. Sister Mary Beth also completed 20 miles in each of the 50 states, not wearing running gear but wearing a full habit consisting of a black wool tunic over a white shirt and underskirt, black headpiece and a black woolen belt... and sneakers. In 2012 Lisa was inducted into the Badwater Hall of Fame.

In 2008 Marshall Ulrich completed a 3,063-mile run (equivalent to 117 marathons) across America in just over 52 days. The film *Running America*, which also features 2003 Badwater finisher Charlie Engle, chronicles their joint attempt to set a new world record for running across the continental United States. Marshall wrote a book chronicling his cross-country adventure (*Running on Empty*, the profits of which he will share with AIDS Orphans Rising) and is planning on a never-before done project in Death Valley. What else would you expect from the Desert Fox? As for Charlie, in 2006 he, along with fellow ultrarunners Kevin Lin and Ray Zahab ran across the Sahara Desert, a 4,300-mile journey that took 111 days to complete. The run was to support water.org, a clean water initiative supporting the water crisis in Africa.

I have yet to return to Death Valley, although running continues to play a prominent role in my life. On November 30, 2011 I completed the 33rd year of my consecutive-days running streak, something I began shortly after I got married to the former Cindy Johnson. This, my third book, is another labor of love I hope serves to not only enlighten but excite others about the wonder and amazement that is the Badwater Ultramarathon. There is no other race like it.

In the 2003 Badwater Ultramarathon 73 runners representing 12 different countries ranging in age from 31 to 70 started the race; only 46 would finish. Approximately 40% of those treated by the medical team (2003 was the first year the race provided roving medical support) were crewmembers. The race was arguably the most difficult in the 20-year history of the 134.4-mile version of the event.

Denise Jones, wife of Ben has this to say about Badwater from her many experiences in Death Valley as both runner and crewmember:

"During Badwater, the things we so carefully hide in everyday life from others, our "real qualities" come out. It's like peeling an onion: as the layers are peeled off, if that runner is a brat, it shows and it is NOT PURDY! In contrast, there are runners who remain polite and kind in the worst of circumstances."

I believe you'll agree you just finished reading about 25 runners who fit Denise's latter description. They came from all walks of life and had many different reasons for competing in the toughest footrace in the planet.

But one thing we all had in common:

In the summer of 2003 each of us left a small piece of our soul in Death Valley.

THE AUTHOR

Scott has run every single day since November 30, 1978 and he currently has the 32nd longest streak in the United States. He has run 200 marathons, over 800 races, and accumulated over 130,000 miles in his lifetime.

He began running ultramarathons early in his running career, his first being a 50-miler in 1982. In time he would run ultras ranging from 31 miles to 135 miles (the Badwater Ultramarathon in 2003, in which he would finish in 6th place). In 2002, Scott ran 129 miles in the U.S. National 24-Hour Championships and won the master's (age 40 and over) national championship. In 1992 he ran 280 miles in six days, from the west side to the east side of the state of Georgia, to raise money for charity.

CREDITS

The cover photograph of Luis Escobar was taken by Doug Rich.

Marshall Ulrich, Ben Jones and Emily Pronovost gathered the information regarding the temperature on July 22, 2003 in Death Valley.

Ben Jones provided the photographs of Pam Reed and Monica Scholz, as well as many of the photographs of Death Valley. All other runner photographs were from the respective runners' personal collection.

Editing: Sabine Carduck, Manuel Morschel
Copy Editor: Sebastian Meyer
Layout: Claudia Lo Cicero

FURTHER READING

STUMBLING TOWARDS THE FINISH LINE

Best of Ironman Columnist
Lee Gruenfeld

STUMBLING
TOWARDS THE
FINISH LINE

Edited by Kevin Mackinnon

NEXT
140.6 MILES

MEYER
&MEYER
SPORT

IRONING OUT IRONMAN
How to Improve the World's Toughest Race

Don't get me wrong: I love Ironman. I wouldn't actually *do* one even if wild crows were pecking out my eyeballs, but I love the sport nonetheless, in much the same way I love, say, crocodile wrestling or *Fear Factor 13: Flirting with Plague*. Which is to say, as a spectator.

But I understand Ironman better than most active non-participating fans, being married to someone afflicted with MESS (Maniacal Endurance Sports Syndrome) and knowing an awful lot of MESS-ed up athletes. Having watched otherwise level-headed people compete in Ironman races around the world, I think I'm eminently qualified to comment on how the sport might be improved, if only those pig-iron-headed know-it-alls at WTC would wake up and smell the VOG.

Herewith a sure-fire set of ideas for ensuring that our favorite sport doesn't go the way of *Gigli*.

1 – The first idea is so absurdly obvious it's hard to fathom that no one's thought of it before:

Make it shorter.

I've thought about it a lot and have come to the conclusion that just about everything that's wrong with Ironman is due to its length. What kind of sense does it make to stage a race that's so long some people can't even finish it? *King Kong* is too long also, and there's nothing that can be done about that now because it's a one-shot deal (okay...one-shot and two remakes). But Ironman can still be edited. Just think of all the benefits.

For one thing, you can get rid of the medical tent, relieving psychic turmoil and buying back some finish line space. Upwards of 13% of all entrants end up in the medical tent, making the finale of the world's most prestigious athletic event look more like an airplane crash investigation than a sporting contest. A cot and a puncture wound in a M*A*S*H tent is why 90,000 people a year compete for a slot?

TThe cost savings alone would be enormous, starting with a lot fewer bananas, water bottles and support personnel. Then there's the reduction in wear and tear among spectators, something race directors have failed to take into consideration from the very beginning. Not to mention equivalent (and sometimes even more severe) wear and tear among the athletes, despite their much-ballyhooed conditioning. Basic corporate economics here, WTC: Why pummel your prime customer base so badly that they can only do business with you once or twice a year? Get the distance down low enough to where an athlete can do thirty, forty races a year and we're talking some serious entry fee revenue here, my friend.

As an added benefit, you foster better relationships with the community. Let's be honest: Not everybody in the deceptively tranquil and purportedly Aloha-soaked Kailua-Kona looks at the annual World Championship the way Kirsti Alley looks at a Mallomar. For one thing, they don't like their main roads getting shut down, a frustration they like to vent by inventing their own sports, like the perennial, week-before-race-day favorite, "Let's see who can drive his 40-ton semi closest to a cyclist without getting a ticket." If the Ironman were entirely confined to a four-block area surrounding the corner of Ali'i and Kuakini Highway and set up so that access to the Blockbuster and Starbucks on Palani remained uninterrupted, why, I'm just guessing that there'd be one or two fewer dirty looks from the guy hawking timeshares from that little booth down by Pancho & Lefty's.

2 – Another one I can't believe no one's thought of yet:

Let's beef up the aid stations.

Mine is not a sophisticated palate and has been described by various snobby acquaintances as roughly akin to a hockey puck when it comes to culinary discrimination. But even I can see that slurping some sucrostic glop out of a foil packet hardly ranks among the world's great gustatory experiences (although I'm told that, when mixed with a goodly dollop of sweat, a certain intriguing piquancy may be achieved).

Try to imagine another event where you pay hundreds of dollars to enter, thousands more to travel there, and all they serve you on the "Big Freakin' Day" is glorified candy bars and sugar water. Out of *disposable bottles*, no less.

It doesn't have to be this way. What would be so hard about a slight upgrade of the menu? And speaking of menus, why does every athlete have to ingest the same stuff as every other athlete? We've got people from Ghana, Liberia, Ecuador and Detroit, and we feed them all the same stuff. What happened to this joyous celebration of multiculturalism the Ironman is supposed to represent?

At a lot of golf courses on the Big Island, there's a telephone mounted on the tee box of the ninth hole that's connected to the restaurant at the club house. There's also a printed menu where the phone book would normally go. You use the phone to place an order before teeing off, then pick up your food as you make the turn to the back nine. Simple, effective, and greatly appreciated by patrons.

So here's what I'm thinking. You know those giant Timex mileage markers? Replace them with menus. Then, a hundred yards later, have a bank of telephones. After athletes pass the menus, they'll have plenty of time to mull over their choices and be ready to call them in when they get to the phones. (Revenue-generating idea: Make them pay phones.) By the time they hit the aid station, their orders will be ready to go.

I keep reading in all these triathlon magazines that there's no reason a healthy diet can't be appealing and delicious as well, so even the kind of limited offerings one expects in the middle of a race should reflect that. What exhausted and numbed-out athlete wouldn't appreciate an appetizer of pâté de foie gras garnished with sprigs of parsley and radish curls, followed half a mile later by a little roast venison with mint sauce accompanied by julienne of potatoes and epinards d'Seville?

Which brings me to another thing: Is there anything in the Ironman rule book about alcohol out on the course? Because it seems to me that washing all of this down with a glass or two of '87 Montrachet would be just the ticket in more ways than I can count. The beneficial effects of red wine are well-established and need no elaboration here, and for athletes, the upside of quaffing in general is even more pronounced. You think PowerBars give you a nice glucose jolt? Slam down a few quick brewskis and you'll get an instant chemistry lesson in the three-step conversion of methyl alcohol into glycogen. There's a reason for that line-up of 5,700-litre beer trucks at the finish line of the Ironman European Championship in Frankfurt, and it isn't to keep the oompah band happy.

And, finally: You know how elite athletes don't worry too much about three-minute penalties anymore, having discovered that using the time to stretch a little and collect themselves can actually improve their overall times? Well, why not make the aid station meals sit-down affairs? White tablecloths, lightstick candles after sundown, table-side salad prep? If Ironman is eighty percent mental, I can't think of anything that would better prepare the mind for those last difficult miles than a relaxing dinner with fellow competitors, topped off with a short snifter of Hennessey and a choice Montecristo stogie.

3 – What's the biggest problem for Ironman racers other than not dying?

I'll tell you what it is: It's boredom. Mind-numbing, will-sapping tedium. Hawai'i is gorgeous, but when you're dragging your butt along the Queen K at barely the speed of smell, it's just one damned chunk of lava after another.

People play all sorts of weird mental games to keep themselves in the moment. Or out of it, depending upon your point of view. They count stripes in the road, or try to recall all the lyrics to "Louie, Louie," or attempt to resolve intricate scientific conundrums, like, "Why does my left quadriceps feel like I've just been bitten by a great white?"

None of this is necessary, which brings me to this suggestion: Issue every participant an iPod, a Blackberry and a Bluetooth headset.

Think of it: You're running along feeling like Dick Cheney in an aerobics class. You reach down to your belt and suddenly you've got Bob Marley wailing "You can make it if you really try..." right in your ear. Is that motivational or what?

Concerned that friends and family back home don't know how you're doing because Ironman.com is on the fritz and all they can get is an endless loop of Mark Allen doing Guido Sarducci impressions? Call 'em up! Or check in at the office! Or find out how Brad and Angelina are doing! A few years ago when my wife was having a particularly tough time at mile 9 of the run, I filled her in on the O.J. verdict. Boy, did she appreciate that timely update. Properly equipped, though, she wouldn't have to be so dependent on me for news.

Did you know you can play on-line poker on a Blackberry? Tell me there could be a greater rush in this world than going all-in with two-seven off suit while heading down into the Energy Lab.

And, hey...I just thought of something else: You wouldn't have to stop at those chintzy pay phones to call in your food order!

* * *

Next time: Neutralizing the unfair advantage of stronger and faster racers and other ideas for improving Ironman.

Ed. note: If editing a Gruenfeld column for Ironman.com is painful (which it is), "Ironing Out Ironman" set new records in pain management. In one quick and easy-to-read column he managed to piss off virtually the entire no-sense-of-humor triathlon community. "Make it shorter?" asked one reader. "It's an Ironman, it needs to be 140.6 miles." (I don't think they quite got Lee's humor.) Race officials were hardly impressed with his "take music and a phone" idea, while Ironman officials, who banned Chuckie Veylupek from the world championship for years because he took a few sips of beer from a spectator, were none-too-impressed with the concept of a "glass or two of '87 Montrachet."

Oh, and how'd you think PowerBar and Gatorade reacted to the "glorified candy bars and sugar water" comment?

It's a miracle I still have hair – although my wife says it started to go grey after Lee came on board with his column.

ISBN: 978-1-78255-005-1
*Available in book stores and on **www.m-m-sports.com***